Information Systems Development

An Introduction to Information Systems Engineering

Paul Beynon-Davies
Department of Computer Studies
University of Glamorgan

Second Edition

150th YEAR
M
MACMILLAN

First Edition 1989
Second Edition 1993

Published by
THE MACMILLAN PRESS LTD
Houndmills, Basingstoke, Hampshire RG21 2XS
and London
Companies and representatives
throughout the world.

ISBN 0–333–59506–8

A catalogue record for this book is available
from the British Library.

Printed and bound in Great Britain by
Biddles Ltd, Guildford and King's Lynn

Contents

Part Four: Methods

Part Five: Environment

Preface to the Second Edition

The First Edition

The first edition of this work began with the following paragraph:

> "Most of the conventional material on information systems development is deterministic in the sense that it imposes some prior framework on the use of the techniques available. The present book is designed to be as flexible or non-deterministic as possible. It provides a series of relatively discrete notebooks on important topics in the field. It therefore leaves it largely up to the reader to impose his own determinism."

The general intent of the second edition remains unchanged. Having said this, the second edition constitutes a new, and more extensive, book rather than a revision of the first edition. Comments from readers have generally indicated that the first edition was held to be strong on technical aspects but weak on discussing the organisational and environmental issues associated with information systems development. This new edition provides a more balanced account of the subject.

One of the most important changes is that a more prominent structure is given to the material. The book is divided into five major parts: context, techniques, tools, methods, environmental issues. Within these parts, a number of new chapters are included such as Business Analysis, Project Management, the Social Dimension of Information Systems Development, Object-Oriented programming, and User Interface Development. Finally, a central case study is provided which augments the separate case studies. In particular, each of the major techniques discussed is applied to the central case study to demonstrate how a coherent specification can be built for an information system.

Strategy

The topic of Information Systems Development is a large one. It is a topic which is getting larger by the day as information systems, particularly computerised information systems, impact more and more on our everyday lives.

Therefore, in this work we have parcelled up the field into several parts, primarily for the purposes of presentation. The figure heading each part of the book illustrates how each can be considered a source of pressure or a force determining the shape of contemporary and indeed future information systems development.

1. Context. Here we discuss issues of what is an information system, why we need information systems, how the concept of information is playing an ever more prevalent role in our lives, and how appropriate ways for developing information systems assume ever more importance.
2. Tools. Here we discuss some of the components with which, and from which, contemporary computerised information systems are built.
3. Techniques. Here we discuss some of the major techniques of analysis and design in the armoury of the information systems specialist.
4. Methodologies. Here we discuss some of the contemporary ideas which relate to a number of distinct approaches to building information systems.
5. Environment. Here we discuss some of the contemporary pressures which mould the shape of information systems. In particular, we address the socio-economic context of information systems work.
6. Information Systems Engineering. Here we re-examine the idea that information systems development can be cast as an engineering exercise. In particular, we look at the 'hybridisation' of the profession and what this means for the future of the information systems specialist.

This work is subtitled *An Introduction to Information Systems Engineering*. My main aim in rewriting this work is to contribute to the development of the discipline of information systems. Casting the discipline as engineering, however, does not mean that I agree with the rather limited conception of engineering portrayed in many quarters of computing. Information systems, by their very nature, are open to interpretation from a number of different viewpoints. In this respect I am conducting a similar exercise to Ehn (1989) in trying to focus on a disciplinary base for the interdisciplinary subject matter of designing computer artefacts. It is hoped that some of this diversity is reflected in the current text.

As a final comment, it is hoped that further editions of this work will be produced frequently to keep it up-to-date with ongoing developments. Any suggestions concerning the current edition or material to be included in subsequent editions would be welcomed, addressed to the author, care of the publisher.

Acknowledgements

My thanks to staff and students of the Department of Computer Studies, the University of Glamorgan, particularly Tim Hutchings, Deri Shephard and Douglas Tudhope. Thanks also to Malcolm Stewart at Macmillan for encouraging me to produce this new edition.

References

Ehn P. (1989). The Art and Science of Designing Computer Artefacts. *Scandinavian Journal of Information Systems*. 1(1). 21-42.

Part One
<u>Context</u>

Context
General setting of experience. (*Oxford English Dictionary*)
Circumstances, factors, situation, milieu. (*Roget's Thesaurus*)

In this part, we use three models to organise the material and introduce some of
the variety of debate surrounding information systems work:

1. A model of the primary components of technical information systems.
2. A model of the place of a technical information system within its environment.
3. A model of the process of developing information systems.

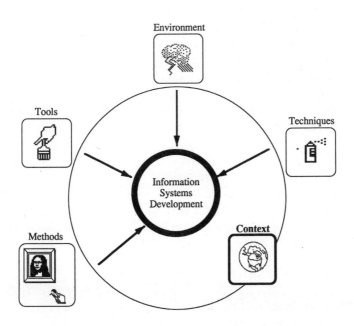

1 Information, Information Systems and Organisations

1.1 Introduction

The concept of information and its exploitation in information systems has been somewhat taken for granted in the contemporary practice of development. Information has been treated in many respects as a mystical fluid which emanates as if by magic from the development of computerised information systems.

As an attempt to combat this simplistic conception there has been a resurgence of interest in the philosophical and sociological underpinnings of information systems work. As such, a discipline of information systems is emerging which has boundaries with management, business studies, behavioural science, computing and many other areas. This chapter provides an introduction to this material.

1.2 What is Information?

The concept of information is an extremely vague one open to many different interpretations (Stamper, 1985). One conception popular in the computing literature is that information results from the processing of data — the assembly, analysis or summarisation of data. This conception of information as analagous to chemical distillation is useful, but ignores the important place of human interpretation.

In this section we shall define a workable definition of information based upon the distinction between data, information and knowledge. We shall elaborate on this definition in further sections, particularly putting people in the picture.

Tsitchizris and Lochovsky define information as being "an increment of knowledge which can be inferred from data" (1982). Information therefore increases a person's knowledge of something. Note that this definition interrelates the concepts of data, information, knowledge and people (see figure 1.1):

1. Data is facts. A datum, a unit of data, is one or more symbols that are used to represent something.
2. Information is interpreted data. Information is data placed within a meaningful context.

1

3. Knowledge is derived from information by integrating information with existing knowledge.
4. Information is necessarily subjective. Information must always be set in the context of its recipient. The same data may be interpreted differently by different people depending on their existing knowledge.

Consider the string of symbols 43. Taken together these symbols form a datum. Taken together however they are meaningless. To turn them into information we have to supply a meaningful context. We have to interpret them. This might be that they constitute an employee number, a person's age, or the quantity of a product sold. Information of this sort will contribute to our knowledge of a particular domain. It might add, for instance, to our understanding of the total number of products of a particular type sold.

Another potent example of sign production is the cryptanalytic work conducted at Bletchley Park in the UK during the second world war (Hodges, 1983). Here the data constituted encrypted signals from the German war machine. Decryption involved translating the signals into referents such as German U-boat positions and movements. The information gleaned was then incorporated into the total knowledge available to allied intelligence on military movements and strategy.

1.3 Semiotics

Liebenau and Backhouse (1990), following Stamper (1973, 1985), have discussed information in terms of semiotics. Semiotics or semiology is the study of signs.

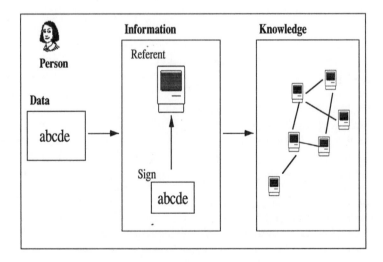

Figure 1.1   Data, Information and Knowledge

Stamper portrays semiotics as "not so much a new subject as a regrouping of ideas from many disciplines having their own private jargons, and little intercommunication" (1973).

One of the most important types of sign can be considered as a convention linking the signifier (the symbol) to that which it is representing (the signified). The fundamental model of sign use can be portrayed in terms of a meaning triangle (Sowa, 1984). The left corner of the triangle is the symbol; the peak is the concept; and the right corner is the referent. In figure 1.2 the symbol is the word 'macintosh', the concept is the idea of a computer, and the referent is the machine sitting on my desk. A given sign can be considered on a number of different levels:

1. Pragmatics. The study of the general context and culture of communication. The shared assumptions underlying communication and understanding.
2. Semantics. The study of the meaning of signs. The association between signs and behaviour.
3. Syntactics. The logic and grammar of sign systems.
4. Empirics. The physical characteristics of the medium of communication.

Pragmatics and semantics study the purpose and content of communication. Syntactics and empirics study the forms and means of communication. Pragmatics and semantics clearly impinge upon other disciplines such as sociology and politics. Syntactics and empirics impinge upon the domain of psychology and indeed even electronics.

Consider, for instance, a mail message transmitted on an office automation system. The mail message is something which exists within a social setting. It

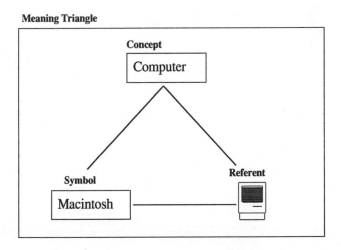

Figure 1.2   Components of a Sign

therefore exists within an environment of expectations, commitments and obligations. At the pragmatic level there must be some reason for sending the message which is presumably expressed in terms of the culture and context in which the information is used. At the semantic level the focus shifts to the subject matter of the message; what meaning is being transmitted by the message. At the syntactic level the language used to express the message is of concern. In so far as the communication takes place along electronic communication lines issues such as bandwiths and other properties of signal transmission will be the concern of the empirics level.

Recently Backhouse *et al.* have called for a focus for information Systems research which draws on much of the work of Stamper. They have proposed an organising framework based on the disciplines of sociology and semiology:

> "Two well-established areas of study provide us with a firm foundation on which to build. These are sociology on the one hand and semiology on the other. The former already constitutes the main thrust of research into social organisation, institutional dynamics, group interaction, working conditions and social policy. The latter brings together the range of studies associated with contexts of language and communication, meanings, grammars, signs and codes". (Backhouse, *et al.* 1991)

1.4 What is an Information System?

The term information system is used in a number of different contexts in the literature. This section attempts to build a workable definition of the term and in the process introduces a number of important distinctions which impinge on the material in further chapters.

A system might be defined as a coherent set of interdependent components which exists for some purpose, has some stability, and can be usefully viewed as a whole. Systems are generally portrayed in terms of an input-process-output model existing within a given environment. The environment of a system might be defined as anything outside a system which has an effect on the way the system operates. The inputs to the system are the resources it gains from its environment or other systems. The outputs from the system are that which it supplies back to its environment or other systems. The process of the system is the activity which transforms the system inputs into system outputs. Most organisations are open systems in that they are affected by their environment and other systems.

The idea of a system has been applied in many fields as diverse as physics, biology and electronics. The class of systems to which computing is generally applied have been referred to as human activity systems (Checkland, 1980). Such systems have an additional component added to the input-process-output model described above: people. Human activity systems consist of people, conventions and artefacts designed to serve human needs.

Every human activity system will have an information system. The purpose of this information system is to manage the human activity system.

1.5 A Simple Human Activity System

Take the example of a simple business which handles claims made against insurance companies as the result of motor accidents. The environment of this system comprises its relationship to its parent company, other insurance companies and the financial industry at large. The main inputs to the system are the claims made against insurers. The main outputs from the system are payments made to other insurers. The main activity of the system is the resolution of claims. The primary people involved in the system are the claims clerks which take a particular claim from inception through to resolution. The system is also made up of a vast range of conventions governing the appropriate ways of processing claims. Most of these conventions govern the flow of information through the system: the information system.

1.6 Formal, Informal and Technical Information Systems

Information systems may be formal, informal, or technical (see figure 1.3). Stamper (1973) cogently makes the distinction as follows:

> "To understand an organisation we must recognise three layers corresponding to the formal, informal and technical levels at which culture is transmitted and behaviour determined. At the formal level are the explicitly recognised precepts of behaviour which may be a part of the wider culture in which the organisation operates; on the other hand they may be expressed in the rules, regulations and official structure of authority. At the informal level, an organisation will gradually evolve complex patterns of behaviour which are never formulated, but which must be learnt by newcomers. The informal culture will be vital to the effectiveness of the organisation; in some respects it may aid, and in others impede, the attainment of organisational objectives... At the technical level an organisation must be described in terms of its flows of messages about the transactions performed, plans made, problems investigated, and in terms of the data-processing activities necessary to accomplish organisational tasks."

1.7 Formal Information Systems

The primary purpose for creating an organised information system is to serve real-world action. The provision of information in organisations is always linked to action: to deciding to do things, accomplishing them, observing and recording the results and if necessary iteratively repeating this process. From the definition of information as data to which meaning has been attributed and the objective of information systems as servers for action a number of consequences follow:

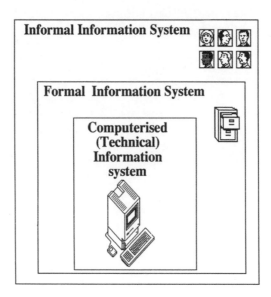

Figure 1.3   Levels of Information System

1. The boundary of information systems will always have to include the attribution of meaning, which is a uniquely human act. An information system will consist of both data manipulation and the attribution of meaning by humans (see figure 1.4).
2. The process of developing an information system requires explicit attention to the purposeful action which the information system is meant to serve. This involves understanding how the people in the organisation conceptualise their world: how they attribute meaning, and how this meaning drives action.

The social dimension of information systems is considered in more detail in chapter 29.

1.8 The Importance of Informal Information Systems

On the morning of 27th October 1986 the new computerised price and dealing information system of the London stock market went down. Breakdowns and suspensions of trading occurred on the system for the following month. When an evaluation was conducted the source of the problem proved to be a massive underestimation of the volume and timing of system usage. On the first day, everybody logged onto the system out of curiousity. Thereafter, regular massive early loading of the system was commonplace as dealers struggled to get their share prices right as early in the day as possible (Willcocks and Mason, 1987).

Information System

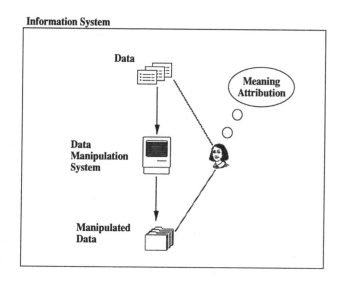

Figure 1.4   Components of an Information System

The analysis of the formal system of stock market information was done well. The price and dealing information system (the technical system) was produced on time. However, the analysis of the informal system of share dealing was done badly.

The main importance of informal information systems is that they can be more robust than information systems established on formal and particularly technical grounds. An informal information system, because of its very nature, is likely to be better able to adapt to the changes in the external environment.

1.9 Soft Systems Analysis

In the same way that we distinguish between a formal and an informal information system we may likewise distinguish between formal and informal systems analysis. Formal or 'hard' systems analysis is the process of investigating and documenting the formal information systems of organisations. Informal or 'soft' systems analysis is the process of investigating and documenting the informal information systems of organisations.

Soft systems analysis equates quite closely with idea of business analysis: of analysing the overall objectives and needs of an organisation and identifying the place of the organisation within its environment (Checkland and Scholes, 1990). The topic of business analysis is discussed in chapter 20.

1.10 The Information Systems Specialist

Institutions like the British Computer Society have recently become interested in broadening the skills expected of information systems engineers. The idea of a hybrid manager — a person with both business and technical knowledge — has been much discussed (Palmer, 1990). In a sense, this initiative is merely echoing a sentiment first expressed by Stamper in the 1970s:

> "The demands of society and the opportunities of technology are now changing so quickly that we must learn to construct organisations that are responsive to our needs. Organisations cannot be left to evolve; as far as it is possible they must be designed. Many people are working on these problems: managers, administrators and staff specialists. In one way or another they are all trying to make organisations use information effectively. It is information that holds organisations together and drives them along. What we urgently need therefore, are information specialists who are as thoroughly acquainted with the information needs of organisations as they are with the capabilities of modern information technology" (Stamper, 1973).

We consider the issue of hyrid managers again in chapter 30.

1.11 The Information Society

In the 1970s Daniel Bell (1970), a US sociologist, wrote an influential book entitled *The Coming of Post-Industrial Society*. In this work, Bell made a series of predictions about the state of Western societies. His premise is now generally accepted: that Western societies are becoming information societies. That whereas the revolution of the latter part of the nineteenth century was an industrial revolution, the revolution of the latter part of the twentieth century is an information revolution.

There is some debate however about whether information technology will bring about the same level of changes in society as characterised the industrial revolution. One school of thought believes that we are clearly moving out of the stage of an industrial society and into the stage of a post-industrial society. They point to a number of indicators to support this thesis:

1. Change from a goods-producing society to a service society.
2. Information becoming a major commodity of organisations.
3. The information explosion.

The second indicator is evident, for instance, in the advertising industry. Advertisements for particular products will be placed within television programmes which are watched by a significant proportion of people who are likely to buy such products. The advertising company derives such information from market researchers who conduct detailed surveys of viewing behaviour. In this context, information has become a currency which determines the cost of particular advertisements.

The second school of thought believes that the magnitude and speed of changes in society have been heavily exaggerated. They maintain that we are seeing just one more stage in the development of industry comparable to developments that have gone before.

1.12 Information Management

One consequence of the information society is the increasing importance of information to modern organisations. Not many years ago, information systems was seen largely as a service activity that facilitated, but did not greatly influence the operation of the majority of companies. With the exception of companies that were in the information systems business themselves, companies tended to treat computing as a necessary expense item to be controlled in a similar manner to heat and electricity.

Over the past few years this conception of information systems as service tools has begun to change. Businesses have begun to consider how information technology can enhance the strategic competitiveness of companies in a rapidly changing market (chapter 23).

A much cited example of this is the case of the US medical supplies company American Hospitals Supply (Earl, 1988). This company was able to increase its market share by setting up computer-based ordering links with customers and suppliers and exploiting a large product range.

Earl (1989) has plotted some of the micro-revolutions making up the global information revolution in companies. He characterises the history of business computing into two eras: what he calls the era of data processing (DP) and the era of information technology (IT). Each era is distinguished by its position on nine dimensions.

1. Financial attitude to IT. In the DP era the financial attitude towards computing was one of cost; in the IT era it is one of investment.
2. Business Role of IT. In the DP era computing was seen as mainly a support activity for company business; in the IT era it is seen as critical to company performance.
3. Applications Orientation of IT. In the DP era the applications orientation was primarily tactical; in the IT era it is strategic.
4. Economic Context for IT. In the DP era computing had a neutral role in changes in the business sectors of national and international economies; in the IT era computing and communications form one of the most important enabling technologies for economic change.
5. Social Impact of IT. In the DP era the social impact of IT was limited; in the IT era it is all pervasive.

6. MIS Thinking on IT. In the DP era management information was seen as secondary to the major information areas of business; in the IT era, management information systems are seen as central.
7. Stakeholders Concerned with IT. In the DP era few people were involved in, or wished to be involved in, deciding information systems strategy; in the IT era the stakeholders are many and various.
8. Technologies Involved in IT. In the DP era IT meant computing; in the IT era it means any technology concerned with information.
9. Management Posture to IT. In the DP era the management posture was one of delegation; in the IT era it is one of leadership.

Earl and many others have been particularly interested in the last change. The discipline of information management directs itself to answering the question: what knowledge will enable management to take an effective role in determining the strategic employment of IT?

1.13 Goronwy Galvanising: A Case Study

To provide some context for many aspects of the discussion of information systems development which follows we begin portraying here the elements of a central case study. The aim is to illustrate how an information system which is to be developed for a small manufacturing company can be viewed from a number of different perspectives. In particular, the case study forms a central part of the techniques section where we illustrate the application of each technique to an aspect of the system. In this chapter we mainly consider the broad implications of the informal and formal information systems at the company. In chapter 2 we inspect the detail of the formal system specific to the proposed technical information system.

Goronwy Galvanising Ltd are a small company specialising in treating steel products such as lintels, crash barriers, and palisades etc., produced by other manufacturers. Goronwy are a subsidiary of a large multi-national whose primary business is the production of various alloys. The multi-national maintains 10 plants on similar lines to Goronwy around the UK. Each plant is relatively autonomous in terms of managing its day-to-day business. Head office coordinates administrative activities such as accounting, finance and the dissemination of information.

Galvanising, in very simplistic terms, involves dipping steel products into baths of molten zinc to provide a rust-proof coating. Untreated steel products are described as being 'black'. Treated steel products are referred to as 'white'. There is a slight gain in weight as a result of the galvanising process.

Goronwy mainly process steel for a major manufacturer known as Blackheads. More than 80% of their business is with Blackheads which places a regular set of orders with Goronwy. Other manufacturers, such as Pimples, order galvanised steel on an irregular basis.

The staff at Goronwy consist of a plant manager, a production controller, an office clerk, 3 shift foremen and 50 shop-floor workers. The plant remains open 24 hours per day, seven days a week. Most of the production workers including the foremen work a shift-pattern.

1.14 Conclusion

In this chapter we have sought to criticise some of the accepted wisdom surrounding the terms information and information system. Information is data placed within a meaningful context. Information is signs. Signs are inherently associated with human interpretation, understanding, and communication. Therefore, in semiotic terms, information can be considered at a number of different levels: pragmatics, semantics, syntactics and empirics.

An information system is a system designed to support human activity. We distinguished between three levels of information system: informal, formal and technical information systems. Informal information systems consist of systems of norms, values and beliefs. Formal information systems consist of systems of rules and regulations. Technical information systems are systems of data and process.

In the next chapter we take forward these distinctions in a discussion of approaches for building technical information systems.

1.15 References

Backhouse J., Liebenau J. and Land F. (1991). On the Discipline of Information Systems. *Journal of Information Systems.* 1(1). January. 19-27.

Bell D. (1976). *The Coming of Post-Industrial Society.* Harper and Row, New York.

Bell D. (1979). The Social Framework of the Information Society. In Dertouzos M.L. and Moses J. *The Computer Age: A Twenty Year View.* MIT Press. Cambridge, Mass.

Checkland P. (1980). *Systems Thinking, Systems Practice.* John Wiley, Chichester.

Checkland P. and Scholes J. (1990). *Soft Systems Methodology in Action.* John Wiley, Chichester.

Earl M.J. (Ed.). (1988). *Information Management: The Strategic Dimension.* Clarendon Press, Oxford.

Earl M.J. (1989). *Management Strategies for Information Technology.* Prentice-Hall, Hemel Hempstead, UK.

Hodges A. (1983). *Alan Turing: the Enigma.* Hutchinson, London.

Liebenau J. and Backhouse J. (1990). *Understanding Information: An Introduction.* Macmillan, Houndmills, Basingstoke.

Palmer C. (1990). Hybrids - A Growing Initiative. *The Computer Bulletin.* 2(6). August.

Sowa J.F. (1984). *Conceptual Structures: Information Processing in Mind and Machine.* Addison-Wesley. Reading, Mass.

Stamper R.K. (1973). *Information in Business and Administrative Systems*. Batsford, London.

Stamper R.K. (1985). Information: Mystical Fluid or a Subject for Scientific Enquiry? *The Computer Journal*. 28(3).

Tsitchizris D.C. and Lochovsky F.H. (1982). *Data Models*. Prentice-Hall, Englewood Cliffs, NJ.

Wilcocks L. and Mason D. (1987). *Computerising Work: People, Systems Design and Workplace Relations*. Paradigm, London.

1.16 Keywords

Data
Empirics
Formal Information System
Human Activity System
Informal Information System
Information
Information Society
Information Management
Knowledge
Pragmatics
Semantics
Semiotics
Sign
Soft Systems Analysis
Syntactics
Technical Information System

1.17 Exercises

1. An insurance society wishes to produce a list of all the claims made against policies. Analyse this report in terms of the distinction between data, information and knowledge.
2. Analyse the claims report in terms of Stamper's distinction between semantics, syntactics, pragmatics and empirics.
3. Discuss the concept of a university in terms of a human activity system.
4. Are we, or are we not, an information society?
5. Detail some of the ways information technology might affect business strategy.
6. If all the products of information systems can be regarded as signs, discuss the problems involved in individuals and groups misinterpreting certain of these signs.
7. Discuss the effectiveness of the highway code as a sign system.

2 Information Systems Engineering

2.1 Introduction

In the previous chapter we introduced the context for information systems development in terms of preliminary definitions for the terms information and information system. We also discussed some of the consequences of information and information systems for organisations, the economy and society.

In this chapter we introduce some of the major themes affecting the development of technical (computerised) information systems. We particularly consider the major ideas concerning appropriate ways of developing technical information systems.

2.2 The Software Problem

Over the last 20 to 30 years the performance of computer hardware has increased by an order of 100. In the same period, software performance has increased only by an order of 10. This is usually described as 'the software problem', 'the applications backlog', 'the software bottleneck' or the 'hardware-software gap' (Boehm, 1981).

The software bottleneck is really the high-level representation of a series of smaller problems, such as:

1. Users cannot obtain applications when they want them. There is often a delay of years.
2. It is difficult, if not impossible, to obtain changes to systems in a reasonable amount of time.
3. Systems have errors in them, or often do not work.
4. Systems delivered do not match user requirements.
5. Systems cost much more to develop and maintain than anticipated.

Figure 2.1 illustrates the software problem in more humorous form.

2.3 Information Systems Development as Engineering

Stimulated by problems such as those above, in recent years there has been an attempt to establish information systems development as an engineering discipline.

13

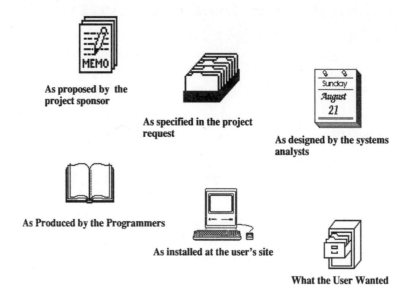

As proposed by the project sponsor

As specified in the project request

As designed by the systems analysts

As Produced by the Programmers

As installed at the user's site

What the User Wanted

Figure 2.1   The Software Problem

The British Computer Society, for instance, has long seen itself as the professional body for information systems engineering in the UK.

In this section we seek to define the remit of the information systems engineer. In particular we define information systems engineering as a discipline which encompasses three interrelated areas of computing: software engineering, information engineering and knowledge engineering.

2.3.1 Software Engineering

Many solutions to the software problem have been proposed. One of the most influential has been to try to cast software development as an engineering exercise. Boehm (1976) defines software engineering in the following terms:

"Software engineering is the practical application of scientific knowledge to the design and construction of computer programs and the associated documentation required to develop, operate and maintain them."

This rather general definition captures the all-encompassing nature of the term software engineering. This definition is however somewhat vague. It contains at least one term — scientific knowledge — which is subject to a number of different interpretations. A more pragmatic definition of software engineering is given below:

Software engineering is the systematic application of an appropriate set of techniques to the whole process of software development.

This definition concisely states the three most important principles of software engineering:

1. A set of techniques is used to increase quality and productivity.
2. The techniques are applied in a disciplined, not a haphazard way.
3. The techniques are applied to the whole process of software development.

One of the important themes of software engineering is the emphasis on a clear structure for software development. This is usually contrasted with the traditional, ad-hoc, approach to software development (see section 2.4.1).

2.3.2 Information Engineering

Originating in the work of Finklestein and Martin (Martin, 1984), information engineering has been an effective complement to software engineering. Information engineering is defined by Martin in the following terms:

> "The term software engineering refers to the set of disciplines used for specifying, designing and programming computer software. The term information engineering refers to the set of interrelated disciplines which are needed to build a computerised enterprise based on data systems. The primary focus of information engineering is on the data that are stored and maintained by computers and the information that is distilled from these data."

Martin discusses the way in which information engineering builds itself on a number of premises:

1. That data lie at the centre of modern data processing.
2. That the types of, or structure of, data used in an organisation do not change very much.
3. That given a collection of data, we can find a way to represent it logically.
4. That data are relatively stable, but processes that use this data change rapidly.
5. That because data remain relatively stable, whereas processes are subject to rapid change, data-oriented techniques succeed if correctly applied where process-oriented techniques have failed.

Figure 2.2 illustrates the basic idea underlying these premises. The skyscraper blocks represent individual applications or processes (the life-blood of software engineering) which are subject to rapid change. All such processes are built on the same bedrock, information engineered foundations, which, by their very nature, must remain relatively stable.

The term information engineering is also used to indicate a particular commercial information systems development methodology (see chapter 21).

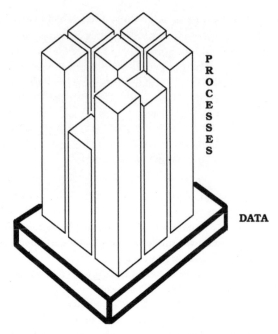

Figure 2.2   Data as a Stable Foundation

2.3.3 Knowledge Engineering

Knowledge engineering is the discipline devoted to the effective construction of knowledgebase systems, i.e., systems that represent knowledge. One of the main conclusions we shall come to is that information systems specialists are not simply software engineers or information engineers, they are also knowledge engineers. The fundamental problem of information systems development is how to represent some subset of organisational knowledge in a computational medium. This is the issue of knowledge representation — a well-discussed topic in Artificial Intelligence. It is for this reason that we include a chapter on knowledgebase systems in our tools section. The information systems developer needs better tools for knowledge representation, and knowledgebase systems are one such tool (Beynon-Davies, 1992).

2.4 Paradigms in Information Systems Development

Kuhn (1970) defines a paradigm as being a set of "universally recognised scientific achievements that for a time provide model problems and solutions to a community of practitioners". Although Kuhn uses this construct to explain the social nature of revolutions in the mature natural sciences, the concept is useful for our purposes in describing the structure of modern-day information systems development.

In our terms, a paradigm might be defined as a sometimes loosely organised framework of concepts which guides activity. Kuhn says that "men whose research is based on shared paradigms are committed to the same rules and standards for scientific practice". In information systems development we normally mean by a paradigm a suggested approach to building information systems. The approach might incorporate a particular philosophy, use particular tools, techniques and methods and even have a suggested area of application.

Most inventions in computing, particularly the paradigmatic shifts of commercial computing, are subject to a phenomenon which we might call the hype curve. Figure 2.3 is meant to illustrate the idea of plotting the degree of 'hype' against time. Any paradigm initially receives an enormous amount of attention, the usual state of affairs being to portray it as the saviour of computing. After a while, (5 years seems average), the amount of 'hype' seems to diminish. Lessons are learned about the true place of the techniques, tools and methods embodied in a paradigm. Much of the paradigm becomes incorporated into the established practice of computing. Note however that no paradigm loses all of its hype.

All five of the paradigms addressed in this chapter have been subject to a form of hype curve. At least one, object-oriented development, is still very much on the upward swing of its curve. Hype seems to be a necessary component of most commercial computing concepts.

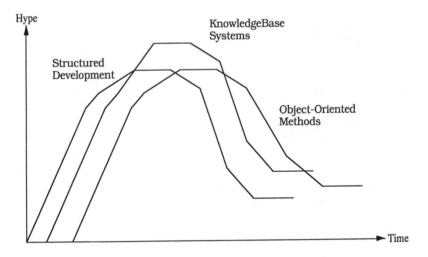

Figure 2.3   Hype Curves

2.4.1 The Ad-Hoc Approach

The traditional approach to information systems development is normally portrayed in the following terms:

1. Applications were developed in a piecemeal manner.
2. Applications primarily addressed the operational levels of business.
3. Analysis was driven by the conventional activities of business.
4. Documentation was in terms of flow-charts and narrative.
5. No formal guidance was given on what to do.
6. There was a concentration on description of a solution in computing terms.

In contrast, contemporary information systems development is normally portrayed in the following terms:

1. Emphasis on integrated applications.
2. Applications at the tactical and strategic levels of business.
3. Emphasis on structure.
4. Emphasis on both data and process concerns.
5. Vast array of graphically-based techniques available.
6. Emphasis on a step-by-step approach to development.
7. Emphasis on documenting the problem domain in terms of logical and conceptual models.

In this sense, the ad-hoc approach is normally used as a base-line from which to compare other, more systematic approaches to systems development.

2.4.2 Structured Programming, Design and Analysis

In response to a dissatisfaction with traditional approaches to systems development three more rigorous areas of computing have been developed (King, 1984):

1. Structured Programming. The attempt to construct a disciplined programming methodology based upon clear ideas as to the appropriate syntax for procedural programming languages. This was the emphasis of the late 1960s and early 1970s in the computing world.
2. Structured Design. The discipline of building hierarchical systems of modular software. This was the emphasis of the mid to late 1970s.
3. Structured Analysis. An attempt to separate the logical from the physical description of information systems. The emphasis of the early 1980s.

These three areas, traditionally seen as sub-disciplines of software engineering, have now become accepted practice within conventional information systems development. They correspond roughly to the three major stages of the software development process: analysis, design and implementation.

2.4.3 Information Management

Whereas structured programming, design and analysis may be seen as sub-disciplines of software engineering, information management is clearly a sub-discipline of information engineering.

In recent years it has become clear that information is a resource of high value to organisations. In this sense, data, viewed as a corporate asset, must be managed in the same way as any other corporate resource. In other words, information resource management pertains to data in the same way as human resource management pertains to people. Data, like people, are subject to sound management principles.

Information resource management has emerged as a discipline for managing not only the data needed to support the activities of an organisation, but also for planning the use of information for competitive advantage. The aim of information resource management is to develop a complete corporate information architecture. This architecture defines the structure of a company's data. It defines a data model for the entire enterprise (see chapter 23).

No longer is it sufficient to see data merely as a means of handling the routine, administrative tasks of the organisation. Data can also be used in a more proactive role as a means of strategically improving the market share of a company. Earl (1989), for instance, cites numerous examples of the way in which data embodied in information technology can take on a more strategic and tactical role.

2.4.4 Object-Oriented Development

Many information systems approaches, such as information mangement, concentrate on data rather than process. This means that the prime area of concern is the data needed to support organisational behaviour. The processes undertaken in any enterprise are seen to be by-products of, or reliant upon, organisational data. This emphasis encourages a global integrated view of organisational data.

However, no consensus has been reached in the information systems development world as to the best way of producing information systems. An equal number of methods concentrate on process rather than data. Organisational activities are seen to be the driving force of any enterprise. Organisational data is seen to derive from an analysis of these activities.

Recently an object-oriented approach has been proposed. The main objective of object-orientation is to attempt to integrate the process and data views of information systems. We shall consider this integrative role in chapter 25.

2.4.5 Formal Methods

One of the major emphases of structured approaches to software development is the attempt to improve the correspondence between the specification of a problem and the implementation of a solution in terms of some information system. Making a specification more precise in this manner usually means searching for ways to make unambiguous statements about what a program or system should achieve.

Because the most unambiguous language available to us is that of mathematics, a recent trend has been towards more mathematical and hence provable methods of system specification. These are the so-called formal methods of system specification, a brief overview of which is given in chapter 17.

2.4.6 Soft Systems Analysis

All stages of the information systems development process are now seen as subject to some form of user group review. User involvement has been shown to produce better systems in terms of a closer match between user requirements and finalised systems.

We shall particularly emphasise how an analysis of the informal systems of organisations (what we might call 'soft' systems analysis) is as equally as important as analysis of the formal information systems of organisations ('hard' systems analysis). We shall equate the term soft systems analysis with the term business analysis (see chapter 20).

2.5 Models of the Development Process

The most developed contemporary paradigm for information systems development is undoubtedly that of structured programming, analysis and design. In this section we examine the dominant model of development associated with this paradigm and briefly contrast it with a number of alternatives.

Structured information systems development is usually seen as being made up of a series of well-defined stages, with well-defined inputs to each stage, and well-defined outputs from each stage (see figure 2.4).

In large organisations, there are usually a large number of requests for applications. To handle such a diversity of applications formally, most such enterprises engage in some form of project selection process. The purpose of such a selection process is to identify the most suitable applications for development in terms of organisational objectives.

The primary mechanism of the project selection process is the project selection committee. This committee does not examine each project in detail. This is the responsibility of the feasibility study. Here, a systems analyst, or team of systems analysts, identifies the initial framework for the application, and investigates whether it is feasible to tackle the project given the available organisational resources. The end-result of the feasibility study is the feasibility report. This report is presented to relevant users who offer their comments and opinions. This user input may then be fed back into the feasibility study which produces a revised report.

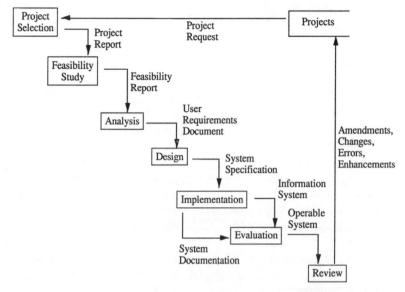

Figure 2.4   The Waterfall Model of Development

In a sense, the project selection process and the feasibility study act as two 'filters' at the beginning of the development life-cycle. Project selection is a coarse-grained filter. Its objective is to reject those projects which are patently unsuitable. The feasibility study is a fine-grained filter. Its objective is to reject projects on more detailed grounds. This 'project hopper' is illustrated in figure 2.5.

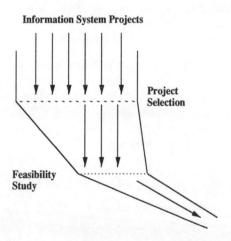

Figure 2.5   Project Selection and Feasibility Study

A typical feasibility report will contain a list of problems in the current environment, a list of requirements for the proposed system, an overview analysis of the major activities and data of the proposed systems, a list of possible technical options for implementation, and a summary of the costs and benefits of the system.

Once the users are satisfed with the feasibility report, it is fed into the analysis phase. The end-result of this phase is the user specification or user requirements document. Elements of this requirements specification are continually reviewed with end-users until they are satisfied that the requirements adequately describe their needs. Most contemporary requirements documents exploit a series of graphic notations for expressing processing and data details. A 'tool-kit' of such techniques is presented in part two.

The requirements document is a logical or implementation-independent view of the proposed information system. This must be turned into a physical or implementation-dependent view of the system through the process of design. The end-result of the design phase, the systems specification, is again reviewed with users until all interested parties are happy with progress.

The completed design document is used to direct the production of the application system. Programmers are given specifications for the various modules of the system, and proceed to program them in the language and on the hardware chosen for the implementation. Another important product of the implementation phase is documentation. This must describe the working system both for technical staff and for the end-user.

The system, once written and tested, must be subject to a critical evaluation phase. This primarily means comparing the system produced with elements of the original requirements document to check that the system has achieved its objectives.

Once the system is in operation, it is usually subject to a whole series of user reviews. Such reviews are likely to generate a whole series of further project requests - amendments to the existing system, suggestions for new systems etc. - which feed back into the project selection process.

Software development is often referred to as a cycle for two major reasons:

1. It is subject to a whole series of small iterations surrounding the user reviews, both within phases and between phases.
2. A system is seldom 100% complete. Users will continually want errors in the system corrected, parts of the system changed, or major extensions added. Software maintenance is therefore a critical factor which should influence all aspects of the development process.

2.5.1 *Alternative Models of the Development Process*

The linear or 'waterfall' model of information systems development as described above is the one that has achieved a certain pre-eminence in recent times. There are however a number of other contrasting models that have been proposed:

1. Rapid Prototyping. A more incremental method of systems development, usually called prototyping, or sometimes rapid prototyping, has come back into favour. Figure 2.6a illustrates the essential elements of a pure prototyping approach. Here, the emphasis is on rapidly developing elements of a working system and continuously feeding back the results of user evaluation. The prototype that emerges from this exercise is regarded as the working system.
2. Structured Prototyping. A more cautious vision of prototyping is illustrated in figure 2.6b. Here prototyping is seen primarily as a requirements elicitation tool. A working version of the technical information system is not expected as the result of the prototyping exercise. Instead, the prototype is documented in a requirements specification before undertaking design.

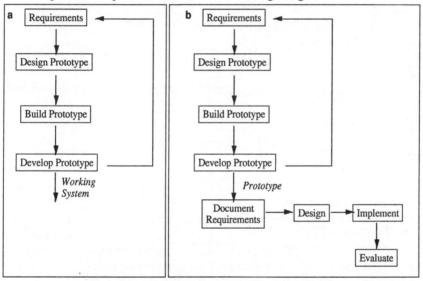

Figure 2.6   Rapid and Structured Prototyping

3. Evolutionary Development. In contrast to the monolithic nature of the waterfall model, this approach calls for a series of development efforts, each of which leads to a delivered product. Each delivered product provides some needed operational capability while also generating further requirements (Crinnion 1991). Figure 2.7 illustrates this idea.
4. Boehm (1987) has proposed a hybrid approach known as the spiralist model. The radial coordinate in figure 2.8 represents the total cost incurred on a project to date. Each loop of the spiral, from the X axis clockwise through 360 degrees represents one phase of development. A phase may be waterfall-based, prototyping-based, or evolutionary-based. The decision as to which model to use, or whether to terminate the project, is made at each crossing of the X axis.

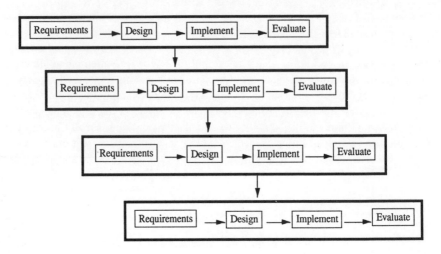

Figure 2.7   Evolutionary Development

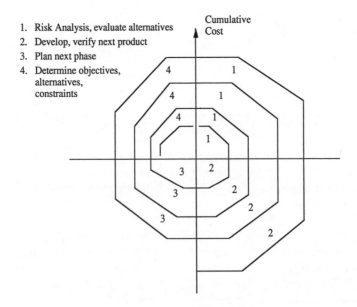

Figure 2.8   The Spiral Model of Development

2.6 Conclusion

In this chapter we have laid some of the groundwork for considering information systems development as an engineering discipline. We first identified the primary problem, the mismatch between developments in hardware and software. We then distinguished between three major sub-disciplines which are attempts to alleviate this problem: software engineering, information engineering and knowledge engineering. A number of paradigms are identifiable under the umbrella of these three: structured programming, design and analysis; information management; object-oriented development; formal methods; soft systems analysis. Finally, we turned attention to a number of models of the development process: the waterfall model; rapid prototyping; structured prototyping; evolutionary development and the spiral-ist model.

2.7 References

Beynon-Davies P. (1992). *Knowledge Engineering for Information Systems.* McGraw-Hill, London.

Boehm B.W. (1976). Software Engineering. *IEEE Transactions on Computers.* 25. 1226-1241.

Boehm B.W. (1981). *Software Engineering Economics.* Prentice-Hall, Englewood-Cliffs, NJ.

Boehm B.W. (1987). The Spiral Model of Software Development and Enhancement. In R.H.Thayer (Ed.) *Software Engineering Project Management.* 128-142. IEEE Press, California.

Crinnion J. (1991). *Evolutionary Systems Development.* Pitman, London.

Earl M.J. (1989). *Management Strategies for Information Technology.* Prentice-Hall, Hemel Hempstead, UK.

King D. (1984). *Current Practices in Software Development: A Guide to Successful Systems.* Yourdon Press, New York.

Kuhn T.S. (1970). *The Structure of Scientific Revolutions.* (2nd Ed.). University of Chicago Press, London.

Martin J. (1984). *An Information Systems Manifesto.* Prentice-Hall, Englewood-Cliffs, NJ.

2.8 Keywords

Evolutionary Development
Hype Curve
Information Engineering

Information Management
Information Systems Engineering
Knowledge Engineering
Rapid Prototyping
Soft Systems Analysis
Software Problem
Software Engineering
Spiralist Model
Structured Analysis
Structured Design
Structured Programming
Structured Prototyping
Waterfall Model

2.9 Exercises

1. Detail three problems, other than those mentioned, associated with the software bottleneck.
2. Distinguish between software and information engineering.
3. Why do you think so many developments in computing are subject to the hype curve?
4. Why do you think information systems developers aspire to be engineers?
5. Why do you think there are so many different models of information systems development?
6. Kuhn's idea of a paradigm relates to a research consensus. In this sense, do the streams discussed in section 2.4 really constitute paradigms?

3 Technical Information Systems

3.1 Introduction

In chapter one we discussed a three-fold division of information systems into informal information systems, formal information systems and technical information systems. In this chapter we discuss an abstract model of a technical information system.

It is useful to divide a technical information system into four major subsystems. Each subsystem is characterised in terms of its responsibilities (see figure 3.1):

1. Data Subsystem. This subsystem is responsible for managing the underlying data needed by an application.
2. Process Subsystem. This subsystem is responsible for managing the processes that transform data.
3. User Interface Subsystem. This subsystem is responsible for maintaining all interaction with the user.
4. Control Subsystem. This subsystem is responsible for controlling the operation of the processing, data and interface subsystems.

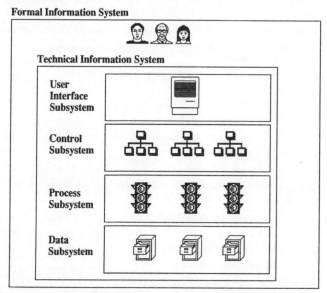

Figure 3.1   Architecture of a Technical Information System

27

Take the example of a technical information system set up for the business which handles claims made against insurance companies as the result of motor accidents.

1. The data subsystem of this information system will encompass the various files on insurance brokers, claims, solicitors, etc. All interaction with these files occurs via this subsystem. In other words, files will be read, written to and updated.
2. The process subsystem of this information system will be made up of various sets of file maintenance operations such as record retrieval, insertion, update and deletion. The production of derived data needed on reports is a further responsibility of this subsystem.
3. The user interface is normally made up of strategies for managing screens, keyboards and printers. Data might be entered into the system via form-like screens and reports produced on printers.
4. The control subsystem will be made up of an architecture of components and an appropriate strategy for combining components. For instance, the control system will associate given data entry screens with given processes with given files.

3.2 Building Technical Information Systems

For many years the four component parts of a technical information system have been built using one tool — the high-level programming language (see chapter 4). A language such as COBOL is used to declare appropriate file structures, encode the necessary operations on files, embed the operations in control structures and manage the terminal screen for user entry and retrieval.

However, over the last twenty years there has been a tendency to attempt to seperate out each component, and provide a separate tool for each job:

1. For instance, database management systems (chapter 6) have been developed primarily as a means of enhancing program-data independence. This is the ideal of separating programs and data such that changes to data structures have a limited effect on data, and vice versa.
2. Knowledgebase systems (chapter 9) can be seen as an attempt to further separate control mechanisms (inference engines) from processes (rules) and data (facts).
3. With the development of direct manipulation interfaces (chapter 19), the tendency has been to supply GUI (Graphic User Interface) tools for the production of specialised interfaces.
4. Many modern analysis and design methods (see part 3), particularly those under the umbrella of object-orientation (see chapter 25) propose the separate development of the four components described above.

All of these developments mean that it is likely that the technical information system of the future will be a hybrid. In other words, it will be built using a range of distinct technologies. This issue is discussed in chapter 30.

3.3 Hardware

This book is primarily devoted to the process of developing information systems from software, data and people components. The other component in the equation, namely hardware or electronic computing machinery, is discussed in numerous other texts (Wright, 1984). In this section we discuss the minimum of concepts necessary to appreciate the hardware side of technical information systems.

3.3.1 Turing Machines

A modern-day computer is a physical implementation of an abstract machine known as a Turing machine, so-called because it was proposed by Alan Turing in the 1930s (Hodges, 1983). Turing conjectured that a Turing machine possesses the power to solve any problem that is solvable by computational means. Hence, Turing machines are generally described as being 'universal' machines.

A Turing machine is made up of two parts: a control mechanism and an input medium (Brookshear, 1989). The control mechanism can be in one of a finite number of states at any time. One of these states is deemed to be the initial state and another the halt state of the machine.

The input medium is normally characterised as an infinitely long piece of paper tape. The machine is equipped with a tape head which is used to both read and write symbols on the paper tape. A machine can move the tape both backwards and forwards through the tape head.

The individual actions that can be performed by a Turing machine consist of write actions and move actions. A write operation consists of replacing a symbol on the tape with another symbol and then shifting to a new state. A move operation consists of moving the tape head one cell to the right or one cell to the left and then shifting to a new state. Which action will be performed at a particular time depends on the current symbol in the cell visible to the tape head as well as the current state of the the machine's control mechanism.

Turing's original 'machine' was a human acting with pencil and paper. It was only with the advent of electronic equipment that the Turing machines could be practically realised. However, the important point is that the theoretical computational abilities of the system remain the same regardless of the technology. In fact, Turing's model is more general than today's electronic computers, since a Turing machine is never restricted by lack of storage space (it uses a tape of infinite length), whereas an actual machine must employ finite storage, however great.

The other important characteristic of a Turing machine is that it demonstrated that any computational process can be 'programmed'. That is, a set of instructions can be given to such a machine to determine its behaviour.

3.3.2 The Components of Hardware

Figure 3.2 illustrates the four primary components of computing hardware:

1. Input. Usually via a keyboard.
2. Processing. The central processing unit (CPU).
3. Storage. Secondary storage devices such as disk drives.
4. Output. Usually via monitors or printers.

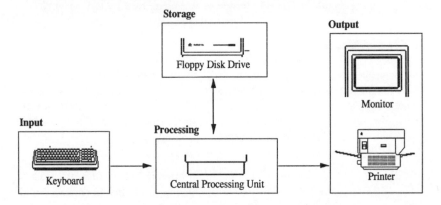

Figure 3.2   The Components of a Computer System

To this we might add that modern-day computers are seldom purely standalone devices. Most computers, particularly in business organisations, are connected to other machines via short-haul or long-haul communication lines. A collection of machines connected by short-haul communication lines is known as a local area network. A collection joined by long-haul communication lines is known as a wide area network. Computer networks are a major component in the prevalent strategy of distributed computing — i.e., siting computer power where it is needed.

The workhorse of a computing machine is the CPU. The central processing unit can be subdivided into the following components (figure 3.3):

1. The Control Unit directs and coordinates the rest of the system in carrying out program instructions.
2. The Logic Unit calculates and compares data, based on instructions from the controller.
3. The Primary Storage Unit holds data for processing, instructions for processing and processed data waiting to be output.
4. Communication between these three components is effected by physical connections known as buses.

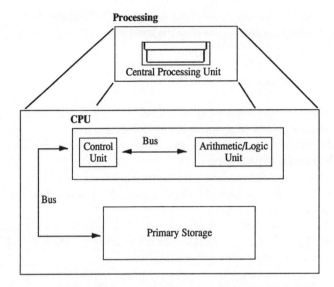

Figure 3.3   The Central Processing Unit

3.4 Software

Software is computer programs. A computer program is a series of instructions for hardware. Programs transform the universal machine embodied in hardware into a machine specialised for some task.

It is useful to delineate a number of different levels of software, of which the most important are:

1. Operating systems. These are programs which supervise the running of all other programs on some hardware. The operating system schedules the running of programs, controls input and output to each program, and manages files on secondary storage.
2. Program Languages. These are formal languages for writing instructions. There are various levels of program languages as discussed in chapter 4.
3. Applications. This is another term for technical information system. An application system is a system, normally written using some language, and designed to perform a particular task.

3.5 Data Analysis and Process Analysis

Our model of technical information systems is useful in identifying a number of different streams of information systems analysis.

Any technical information system can be viewed in two distinct but complementary modes: the dynamic view and the static view.

1. The dynamic view emphasises the importance of process. How data flows through an information system and is transformed by the various processes making up the information system.
2. The static view emphasises data. How data is or should be organised in order to support organisational processes.

We document the dynamic view of an information system in a process model. We document the static view of an information system in a data model. Both the data model and the process model are needed to form a complete information systems model. The activity of producing a data model is known as data analysis (Part 3, section 1). The activity of producing a process model is known as process analysis (Part 3, section 2). The analysis of control subsystems is usually subsumed under process analysis.

To the process model and data model we should also add the user interface model. A great deal of literature has now developed surrounding the analysis and design of user interfaces. We discuss this material in chapter 19.

3.6 A Standard Application System

A standard application system will be made up of the following components, many of which will cross the boundaries of the four subsystems discussed above:

1. Menus. Normally used as a means of allowing users to navigate around the system.
2. Data entry screens. These allow users to enter data into the files making up the data subsystem.
3. Data retrieval screens. These allow users normally to select given records from the system based on various criteria.
4. Reports. Complex retrieval functions are normally produced as reports output to printers.
5. Internal modules. These are routines designed to perform processing internal to the system. An example might be a routine which updated customers' balances overnight.

3.7 Goronwy Galvanising

In this section we discuss further the current system at Goronwy Galvanising.

Black products are delivered to Goronwy on large trailers in bundles referred to as batches. Each trailer may be loaded with a number of different types of steel product. Each batch is labelled with a unique job number. Each trailer is given its own advice note detailing all the associated jobs on the trailer.

Goronwy mainly process lintels for a major steel manufacturer, Blackheads. The advice note supplied with lintels is identified by an advice number specific to this manufacturer. Each job is identified on the advice note by a job number generated through Blackheads' check digit routine. Figure 3.4 represents a typical advice note received from Blackheads detailing the black material on a trailer.

Smaller manufacturers like Pimples supply an advice note in which jobs are identified by a concatenation of an advice number and line number on which the job appears. Each job, whether it be for Blackheads or Pimples, is also described on the advice note in terms of a product code, description, item length, order quantity and batch weight. Each advice is dated.

On arrival at the plant the material is unpacked and checked for discrepancies between the material indicated on the advice note and the material actually on the trailer. Two major types of discrepancy are important. A count discrepancy occurs when the number of steel items actually found is less than or greater than the amount indicated. A non-conforming black discrepancy arises when some of the material is unsuitable for galvanising. For instance, a steel lintel may be bent. Such discrepancies are written as annotations to the advice note.

When all material has been checked, the advice note is given to the production controller. He and the office clerk transcribe details, including any discrepancies, from the advice note onto job sheets. An example job sheet is illustrated in figure 3.5. The job sheet is passed down onto the shop floor where the shift foreman uses it to record details of processing.

Most jobs will pass through the system smoothly. The steel items will be placed

Blackheads Steel Products				Despatch Advice		
Advice No. *A3137*				**Date** *11-1-88*		
Customer & Address				**Instructions**		
Goronwy Galvanising, Cardiff				*Galvanise & Return*		
Order Number	Description	Product Code	Item Length	Number This Delivery	Weight (tonnes)	
13/1193G	*Lintels*		*1500*	*20*		
44/2404G			*1500*	*20*		
70/2517P			*1350*	*20*		
23/2474P			*1200*	*16*		
Hauliers Name *International 5*		**Received in Good Order and Sound Condition**				

Figure 3.4   Goronwy Delivery Advice

Job Sheet					
Advice No. *A3137*			**Date** 11/1/92		

Order Number	Description	Product Code	Item Length	Order Qty	Batch Weight
13/1193G	*Lintels*	*UL15*	*1500*	*20*	

Count discrepancy	Non-Conforming Black	Non-Conforming White	Non-Conforming No Charge

Galvanised	Despatches			
Y	Despatch Number	Despatch Date	Qty Returned	Weight Returned

Figure 3.5   Goronwy Job Sheet

on racks, dipped in the zinc bath and left to cool. The site foreman will then check the condition of the job. If all items have galvanised properly he will tick the job completed box on the job sheet and pass it back to the production controller.

Occasionally, some of the items will not have galvanised properly. Such items are then classed as non-conforming white, and indicated as such on the job sheet. These items will normally be re-galvanised at some later date.

When Goronwy have treated a series of jobs the production controller will issue a despatch note and send it down to the shop-floor. Workers will then stack the white material on trailers ready to be returned to the associated manufacturers. Each trailer will have an associated advice note detailing the material on the trailer. Partial despatches may be made from one job. This means that the trailer of white material need not correspond to the trailer of black material originally supplied to Goronwy. The despatch advice is given a unique advice number and is dated. Each despatch details the job number, product code, description, item length, batch weight, returned quantity and returned weight. Figure 3.6 represents a despatch advice prepared for Goronwy for a collection of white material.

3.8 References

Brookshear J.G. (1989). *Theory of Computation: Formal Languages, Automata and Complexity*. Benjamin-Cummings, Redwood City.

Hodges A. (1983). *Alan Turing: The Enigma*. Hutchinson, London.

Goronwy Galvanising		Despatch Advice					
Advice No. *101*			**Date** *12/02/90*				
Customer & Address *Blackheads,* *Cardiff*							
Order Number	**Description**	**Product Code**	**Item Length**	**Order Qty**	**Batch Weight**	**Returned Qty**	**Returned Weight**
13/1193G	*Lintels*	*UL15*	*1500*	*20*	*150*	*20*	*150*
44/2404G		*UL15*	*1500*	*20*	*150*	*20*	*150*
70/2517P		*UL135*	*1350*	*20*	*135*	*20*	*135*
23/2474P		*UL12*	*1200*	*16*	*100*	*14*	*82*
Driver		**Received By**					

Figure 3.6   Goronwy Despatch Advice

Wright G.G.L. (1984). *Mastering Computers*. 2nd Ed. Macmillan, London.

3.9 Keywords

Control Subsystem
Data Subsystem
Hardware
Process Subsystem
Technical Information System
Turing Machine
User Interface Subsystem

3.10 Exercises

1. Why are computers referred to as 'universal' machines?
2. Try de-coupling the data, process, user interface, and control subsystems of some technical information system with which you are familiar.
3. What advantages do you think arise from separating out the four components of a technical information system?
4. Discuss in which of the four subsystems each of the standard components of an application system would need to be placed.

Part Two
Tools

Tool

Thing designed to help or enable the hand to apply force. (*Oxford English Dictionary*)

Implement, instrument, apparatus, appliance. (*Roget's Thesaurus*)

This part discusses a common set of tools used to build contemporary technical information systems. We also discuss a number of elements of technology, such as object-oriented programming languages, hypermedia systems and knowledgebase systems, which are beginning to impact on the process of information systems development.

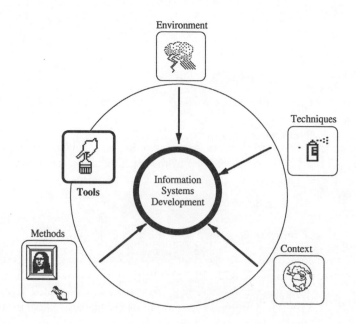

4 Structured Programming Languages

4.1 Introduction

Programming languages are used to describe algorithms — i.e. sequences of steps that lead to the solution of problems. Programming languages are broadly classified into two groups: low-level languages and high-level languages. Low-level languages are close to machine languages. They demonstrate a strong correspondence between the operations implemented by the language and the operations implemented by the underlying hardware. High-level languages in contrast are closer to human languages. Each statement in a high-level language will be equivalent to many statements of a low-level language. The key advantage offered by high-level languages is therefore abstraction. As the level of abstraction increases the programmer needs to be less and less concerned about the hardware on which a program runs and more and more concerned with the problems of the application. Hence, the trend has been to build more and more abstraction into programming languages.

In this chapter we concentrate primarily on high-level languages, illustrating concepts using the language Pascal. In chapter 5 we look at a particular set of languages known as object-oriented languages, and in chapter 7 we look at fourth generation languages.

4.2 Generations of Programming Languages

There is some consensus that there have been at least three generations of programming languages:

1. Machine code. This is the earliest form of programming language, only one step removed from the binary code used by the machine to perform instructions.
2. Assembly language. This was the first attempt to abstract out detail of the machine and provide the programmer with a more powerful set of symbolic instructions with which to write programs.
3. High-level languages (also known as third generation languages). These are meant to be general-purpose programming languages removed from machine implementation. Such languages can be divided into further groupings such as imperative languages (FORTRAN, COBOL, C), functional languages (LISP), logic programming languages (PROLOG), and object-oriented languages (Smalltalk, C++). Imperative languages are by far the most widely used for

37

information systems development, although object-oriented languages in particular are beginning to have an influence. Figure 4.1 illustrates a family tree of high-level languages.

Some people talk of fourth generation languages and some even of fifth generation languages. Fourth generation languages and environments are the topic of chapter 7. Fifth generation languages are discussed in chapter 9.

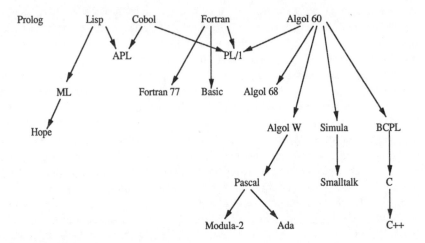

Figure 4.1   A Family Tree of High-Level Languages

4.3 Structured Languages

In 1965, a Dutch academic named Edsgar Dijkstra presented a paper in which he described how programming could be reduced to a few basic rules. One of these rules called for the elimination of GOTOs from programming languages. The other rules detailed how programs could be built from three basic constructs: sequence, selection and iteration. This, in essence, stimulated the structured programming movement.

During the 1970s and early 1980s a series of so-called structured languages emerged. The intention was to provide a more rigorous tool-set with which to build information systems. The earliest of such languages were a group of languages known as the ALGOL family. Kernighan and Plauger (1976) brought out an influential, minimalist language at Bell labs known as C. This is currently one of the most popular of the modern-day programming languages.

4.4 The Major Constructs of Structured Programming Languages

In this section we discuss the basic building blocks of most structured programming languages. We illustrate the concepts using a simple dialect of the language Pascal, a language much-used in educational circles and a derivative of ALGOL.

Most conventional programming languages are built out of two constructs: statements and control structures.

4.4.1 Statements

Statements are the basic instructions of high-level languages. Statements are command lines built from a mixture of keywords, variables and constants. Examples of valid Pascal statements are:

```
balance := balance + credit;
READ (credit);
WRITELN ('Balance is',balance);
```

The first statement assigns the summation of the values held in the two placeholders or variables, balance and credit, to the placeholder on the left of the ':=' sign. The second statement reads a value from a file into a variable. The third statement writes a string to the terminal screen.

4.4.2 Control Structures

Control structures are used to control the flow of execution of statements. Control structures come in three major forms: sequences; conditions; and loops.

Sequences

Sequences are logical sets of statements. In Pascal it is usual to encase sequences in the keywords BEGIN and END, called a block, e.g.,

```
BEGIN
    balance := balance + credit;
    WRITELN ('Balance is',balance);
END;

BEGIN
    balance := balance – debit;
    WRITELN ('Balance is',balance);
END;
```

Note how each statement is terminated with a semicolon. Keywords are written here in uppercase merely to distinguish them from application-specific words, such as variable names.

Conditions

Conditions allow selection among alternatives. There are three forms of conditions:

1. Single-branched

```
IF credit > 0 THEN  balance := balance + credit;
```

2. Double-branched

```
IF transactionType = 'C' THEN
        balance := balance + credit
ELSE
        balance := balance – debit;
```

3. Multiple-branched

```
CASE transactionType OF
        'C': balance := balance + credit;
        'D': balance := balance – debit;
        'P': WRITELN ('Balance is',balance);
END;
```

The multiple-branched condition can be emulated by a series of deeply nested IF THEN ELSE statements. The CASE construct is however generally held to be more readable in these situations.

Loops

Loops are the mechanisms of iteration. Iterative statements come in three forms:

1. Countable loop. This form of loop is performed a specified number of times.

```
FOR count := 1 to 10 DO
    BEGIN
            READ (credit);
            balance := balance + credit;
            count := count + 1
    END;
```

2. While loop. A test is performed at the start of each iteration. If the condition specified is true the loop continues. If the condition is false, the loop terminates.

```
count := 1
WHILE count < 11 DO
    BEGIN
        READ (credit);
        balance := balance + credit;
        count := count + 1
    END;
```

3. Repeat loop. This works in a similar manner to the while loop, except that the test is performed at the end of each iteration rather than at the start.

```
count := 1
REPEAT
    READ (credit);
    balance := balance + credit;
    count := count + 1
UNTIL count = 10;
```

Other Component Parts

There are many other component parts to modern programming languages. We discuss three important parts below:

1. Declarations. Pascal programs are made up of two parts: a heading and a body. The heading provides the program name and lists the program's interfaces with its environment. The body consists of a declaration part and a statement part. All variables used in a Pascal program must be declared to be of a given data type, e.g.,

```
PROGRAM BankAccount (input, output);

VAR
balance, credit, debit: REAL;
age: INTEGER;
transactionType: CHAR;
```

The parameters of the program declared between parentheses indicate that input should be taken from the keyboard and output should be made to the

```
TYPE
    Account = RECORD
            AccountId: INTEGER;
            Balance: REAL;
    end;
```

2. Input/output. The default input/output is reading via the keyboard and writing to the screen. To read from an external file, the filename has to be specified in the parameters of the program. The simple program below reads customer identifiers from a text file named customers and displays them on the screen.

```
PROGRAM CustomersDisplay (Customers, OUTPUT);

VAR
    Customers: TEXT;
    CID: PACKED ARRAY [1..10] OF CHAR;
    Count: INTEGER;

BEGIN

    RESET (Customers);

    FOR count := 1 to 100 DO
            READLN (Customers, CID);
            WRITELN ('Customer: ':CID)
    END;

END.
```

The RESET command initialises the file pointer to the first line of the Customers file. READLN reads a customer identifier into a string of 10 characters long, and moves to the next line in the file.

3. Procedures. As we shall see in chapter 18, one of the main tenets of structured development is that any system should be built out of a series of highly cohesive but loosely coupled modules. Modules are declared in Pascal as procedures.

   A procedure is made up of three parts: a procedure heading which specifies a name for the procedure and parameters to be passed to the procedure; a series of local variable declarations; and a procedure body.

   The simple program below contains an embedded procedure. It prints out a percentage of the amount owed on a chargecard.

```
PROGRAM ChargeCard (OUTPUT);

PROCEDURE PrintOwed(Balance, Percentage:INTEGER);

VAR
    Payment: INTEGER;

BEGIN
    Payment : = Balance * Percentage DIV 100;
    WRITELN ('Pay £ ',Payment)
END;

END.
```

4.5 Conclusion

The high-level programming language is still the medium in which most commercial information systems are constructed. COBOL, originally an unstructured language, still maintains its place as the dominant language for commercial development. However, the lessons of good structure have influenced much of the style of modern-day COBOL programming.

Having said this, much modern development occurs in structured languages. By far the most prevalent is the language C. Because of its portability, many other tools such as DBMS and 4GLs are written in this language. In the next chapter we consider a number of concepts embodied in a popular superset of C known as C++.

4.6 References

Kernighan B.W. and Plauger P.J. (1976). *Software Tools*. Addison-Wesley, Reading, Mass.

4.7 Keywords

Assembly Language
Block
Condition
Control Structure
Declaration
High-Level Language

Imperative Language
Loop
Machine Code
Procedure
Sequence
Statement
Structured Language

4.8 Exercises

1. What is meant by describing a language as imperative?
2. The GOTO statement is sometimes referred to as an unconditional jump. What do you think is meant by this description?
3. Discuss some of the reasons why the GOTO statement is generally considered a dangerous programming construct.
4. Why is it useful to have both a do while and repeat until statement in modern programming languages?
5. Discuss some of the advantages of being able to build systems out of a series of related program modules.
6. Many unstructured variants of COBOL are still very much used for systems development. Why do you think this is?

5 Object-Oriented Programming Languages

5.1 Introduction

The fundamental difference between conventional and object-oriented programming (OOP) relates to the way each approach treats data and process. In conventional programming (chapter 4) data and process are separate things. To create an information system we define our data structures and then we define routines to operate upon them.

In OOP, process and data are intertwined. When we build an information system using OOP we define both data and processes to be the characteristic of objects. In this approach, information systems are seen as being composed of a large set of interacting objects.

This chapter presents an overview of OOP. We first discuss some of the major concepts of OOP. Then we discuss the development of object-oriented programming languages. Finally, we illustrate OOP with an extension to Pascal.

5.2 Objects, Methods, Messages, and Encapsulation

An object is some entity that contains data and the associated set of routines that operate on data. The data associated with an object are said to be the attributes or instance variables of an object. The routines associated with an object are referred to as an object's methods. To make an object perform one of its methods we have to send an object a message. OOP is fundamentally message-passing.

For example, we might create an object that represents a rectangle. Its attributes constitute the four corners of the rectangle. Its methods constitute routines for drawing, erasing and moving rectangles. To actually draw a rectangle, you send the object a draw message. This binding together of attributes and methods with a common interface is referred to as encapsulation.

Contrast this approach with the way we would handle rectangles using a conventional programming approach. First we would probably define a data structure that represents the four corners of the rectangle. Then we would build routines to draw, to erase and to move a rectangle. Each of these routines will take a rectangle data structure as an argument.

45

5.3 Classes

Every object belongs to an object class. The class defines the implementation of a particular kind of object. We normally say that every object is a member or instance of a class. Hence, every instance of a rectangle is a member of the class Rectangle. We might define the class Rectangle as below:

Class
Rectangle

Instance Variables
top, left, bottom, right

Methods
draw line from point to point
erase lines
offset points

Messages
Draw, Erase, Move

5.4 Inheritance and Polymorphism

We can define a class to be an instance of an existing class. The new class is called the subclass, and the existing class is called the superclass. A class without a superclass is said to be the root class of the hierarchy.

A class hierarchy is used to support the concept of inheritance. A subclass is said to inherit all the instance variables and methods of its superclass. Subclasses can also define additional instance variables and methods or override the methods defined in the superclass. Overriding a method means that the subclass responds to the same message as the superclass, but uses its own routine to respond to the message.

For example, suppose we create a class to represent employees of a company. We define the class as below:

Class
Employee

Methods
return name
return (today - dateOfBirth)
return 0

Superclass
none

Instance Variables
name, dateOfBirth

Messages
GetName, GetAge, GetPay

We can now define two subclasses: HourlyEmployee and WeeklyEmployee. Both subclasses inherit all the instance variables and methods of the Employee class. Each subclass however defines a new instance variable to store the appropriate salary, and each subclass overrides the GetPay method to return the appropriate weekly salary. The definitions are given below:

Class	**Class**
HourlyEmployee	WeeklyEmployee
Superclass	**Superclass**
Employee	Employee
Instance Variables	**Instance Variables**
hourlySalary	YearlySalary
Methods	**Methods**
return (hourlySalary * 40)	return (YearlySalary / 52)
Messages	**Messages**
GetPay	GetPay

Sending the same message, GetPay, to the two classes HourlyEmployee and WeeklyEmployee will therefore get the same response, but will have been implemented in different ways. This ability to send the same message to objects of different classes is known as polymorphism.

5.5 Object-Oriented Programming Languages

A vast range of contemporary programming languages claim to be object-oriented. Not all such languages however support the concepts described in sections 5.2 to 5.3. Wegner makes a useful distinction between what he calls object-based, class-based and true object-oriented languages (Wegner, 1989). Object-based languages are those languages that support the concept of an object in the sense that data and processes are encapsulated together, but do not support the concept of classes or inheritance. An example of a class-based language is Ada. Class-based languages offer support for objects and classes. An example is the language CLU. True object-oriented languages offer support for objects, classes, inheritance and the related concepts of encapsulation and polymorphism. The foremost example is SmallTalk.

5.6 Object Pascal

Many examples of conventional programming languages now offer object-oriented extensions. The advantage of this approach is that the programmer can gradually migrate from conventional to object-oriented programming. One of the most popular of such languages is C++, an object-oriented superset of C (Jordan, 1990).

To maintain consistency, in this section we consider how objects might be implemented in extensions to the language Pascal (chapter 4).

We will assume that a class declaration is similar to a record declaration. We give the class a name, specify its superclass, and declare its instance variables and methods as below:

```
TYPE
    <className> = OBJECT (<superclassName>)
        <instanceVariableDeclaration>;
            .
        <methodDeclaration>;
            .
END;
```

Suppose, for instance, we wish to create an object representing companies with which our business corresponds. We might declare it as below:

```
TYPE
    Company = OBJECT
    name: STRING;
    address: STRING;
    VATNo: INTEGER;
    CONSTRUCTOR Init(initName, initAddress: STRING,
    initVat: INTEGER);
    FUNCTION GetName: STRING;
    PROCEDURE PrintLabel;
END;
```

Note that this represents the root class of our hierarchy, since no superclass is specified. Note also that methods are defined as standard Pascal procedures and functions. Each procedure or function must then be prefixed with the class name to which it applies. For example:

```
PROCEDURE Company.PrintLabel;
BEGIN
    WRITELN (name);
    WRITELN (address)
```

```
END;
FUNCTION Company.GetName: STRING;
BEGIN
     GetName := name
END;
```

Two special types of procedure are also required: constructor and destructor. Constructor creates new instances of objects, destructor removes instances of objects. For example:

```
CONSTRUCTOR Company.Init(initName, initAddress: STRING);
BEGIN
     name := initName;
     address := initAddress;
     vatNo := initVat
END;
```

Two subclasses of the class Company can now be declared:

```
TYPE
     Supplier = OBJECT(Company)
     reliabilityRating: INTEGER;
     PROCEDURE MakeSupply(RM: RawMaterial)
END;
```

```
TYPE
     Customer = OBJECT(Company)
     creditRating: INTEGER;
     PROCEDURE MakeOrder(P: Product)
END;
```

Supplier and Customer will now inherit the instance variables and methods of the superclass Company. Each subclass also has its own instance variable and method defined for it. MakeSupply is specific to Supplier, MakeOrder is specific to Customer. If a subclass wanted to override any of the methods of a superclass then we would have to include the keyword 'override' as an additional clause in a method declaration. Suppose, for instance, we wished to produce a special form of printed label for customers. We would then override the PrintLabel method as below:

```
TYPE
     Customer = OBJECT(Company)
     creditRating: INTEGER;
     PROCEDURE MakeOrder(P: Product);
```

```
        PROCEDURE PrintLabel OVERRIDE
    END;
```

Having declared the class hierarchy, processing involves sending messages (calls) to the methods of classes. Suppose, for instance, we wish to process new customer. We might do this as follows:

```
    VAR smiths: Customer;
    .
    .
    smiths.Init('Smiths and Sons Ltd.','The Grove, Pontypridd',1234);
    .
    smiths.PrintLabel;
```

5.7 Advantages of Object-Oriented Programming

A number of advantages are claimed for OOP:

1. It is claimed that encapsulation aids maintenance in the sense that changing the implementation of a given object is relatively straightforward.
2. The emphasis of OO is on software reuse. The idea is to allow the system builder to create a framework for the new system out of readily available classes.
3. OO approaches have been proposed as a unifying paradigm for systems analysis, design and implementation. As we shall see in chapter 25, OO concepts such as encapsulation, inheritance, etc. are equally relevant to the analysis and design of systems as they are to programming.

5.8 Disadvantages of OOP

1. Resuse is only feasible if the programmer knows of the existence of existing classes. The overhead of searching and overriding existing classes may be as great as that involved in writing new code.
2. Although a number of proposals are being made, no consensus has been reached yet on appropriate ways of building OO systems.
3. OO seems particularly suited for problems which involve some aspect of real-world simulation. The case for exploiting OO in the area of traditional data processing still has to be made.

5.9 Conclusion

Object-oriented concepts are having an influence not only on programming languages but also on other varieties of software such as operating systems and DBMS. In chapter 9 we look at some related ideas in the area of knowledgebase systems. The idea of producing systems from hierarchically organised collections of classes have even influenced the areas of systems analysis and design. We discuss these issues in chapter 25.

5.10 References

Wegner P. (1989). Learning the Language. *Byte*. March. 245-253.
Jordan D. (1990). Implementation Benefits of C++ Language Mechanisms. *CACM*. 33(9). 61-64

5.11 Keywords

Encapsulation
Inheritance
Instance
Method
Message
Object
Object Class
Polymorphism

5.12 Exercises

1. Identify some of the possible objects in the simple claims insurance system described in section 1.5.
2. Identify candidate methods for these objects and potential messages that we might send to objects.
3. Define at least one of these objects using the syntax of Object Pascal.
4. How much hype do you think there is presently in object-orientation?
5. Discuss the corresponding need for an object-oriented approach to analysis and design.
6. A class browser, a tool for locating appropriate object classes, is a much discussed tool amongst the object-oriented programming fraternity. List some other tools you feel might be important for the object-oriented programmer.
7. The database fraternity (chapter 6) have spent much effort separating programs from data. Object-oriented programming re-integrates these two components. Is this a step back, or a step forward?
8. Discuss the claim that object-oriented programming is in some way more 'natural' than conventional structured programming.
9. How might structured and object-oriented programming be integrated? Is there any benefit in such integration?
10. What advantages arise from polymorphism?
11. Identify some possible objects for the Goronwy Galvanising system.

6 Databases, Database Management Systems and Data Models

6.1 Introduction

When organisations first began to use the computer they naturally adopted a piecemeal approach to information systems development. One manual system at a time was analysed, redesigned and transferred onto the computer with little thought to its position within the organisation as a whole. This piecemeal approach was necessitated by the difficulties experienced in using a new and more powerful organisational tool.

This piecemeal approach by definition produces a number of separate information systems, each with its own program suite, its own files, and its own inputs and outputs. As a result of this:

1. The systems, being self-contained, do not represent the way in which the organisation works, i.e., as a complex set of interacting and interdependent systems.
2. Systems built in this manner often communicate outside the computer. Reports are produced by one system, which then have to be transcribed into a form suitable for another system. This proliferates inputs and outputs, and creates delays.
3. Information obtained from a series of separate files is less valuable to the organisation because it does not provide the complete picture. For example, a sales manager reviewing outstanding orders may not get all the information he needs from the sales system. He may need to collate information about stocks from another file used by the company's stock control system.
4. Data may be duplicated in the numerous files used by different information systems in the organisation. Hence, personnel may maintain data similar to that held by payroll. This creates unnecessary maintenance overheads and increases the risk of inconsistency.

6.2 Databases and Database Management Systems

Because of the many problems inherent in the piecemeal approach, it is nowadays considered desirable to maintain a single centralised pool of organisational data, rather than a series of separate files. Such a pool of data is known as a database.

It is also considered desirable to integrate the systems that use this data around a piece of software which manages all interactions with the database. Such a piece of software is known as a database management system or DBMS.

6.3 What is a Database?

A database in manual terms is analogous to a filing cabinet, or more accurately to a series of filing cabinets. A database is an organised repository for data. The overall purpose of such a system is to maintain data for some set of enterprise objectives. Normally, such objectives fall within the domain of business administration. Most database systems are built to retain the data required for the running of the day-to-day activities of a business.

Organisation usually implies some logical division, usually hierarchical. Hence we speak of a database as being a collection of files. A collection of files containing information on jobs at Goronwy, for instance, would normally constitute a database. Each file in a database is in turn also a structured collection of data. In manual terms, such files would be folders hung in a filing cabinet. Each file in the cabinet consists of a series of records. These might be cards of information, for example, on each job due to be processed. Each record is divided up into a series of areas known as fields such as jobNo, batchWeight, etc. Within each field a specific value is written.

6.4 Properties of a Database

The question of organisation is therefore of fundamental importance to a database system. In database terms organisation further implies a series of properties: data sharing, data integration, data integrity, data security, data abstraction, data independence.

6.4.1 Data Sharing

Database systems were originally developed for use within multi-user environments. In such environments, data held in a database is not usually there solely for the use of one person. A database is normally accessible by more than one person perhaps at the same time. Hence a personnel database might be accessible by members of not only the personnel department but also the payroll department.

6.4. 2 Data Integration

Shared data brings numerous advantages to the organisation. Such advantages, however, only result if the database is treated responsibly. One major responsibility of database usage is to ensure that the data is integrated. This implies that a database should be a collection of data which has no unnecessarily duplicated or redundant data. In the past, separate personnel and payroll systems maintained similar data on company employees such as names, addresses, dates of birth, etc. The aim of a database system is to store one logical item of data in one place only.

6.4. 3 Data Integrity

Another responsibility arising as a consequence of shared data is that a database should display integrity. In other words, that the database accurately reflects the universe of discourse that it is attempting to model. This means that if relationships exist in the real world between objects represented by data in our database then changes made to one partner in such a relationship should be accurately reflected in changes made to other partners in that relationship. Hence, if changes are made to the information stored on a particular company department, for instance, then relevant changes should be made to the information stored on employees of that department.

6.4.4 Data Security

One of the major ways of ensuring the integrity of a database is by restricting access; in other words, securing the database. The main way this is done in contemporary database systems is by defining in some detail a set of authorised users of the whole, or more usually parts of the database. A secure system would be one where the payroll department has access to information for the production of salaries but is prohibited from changing the pay points of company employees. This activity is the sole responsibility of the personnel department.

6.4.5 Data Abstraction

A database can be viewed as a model of reality. The information stored in a database is usually an attempt to represent the properties of some objects in the real world. Hence, for instance, a personnel database is meant to record relevant details of people. We say relevant, because no database can store all the properties of real-world objects. A database is therefore an abstraction of the real world.

6.4.6 Data Independence

One immediate consequence of abstraction is the idea of buffering data from the processes that use such data. The ideal is to achieve a situation where data organisation is transparent to the users or application programs which feed off data. If, for instance, a change is made to some part of the underlying database no application programs using affected data should need to be changed. Also, if a change is made to some part of an application system then this should not affect the structure of the underlying data used by the application.

6.5 What is a Database Management System?

A database management System (DBMS) is an organised set of facilities for accessing and maintaining one or more databases. A DBMS is a shell which surrounds a database and through which all interactions take place (see figure 6.1). The interactions catered for by most existing DBMS fall into 3 main groups:

1. File Maintenance
    a. adding new files to the database.
    b. removing files from the database.
    c. modifying the structure of existing files.
    d. inserting new data into existing files.
    e. updating data in existing files.
    f. deleting data from existing files.
2. Information Retrieval
    a. extracting data from existing files for use by end-users.
    b. extracting data for use by application programs.

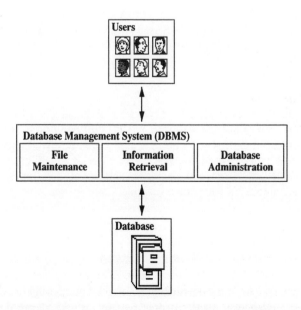

Figure 6.1   Components of a Database System

3. Database Administration
   a. creating and monitoring users of the database.
   b. restricting access to files in the database.
   c. monitoring the performance of databases.

6.6 Data Models

Any database adheres to a particular data model. A data model is an architecture for data. It describes the general structure of how data is organised. A data model is generally held to be made up of three components (Tsitchizris and Lochovsky, 1982):

1. A set of data structures.
2. A set of data operators.
3. A set of inherent integrity rules.

These three components are frequently referred to as data definition, data manipulation and data integrity respectively.

6.7 The Relational Data Model

In this section we provide a brief overview of the relational data model, one of the most popular of the contemporary data models. For a more detailed discussion of this topic the reader is referred to Beynon-Davies (1991, 1992).

We begin our discussion with a definition of the component parts of the relational data model: data definition, data manipulation, and data integrity. We then give a brief overview of what is emerging as the standard core of any relational DBMS - the database sub-language SQL.

6.7.1 Data Definition

A database is effectively a set of data structures for organising and storing data. In any data model we must have a set of principles for exploiting such data structures for business applications. Data definition is the process of exploiting the inherent data structures of a data model for a particular business application. The relational data model has only one data structure - the disciplined table or relation.

Policies

Policy No.	Holder No.	Start Date	Renewal Date	Premium	Policy Type
5432	2001	01/02/85	01/02/93	45.35	Standard Life
5242	2001	01/03/80	01/03/93	300.26	Standard Buildings
5348	2001	01/03/80	01/03/93	98.78	Standard Contents

4289	2189	01/01/76	01/01/93	20.20	Standard Life
4346	2189	01/01/76	01/01/93	156.56	Standard Buildings
4389	1136	31/02/70	31/02/93	11.63	Standard Life

Holders

Holder No.	Holder Name	Holder Address	Holder Tel.
2001	J.F.Davies	2, The Drive, Gabalfa	(0222) 289436
2189	T.Evans	15, Orchard Ave., Penylan	(0222) 543483
1136	L.Jones	1, The Parade, Canton	(0222) 389389

The two tables above are relations because they adhere to a certain restricted set of rules:

1. Every relation in a database must have a distinct name.
2. Every column in a relation must have a distinct name within the relation.
3. All entries in a column must be of the same kind.
4. The ordering of columns in a relation is not significant.
5. Each row in a relation must be distinct. In other words, duplicate rows are not allowed in a relation.
6. The ordering of rows is not significant. There should be no implied order in the storage of rows in a relation.
7. Each cell or column/row intersection in a relation should contain only an atomic value. Multi-values are not allowed in a relation.

To enforce the property that duplicate rows are forbidden each relation must have a so-called primary key. A primary key is one or more columns of a table whose values are used to uniquely identify each of the rows in a table. PolicyNo and holderNo are the primary keys of the tables above. A primary key will be chosen from the set of candidate keys. A candidate key is any column or group of columns which could act in the capacity of a primary key.

The primary unit of data in the relational data model is the data item, for example, a part number, a policy number or a person's date of birth. Such data items are said to be non-decomposable or atomic. A set of such data items of the same type is said to be a domain. For example, the domain of policy numbers is the set of all possible policy numbers. Domains are therefore pools of values from which actual values appearing in the columns of a table are drawn.

Foreign keys are the 'glue' of relational systems. They are the means of interconnecting the information stored in a series of disparate tables. A foreign key is a column or group of columns of some table which draws its values from the same domain as the primary key of some other table in the database. In our insurance database example holderNo is a foreign key in the policies table. This column draws its values from the same domain as the holderNo column - the primary key- of the holders table. This means that when we know the holderNo of some policy we can cross-refer to the holders table to see, for instance, where that customer lives.

6.7.2 Data Manipulation

Data manipulation has four aspects:

1. How we input data into a relation.
2. How we remove data from a relation.
3. How we amend data in a relation.
4. How we retrieve data from a relation.

When Codd first proposed the relational data model by far the most attention was devoted to the final aspect of data manipulation — information retrieval. In his early papers, Codd proposed a collection of operators for manipulating relations (Codd, 1970). He called the entire collection of such operators the relational algebra.

The relational algebra is a set of some eight operators. Each operator takes one or more relations as input and produces one relation as output. The three main operators of the algebra are select, project and join. Using these three operators most of the manipulation required of relational systems can be accomplished. The additional operators — product, union, intersection, difference and division — are modelled on the traditional operators of set theory.

1. Select/Restrict. The select or restrict operator of the relational algebra takes a single relation as input and produces a single relation as output. Select is a 'horizontal slicer'. It extracts rows from the input relation matching a given condition and passes them to the output relation.
2. Project. The project operator takes a single relation as input and produces a single relation as output. Project is a 'vertical slicer'.
3. Join. The join operator takes two relations as input and produces one relation as output. A number of distinct types of join have been identified. Probably the most commonly used is the natural join. The natural join operator combines two tables together but only for records matching a given condition. It also projects out one of the join columns.

6.7.3 Data Integrity

When we say a person has integrity we normally mean we can trust what that person says. We assume, for instance, a close correspondence between what that person says and what he or she does.

When we say a database has integrity we mean much the same thing. We have some trust in what the database tells us. There is a close correspondence between the facts stored in the database and the real world it models. Hence, in terms of our insurance database we believe that the fact — policy 5432 is a life insurance policy — is an accurate reflection of the workings of our enterprise.

Two types of integrity are important to the relational model: entity and referential integrity.

Entity integrity concerns primary keys. Entity integrity is an integrity rule which states that every table must have a primary key and that the column or columns chosen to be the primary key should be unique and not null.

Referential integrity concerns foreign keys. The referential integrity rule states that any foreign key value can be in one of two states. The usual state of affairs is that the foreign key value refers to a primary key value of some table in the database. Occasionally, and this will depend on the rules of the organisation, a foreign key value can be null. In this case we are explicitly saying that either there is no relationship between the objects represented in the database or that this relationship is unknown.

6.8 The Database Sub-language SQL

One of the major formalisms which define the present generation of relational database management systems is Structured Query Language or SQL for short. SQL was originally designed as a query language based on the relational algebra. SQL however is a lot more than simply a query language, it is a database sub-language. This database sub-language is becoming the standard interface to relational and non-relational DBMS.

SQL comes in 3 major parts:

1. A data definition language (DDL) with integrity enhancement.
2. A data manipulation language (DML).
3. A data control language (DCL).

6.8.1 Data Definition Language

Suppose that we have a company requirement to produce a database of information, like the tables given above. The structure for each of the tables in the database can be set up using the create table command. For example:

```
CREATE TABLE holders
(holderNo CHAR(4),
holderName CHAR(20),
address CHAR(30),
telNo CHAR(12))
```

The create table statement allows us to specify a name for a table, and the names, data-types and lengths of each of the attributes in the table. Many contemporary implementations of SQL have no direct mechanism for enforcing the notion of primary and foreign keys. An addendum to the ANSI standard however specifies a primary and foreign key clause:

    CREATE TABLE policies
    (policyNo CHAR(4),
    holderNo CHAR(4),
    startDate DATE,
    renewalDate DATE,policyType CHAR(20))
    PRIMARY KEY (policyNo)
    FOREIGN KEY (holderNo IDENTIFIES holders)

When a table is created information is written to a number of system tables. This is a meta-database which stores information about the structure of tables at the base level. Information about a table can be removed from the system tables by using the DROP command:

    DROP TABLE policies

Only a certain amount of amendment activity is allowed on table structures by SQL. We can add an extra attribute to a table:

    ALTER TABLE holders
    ADD (dateOfBirth, DATE)

We may also modify the size of an existing attribute:

    ALTER TABLE holders
    MODIFY (address char(40))

6.8.2 *Data Manipulation Language*

Having created a structure for the tables in our database, we may enter data into such tables using the INSERT command:

    INSERT INTO holders
    (holderNo, holderName, address, telNo)
    VALUES ('1111', 'P.Beynon-Davies','12, Redrose Hill, Splott', '(0222) 434567')

If the list of values is in the same sequence as the sequence of attributes in the table, the sequence of attribute names can be omitted:

INSERT INTO holders
VALUES
('1111', 'P.Beynon-Davies','12, Redrose Hill, Splott', '(0222) 434567')

We also maintain the ongoing data in the database through use of the update and delete comands:

UPDATE policies
SET policyType = 'SLife'
WHERE policyType = 'Standard Life'

DELETE FROM policies
WHERE holderNo = '5432'

Although SQL has a data definition and file maintenance subset, the language was designed primarily as a means for extracting data from a database. Such extraction is accomplished through use of the select command: a combination of the restrict, project, and join operators of the relational algebra. Simple retrieval is accomplished by a combination of the select, from and where clauses:

SELECT policyNo, holderNo
FROM policies
WHERE policyType = 'Standard Life'

The list of attribute names can be substituted with the wildcard character '*', in which case all the attributes in the table are listed:

SELECT *
FROM policies
WHERE policyType = 'Standard Life'

To produce a sorted list as output we add the order by clause to the select statement:

SELECT policyNo, holderNo
FROM policies
WHERE premium > 75.00
ORDER BY premium

To undertake aggregate work such as computing the average premium of each insurance policy we use the GROUP BY clause:

SELECT avg(premium)

```
FROM policies
WHERE startDate > '01-JAN-80'
GROUP BY premium
```

SQL performs relational joins by indicating common attributes in the where clause of a select statement. For instance, the select statement below extracts data from the policies and holders tables of relevance to life insurance salesmen and orders it by the startDate.

```
SELECT policies.holderNo, holderName, policyNo, startDate
FROM policies, holders
WHERE policies.holderNo = holders.holderNo
AND policyType = 'Standard Life'
ORDER BY startDate
```

6.8.3 Data Control Language

The primary mechanism for enforcing control issues in SQL is through the concept of a view. Views are virtual tables which act as 'windows' on the database of real tables. The view below establishes a virtual table using the query above. Salesmen granted access only to this view would be unable to see information of relevance to other insurance areas.

```
CREATE VIEW life
AS SELECT policies.holderNo, holderName, policyNo, startDate
FROM policies, holders
WHERE policies.holderNo = holders.holderNo
AND policyType = 'Standard Life'
ORDER BY startDate
```

The view becomes a table definition in the system catalog and remains unaffected by updating of the underlying policies and holders table.

Access can be restricted on tables and views to particular users via the grant and revoke facilities of SQL. Grant allows users read and file maintenance privileges on tables or views. Revoke takes such privileges away.

```
GRANT INSERT,UPDATE
ON life TO pbd
```

```
REVOKE SELECT,INSERT
ON life FROM pbd
```

6.9 Conclusion

Databases and DBMSs are important for modern information systems development because they encourage the development of an integrated policy for organisational data. Such a policy more clearly reflects, or models, the organisation as being a set of interdependent subsystems. In chapter 23, we shall discuss how information management is a discipline devoted to this exercise in integration.

Also because of its logical simplicity, the relational database approach has stimulated a whole range of database design techniques. Perhaps the two most prominent are Codd's notion of normalisation (see chapter 11), and Chen's notion of entity-relationship diagramming (see chapter 12).

6.10 References

Beynon-Davies P. (1991). *Relational Database Systems: A Pragmatic Approach.* Blackwell Scientific, Oxford.

Beynon-Davies P. (1992). *Relational Database Design.* Blackwell Scientific, Oxford.

Codd E.F. (1970). A Relational Model for Large Shared Data Banks. *CACM.* 13 (1). 377-387.

Tsitchizris D. and Lochovsky F. (1982). *Data Models.* Prentice-Hall, Englewood Cliffs, NJ.

6.11 Keywords

Candidate Key
Data Definition
Data Integrity
Data Manipulation
Data Model
Database
Database Management System
Domain
Entity Integrity
Foreign Key
Primary Key
Referential Integrity
Relation
Relational Algebra
SQL

6.12 Exercises

1. Define a table to hold insurance brokers' information using the create table command of SQL. The table should contain a broker number, name, address and telephone number.
2. To link brokers to policies we need an extra field in the policies table. What is this field and how do we conduct this modification using SQL?
3. Assuming answers to questions 1 and 2 write an insert statement in SQL to put some data into the brokers' table. Also write an update statement to add appropriate information to the policies table.
4. Write a select statement which will list all the policies relevant to the broker you have created.
5. Package the select statement as a view.
6. Grant retrieval access only on this view to a user named Jones.
7. Start considering the data that we would need to hold for Goronwy Galvanising.
8. What reports would be needed by the production controller at Goronwy?

7 Fourth Generation Environments

7.1 Introduction

Like many terms in computing the concept of fourth generation languages (4GLs) and environments is an extremely hazy one. One way to distinguish between third generation and fourth generation tools is to express the ideal of a non-procedural development environment. It must be remembered however that few if any contemporary products satisfy this ideal.

Third generation languages such as COBOL and C are inherently procedural in nature. That is, the programmer is required to specify not only what is needed but also how the computer is expected to solve the problem in a detailed, step-by-step manner. In contrast, fourth generation languages are ideally designed to be non-procedural. The programmer need only specify what is required. The how is left to the 4GL compiler or interpreter to sort out.

Another way of expressing this is to say that any algorithm is made up of two components: logic and control (Kowalski, 1979). In a third generation language, logic and control are necessarily intertwined. The programmer expresses both the solution to the problem and such things as sequencing and iteration in one medium. In the ideal 4GL some indication of the logic of the process is given: the general structure of the data needed to support the process; the general form of the output expected from the process, and the form of the interface needed between the user and the process. No indication need be given of the detailed control needed to accomplish the processing.

7.2 Components of a Fourth Generation Environment

Given the above definition few if any existing self-styled 4GLs are truly 4GLs. The contemporary form of 4GL is usually a higher-level programming language in the sense that it has in-built functions for information systems, particularly screen and database handling. In this sense, they are more like 31/2 GLs.

The ideal of non-procedurality achieves more ready recognition in the idea of a fourth generation environment (4GE). A fourth generation environment can be conveniently used as an umbrella-term for a collection of distinct products, many of which can be classified as CAISE (see chapter 8):

1. Physical Data Dictionary. A place for storing the specifications both of the data used, and of the databases where this data is physically located.
2. Screen Painter. Used to outline the format of any data entry and retrieval screens needed by an application. Such screens are normally driven from default output produced from the data dictionary.
3. Report Generator. Used primarily to specify the format of printed reports, normally by reference to the database structures stored in the data dictionary.
4. Query Language. A means of flexibly specifying non-procedural queries on a database.
5. Dialogue specifier. Used to indicate the nature of program flow, where this is not apparent from the non-procedural information provided.
6. Code generator. A means of generating 3GL code from data dictionary definitions.

Many environments include a high-level procedural language and other facilities such as spreadsheet and graphics tools within their environments. In section 7.4 we shall look at the offering available from the ORACLE corporation as an instance of a fourth generation environment.

7.3 Application Generators

The term application generator is frequently used as a synonym for fourth generation environment. An application generator is designed to create one or more of the standard pieces of an information system such as menus, data entry screens, enquiry programs, reports or batch programs. They work typically by displaying a series of parameters which can be modified by the developer. These customised parameters are then either interpreted by a shell when the application is run, or compiled into some form of source code, probably COBOL or C.

In the case of an update program, for example, the developer might specify which files are to be updated, the fields from the file that are to be displayed and modified, and the restrictions to be placed on the information to be entered. The application would then run without needing further input from the developer.

This generator approach works well when the data and processes needed by an application are not too complex. It is insufficient however for the more complex applications required by most information systems departments. One approach to solving this problem is to offer more screens in the generator such that the developer can specify the logic of the application in greater detail. Clearly however, this approach is limited by the fact that the parameter screens can become so complex as to be unusable. The answer adopted by most products is therefore to generalise as many of the user requirements as possible using the non-procedural approach, but then offer 'hooks' where the developer can attach modules of 3GL or procedural 4GL Code.

7.4 The ORACLE Kernel and Toolkit

Modern day relational DBMS generally come in two parts, which we shall refer to as the kernel and the toolkit. The kernel comprises the core DBMS functions generally implemented in some dialect of SQL. Around this standard interface most vendors offer a range of additional software tools for producing information systems. Thus the concept of DBMS discussed in chapter 6 is extending ever further outwards to encompass more and more areas of application building.

Figure 7.1 illustrates the architecture available from the ORACLE Corporation.

The kernel comprises a relational database engine and a standard interface known as SQL*Plus. SQL*Plus allows the user to create and modify tables, enter and modify data, and set up ad-hoc queries. SQL*Plus is SQL with additional features for editing, running command files and controlling the format of output.

Around this kernel a range of products are offered:

1. SQL*Forms — a forms-based application development tool. It builds menus and data entry or retrieval screens as a front-end to SQL*Plus.
2. SQL*Calc — a spreadsheet facility that allows data to be retrieved from the database. Spreadsheet cells can also invoke SQL statements.
3. SQL*Graph provides graphic representation (bar, line and pie charts) auto-

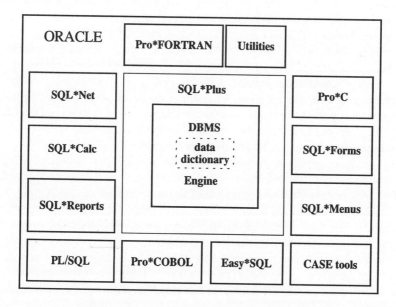

Figure 7.1   The ORACLE Environment

matically for data that is the result of an enquiry on the database.
4. SQL*Net is a tool for building distributed systems.
5. SQL*Menu is the interface through which menus can be developed to reference forms, reports and commands. It is a menu environment to control and provide security in the way tasks are carried out.
6. SQL*Report — a report-writer.
7. A number of links to third generation languages, the most developed of which is to C. This is called PRO*C.
8. SQL*Design Dictionary is a structured system to monitor and control the development of applications at all stages of the development from initial analysis to running and maintenance.

Version 6 of ORACLE also encompasses a procedural 4GL known as PL/SQL and a set of CASE tools based around entity-relationship diagramming.

7.5 Embedded SQL

SQL comes in two forms. It can either be used interpretively or it can be embedded within a host language such as COBOL, FORTRAN, PL/1, C, or PASCAL. It is the former usage that we discussed in chapter 6. The latter usage is primarily for application developers. It is designed to simplify database input and output from application programs via a standard interface. In this section we introduce the concept of SQL as an embedded database language by discussing one simple example in a pseudo-host language modelled on PASCAL.

```
PROGRAM emp_names;

VAR empno: integer;

BEGIN
        EXEC SQL DECLARE employees CURSOR FOR
                SELECT empno
                FROM employees;
        PRINT 'Employee Numbers';
        PRINT '_____';
        EXEC SQL OPEN employees;
        EXEC SQL FETCH employees INTO :empno;
        WHILE SQLCODE = 0 DO
                PRINT empno;
                EXEC SQL FETCH employees INTO :empno;
        EXEC SQL CLOSE employees
END;
```

The program above prints the list of employee numbers in a table named employees. Embedded data language statements are preceded by the keywords EXEC SQL. The DECLARE statement defines a pointer to the employees table known as a cursor. When the open statement is activated, the select statement defined at the declare stage is executed. This creates a copy of all the employee numbers in the base table and places it in a workspace area. To retrieve an actual record from this workspace we use the fetch command. The fetch statement takes an employee number and places it in a program variable empno, indicated by the colon. Sqlcode is a system variable. It returns 0 if the fetch executed successfully, non-zero otherwise. Hence we use it here to act as a terminating condition to traverse the employee numbers in the workspace.

The concept of a cursor is extremely important in that it acts as the cement between the inherently non-procedural nature of SQL and the inherently procedural nature of a third generation language such as Pascal. There is in fact what is usually referred to as an impedance mismatch between SQL and 3GLs. SQL, being relational, works at the file level. It takes tables as input and produces tables as output. 3GLs however work at the record level. They only process one record at a time. We therefore have to have some mechanism for translating from a file-based to a record-based approach. This is provided by the cursor.

A program written in this hybrid manner is normally submitted to a pre-compiler. The exec sql keywords are important in enabling the pre-compiler to identify SQL commands from Pascal commands. The pre-compiler will take the SQL commands and create a database access module. It will also take the Pascal commands and produce a source program suitably modified with database access calls. This modified source is then compiled in the normal manner.

7.6 The DBASE Family

The fourth generation approach has achieved particular fruition in the personal computer end of the information systems market. One of the most popular of fourth generation environments available on personal computers are a range of products originally descended from dBase II. dBase has become almost something of a standard language for application development on PCs. In this section we characterise some of the key features of the dBase language.

The main strength of dBase, and the feature which contributes most to defining it as fourth generation, is its ability to perform database access. Unlike languages such as Pascal (see chapter 4), dBase is designed to interact with a predefined database.

Suppose we wish to create a simple application to maintain the products file for the Goronwy Galvanising system. In dBase, the products file would be constructed using the CREATE command. This would allow us to specify the structure of the file by filling in a template as below:

Field Name	Type	Width	Dec
ProductCode	Char	4	
ProductName	Char	20	
ItemLength		Numeric	8 2
ItemWeight	Numeric	8	2

A record can be added to the products file using the command APPEND. A default data entry screen will then appear as follows:

        Record No. 1
        ProductCode
        ProductName
        ItemLength
        ItemWeight

Data can be retrieved using the command LIST. For instance, the following statement will display the product codes and names of all products more than 1.5 metres long:

        LIST ProductCode, ProductName, FOR ItemLength > 1.5

The procedural programming language of dBase enables the production of data entry/retrieval screens, complex processing, menus and reports. For instance, the program below is given to illustrate the power of the approach. It represents a formatted data entry screen for products information. Comments are lines beginning with an asterisk, or strings beginning with two ampersands.

```
* Products Entry *

USE products INDEX products

* This statement declares the file to be accessed and indicates *
* index to be used - in this case, an index on ProductCode *

CLEAR && clears the screen

SET SPACE(1) TO response
SET SPACE(4) TO p1
SET SPACE(20) TO p2
```

```
    SET 0 to p3
    SET 0 to p4
    * initialise local variables *
    DO WHILE response <> 'Q'
        DO screen && call to the procedure named screen
        DO getdetails && call to the procedure getdetails
        @ 23,10 SAY 'Is this correct (Y/N/Q)?' GET response PICTURE '!'
        CASE response = 'Y'
            DO writedetails
        CASE response = 'N'
            SET SPACE(4) TO p1
            SET SPACE(20) TO p2
            SET 0 to p3
            SET 0 to p4
        CASE response = 'Q'
        OTHERWISE
            @ 23,10 say 'Invalid response, type Y,N, or Q'
            SET space(1) To response
        ENDCASE
    ENDDO


RETURN && This will cause a return to the main body of the program


PROCEDURE Screen
* This procedure uses a series of @ statements to paint the *
* screen with text, having the form @ <row>, <col> SAY '<text>' *


@ 1,30 SAY 'Products Entry'
@ 3,10 SAY 'Product Code'
@ 5,10 SAY 'Product Name'
@ 7,10 SAY 'Item Length'
@ 9,10 SAY 'Item Weight'
RETURN


PROCEDURE GetDetails
* This procedure uses a series of modified @ statements *
* to read input from specified parts of the screen.*
* The statements have the form @ <row>, <col> GET <variable> *


@ 3,50 GET p1
@ 5,50 GET p2
@ 7,50 GET p3 PICTURE '999999.99'
@ 9,50 GET p4 PICTURE '999999.99'
```

```
                 * The PICTURE clause establishes a template for data entry *
                 RETURN

                 PROCEDURE WriteDetails

                 * This procedure replaces the fields in a record with the *
                 * contents of local variables *

                 APPEND BLANK
                 REPLACE ProductCode WITH p1
                 REPLACE ProductName WITH p2
                 REPLACE ItemLength WITH p3
                 REPLACE ItemWeight WITH p4

                 RETURN
```

One of the major problems with dBase and indeed most of the fourth generation environments available on PCs is that their development has run somewhat counter to the mainstream development of SQL-based approaches. Although many packages such as dBase IV include an SQL interface, this is usually merely an add-on to the basic architecture of the system. Because SQL is being proposed as a standard for database access, a question must be placed over the future development of these products.

7.7 Conclusion

There is currently no agreement as to what constitutes a fourth generation language or environment. So far as languages are concerned we have therefore concentrated on explaining the concept of a programming language with an enhanced data management facility. In the PC world, the class of dBase languages is probably the most popular. In terms of an environment we have concentrated on explaining some of the elements of a toolkit designed to enhance the productivity of the developer. The tools surrounding the ORACLE DBMS are characteristic of this sort of framework.

7.8 References

Cobb R.H. (1985). In Praise of 4GLs. *Datamation*. July 15th. 90-96.
Kowalski R. (1979). Algorithm = Logic + Control. *CACM*. 22. 424-436.

7.9 Keywords

Cursor
Embedded SQL
Fourth Generation Language
Physical Data Dictionary
Query Language
Report Generator
Screen Painter

7.10 Exercises

1. Discuss the distinction between a third generation language and a fourth generation language.
2. Discuss the distinction between a fourth generation language and a fourth generation environment.
3. Why do you think a data dictionary is central to a fourth generation environment?
4. In what ways do you think 4GEs may improve programmer productivity?
5. In what ways do you think 4GEs may improve the quality of information systems?
6. Discuss whether you think embedded SQL is an ideal mechanism for interfacing 3GLs with databases.
7. In what way do you think object-orientation is likely to affect the future of 4GE?
8. How is the concept of fourth generation related to CAISE?
9. In what way do you think database systems have influenced the development of fourth generation languages?
10. Modern fourth generation languages are really three and a half generation languages. Discuss.
11. The IT director of Goronwy's holding company is considering purchasing a 4GE. Write a formal memo to him explaining the advantages and disadvantages of using a 4GE.

8 Computer Aided Information Systems Engineering (CAISE)

8.1 Introduction

In this chapter we shall discuss the growing number of automated tools for information systems development. Many people place such tools within the context of CASE — Computer Aided Software Engineering. The author prefers the term CAISE — Computer Aided Information Systems Engineering. CASE may be regarded as a subset of CAISE. Many CAISE tools are involved in the production of software and are hence logically software engineering tools. Many others, particularly those in the database area, are not directly involved in the production of software. Most database design tools, for example, have as their remit the production of structures for storing and manipulating data.

The large number and diversity of CAISE tools makes it impossible to do justice to a representative sample. We have therefore chosen to describe elements of a generic tool-set particularly concentrating on those for database development. Our main aims in discussing this tool-set are:

1. To illustrate some of the main features one would expect to see in contemporary commercial products.
2. To discuss the practical integration of tools to support the entire database development process.
3. To highlight some of the important advantages arising from the use of CAISE in database development.
4. To discuss some of the pitfalls of implementing CAISE within organisations.

8.2 A Model of the Development Process

CAISE is a logical consequence of a recursive or incestuous view of information systems development. It has stimulated the view that information systems development, considered as an information system in itself, should be subject to and benefit from the same sorts of automation that characterise everyday information systems.

CAISE is therefore based upon a particular model of the information systems development process. In this model, the development process is seen as a set of activities operating on objects to produce other objects. The objects manipulated by such activities will frequently be documents, diagrams, file-structures or even programs. Similarly, the activities involved may be relatively formal (e.g., compile a program) or informal (e.g., obtain user's requirements). It is not suprising therefore that the waterfall model of information systems development and the associated adoption of structured techniques (section 2.5) is particularly suited to the application of CAISE (Parkinson, 1991).

8.3 Back-end, Front-end and Integration

A distinction is normally made between back-end CAISE tools and front-end CAISE tools.

Front-end CAISE tools are generally directed at the analysis and design stages of information systems development. In terms of database development, for instance, front-end tools include such products as E-R diagramming editors (chapter 11), determinancy diagramming editors (chapter 12) and data dictionaries (chapter 14).

Back-end CAISE tools are directed at the implementation, testing and maintenance stages of information systems development. Here tools such as physical data dictionaries, performance monitors and other aids for physical database design are relevant.

Many vendors have now attempted to integrate their front-end and back-end tools. The intention is, for instance, to offer assistance at all the stages of information development, and to expect the outputs from each stage to feed as inputs to subsequent stages.

8.4 I-CAISE, C-CAISE and Meta-CAISE

One of the major decisions for potential users of CAISE is whether to use component CAISE (C-CAISE) or integrated CAISE (I-CAISE). Component CAISE, such as IBM's AD/Cycle or DEC's cohesion CAISE, relies on CAISE software from different suppliers being able to work together to cover different parts of the project life-cycle. I-CAISE, such as the Information Engineering Facility from James Martin Associates, is a suite of CAISE tools from one supplier designed to work together. The heavy investment in Integrated Project Support Environments (IPSE) in the late 1980s are the precursors of I-CAISE (McDermid, 1985).

The main advantage of I-CAISE is that it imposes a rigid discipline. Developers have to learn only one tool-set. The main problems with I-CAISE are that many products are not as integrated as one would expect, and that opting for I-CAISE means being locked into one supplier. Hence, the supplier becomes a strategic partner in development plans.

C-CAISE offers a more flexible option in that organisations can pick what best suits their organisational approach. The main problem with C-CAISE is that the different products making up C-CAISE may use incompatible data structures, hence making communication difficult.

The common threads running through many of the techniques of modern systems development has meant that a certain degree of abstraction is possible in CAISE. The foremost example of such abstraction is a group of products collectively known as meta-CAISE tools. Using such tools, an organisation can build its own CAISE toolkit perhaps to suit its own in-house methodology (chapter 21).

8.5 Facilities of CAISE

The objective of an integrated CAISE environment is to improve the effectiveness of an organisation in developing and maintaining information systems. In this sense it will provide facilities for development objects to be created, manipulated and communicated between members of a project team. Facilities for the management of projects (chapter 28) should also be a part, as should facilities for managing inter-project relationships. This can be summarised by saying that CAISE can provide a gearing effect at three different levels:

1. Individual
2. Project
3. Corporate

8.5.1 Individual Gearing

The individual gearing that can be provided by CAISE is concerned with enabling a person to carry out his or her activities more effectively. Examples of the types of facilities provided by CAISE to facilitate individual gearing are:

1. For a programmer, better compilers and higher level languages such as 4GLs (chapter 27).
2. For an analyst better documentation facilities, particularly diagramming editors.
3. For a project manager, control tools such as PERT planners (chapter 28).

8.5.2 Project Gearing

CAISE support at the project level is concerned with providing means for coordinating the activities of a set of individuals. Support at this level includes:

1. Integration of tools to ensure smooth information flow between team members.
2. Support for standards.
3. Maintenance of automatic version control.

8.5.3 Corporate Gearing

In any business reliant on information systems, there will be a number of discrete but interrelated projects. The effectiveness of the company will depend upon its ability to control the interrelationships between projects. Such relationships might be technical (e.g., one project relies on the framework of another), to do with resources (e.g., one project may rely on another project finishing to release key skills) or concerned with business effectiveness. Examples of facilities which relate to gearing at the corporate level include:

1. Tools for strategic information systems planning (chapter 23).
2. Dissemination of working practices, methods, and tools.
3. Construction and utilisation of a corporate 'experience-base' (eg., the availability of component libraries).

8.6 The Advantages of CAISE

Many of the advantages of CAISE arise from automation. Let us examine, for instance, the process of constructing data models in terms of entity-relationship diagrams. It is relatively straightforward to produce small entity models on paper. As soon as we start to scale up the exercise to realistically large levels however many problems emerge. Some paper-based data models end up being displayed at one end of the office and terminate two hundred yards away at the other side of the building! The number of entities, relationships and attributes in such data models makes a paper-based storage mechanism impracticable.

Many of these problems of scale are well known from software engineering. Much work has been invested in building integrated project support environments (IPSE) designed to support large teams of software developers working on long-term projects (Mcdermid, 1985). Some of the key problems which CAISE tools for database work address are:

1. In terms of a large data model we have to ensure that we maintain the integrity of the data model in much the same way as we have to maintain the integrity of an everyday database. CAISE tools will contain automatic checking and error-finding facilities.
2. We have to ensure that all members of the development team are using the same notational devices. A CAISE tool helps to enforce standards.
3. We have to ensure that concurrent access to the model is controlled and that the data model remains an accurate reflection of design decisions. We also have to ensure that a history of design decisions is available for inspection. A version control facility is thereforeessential for most CAISE tools.

8.7 Problems with CAISE

One of the fundamental problems of CAISE is that it has frequently been cast as a panacea for all the ills of systems development. This it is clearly not. Spurr (1989) more accurately portrays CAISE as a culture shock for many organisations.

One of the main lessons that has been learnt by organisations applying CAISE technology is that CAISE demands large investments of time and effort, particularly in the training of staff. Most CAISE tools are inherently linked with given methodologies (chapter 21). Hence, to apply CAISE products effectively one must also adopt the tenets of the methodology the product supports. The consequence of this is that organisations frequently have to invest in changes of methods as well as changes in technology. This forces project management techniques to be reviewed (chapter 28).

8.8 An Illustration of Front-End CAISE

Entity-relationship diagramming editors are common-place tools in the CAISE market. In this section we discuss the functionality of such a tool, and in particular how such tools integrate with database development. Figure 8.1 illustrates the constructs of an E-R diagramming editor. We assume that the editor runs in a windows-based environment (chapter 10). Such an editor would manipulate the following graphic objects: labelled rectangles representing entities; lines representing relationships; ovals representing attributes.

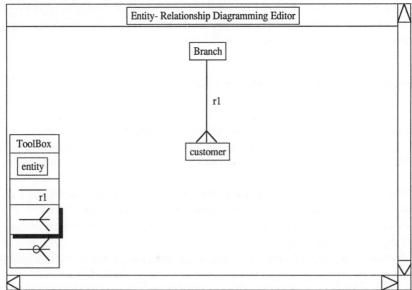

Figure 8.1   Screen from an E-R Diagramming Editor

Crows-feet and optionality circles would be added to a diagram by selecting the end of an existing relationship line and conducting a structured dialogue with the system.

Because of the difficulties involved in validating free-form entry of graphics, most of these tools work in a constrained dialogue with the user, such as the following:

1. The user selects a box (an entity) from the graphics menu. The system then prompts for an entity name. The user enters 'Branch'.
2. The user selects another box from the graphics toolbox. The system then prompts for an entity name. The user enters 'Branch'. The system displays the message, 'Entity Branch already exists'. This is an example of the in-built validation mechanisms in CAISE tools. The user then enters 'Customer'.
3. The user selects a line (a relationship) from the menu. The system prompts for the first entity involved in the relationship. The user selects Branch. The system prompts for the cardinality of the relationship. The user selects 1. The system prompts for optionality. The user selects mandatory. The system prompts for the second entity involved in the relationship. The user selects Customer. The system prompts for the cardinality and optionality of the relationship as above.

Underlying the activities of the E-R diagramming editor we have a meta-database, which for reasons of consistency we have chosen to call our data dictionary system. Here we store all the information about entities, relationships, and attributes relevant to a particular application.

From the information stored in this repository it is feasible for a further CAISE tool to automatically generate a database schema conforming to some data model such as the relational data model. In turn, a physical schema expressed in something like ORACLE's SQL*Plus can be generated (chapter 6).

8.9 Data Dictionaries and Back-end CAISE

A data dictionary is a repository for meta-data. The classic data dictionary is a passive repository. In other words, the first data dictionaries were built as systems external to a database. They were systems built to record the complexities of a given database structure for use by application development staff and DBAs (see chapter 14).

If we equate the term data dictionary with the set of system tables as discussed in chapter 6, then a data dictionary in a relational system is an active repository. It is an inherent, internal part of the database system designed to buffer the user from the base tables.

Many people believe however that the system tables available in most SQL-based products are inherently limited in functionality (Codd, 1990). In particular, they wish to see the inclusion of some representation of inherent and additional integrity mechanisms within the data dictionary.

Traditionally, integrity issues have been external to the database system. Integrity has primarily been the province of application systems written in languages such as COBOL or C which interact with the database. Programs are written in such languages to validate data entered into the database and ensure that any suitable propagation of results occurs (chapter 7).

Many have argued however that the logical place for integrity is within the domain of the data dictionary under control of the DBMS. The argument is that integrity cannot be divorced from the underlying database. Two or more application systems interacting with one database may enforce integrity differently or inconsistently. Hence, there should be only one central resort for monitoring integrity. Integrity should be the responsibility of the DBA. Mechanisms should be available therefore for the DBA to define and enforce integrity via the DBMS.

When the stage at which additional integrity is incorporated within the realms of the DBMS this engine changes somewhat in nature. No longer is it correct to call it a tool for managing a database or a set of databases. The DBMS becomes more of a tool for application building. It is not surprising therefore to find the world of fourth generation languages melding with the realm of relational systems (see chapter 7).

8.10 Conclusion

CAISE by its very nature is an attempt to automate the process of information systems development. Some people see its eventual aim as being the provision of a sufficient range of facilities to make information systems development a factory production process. The aim is to provide an information system for the production of other information systems.

There is however a major problem with this aim. As of now, there is no consensus as to what constitutes a suitable information system for the production of technical information systems. The rise of standard methodologies such as SSADM (see chapter 21) has undoubtedly stimulated a certain degree of communality amongst the key CAISE vendors. In general however, the diversity of CAISE still reflects the diversity of current methods and techniques for information systems development.

8.11 References

Codd E.F. (1990). *The Relational Data Model for Database Management*. Version 2. Addison-Wesley, Reading,Mass.

McDermid J. (1985). (Ed.). *Integrated Project Support Environments*. Peter Peregrinus, London.

Parkinson J. (1991). *Making CASE Work*. NCC Blackwell, Oxford.

Spurr K. (1989). 1(5). CASE: A Culture Shock. *The Computer Bulletin*. June. 9.

8.12 Keywords

Active Data Dictionary
Back-End CAISE
CAISE
Component-CAISE
Data Dictionary
Integrated-CAISE
Front-End CAISE
Meta-CAISE
Passive Data Dictionary

8.13 Exercises

1. What is CAISE?
2. Describe the distinction between front-end and back-end CAISE tools.
3. Discuss the distinction between Component-CAISE, Integrated-CAISE and Meta-CAISE.
4. What are the advantages of CAISE?
5. You are given the remit to assess the potential of CAISE tools for the IT needs of your organisation.. Produce a short report stating the desirability and feasibility of applying CAISE.
6. CAISE is a logical development of the structured methods movement. Discuss.
7. Discuss whether the idea of an information systems factory is feasible.
8. Is it reasonable to expect a coherent end-product from a set of component CAISE tools?
9. How might be CAISE be applicable to the Goronwy Galvanising project?

9 KnowledgeBase Systems

9.1 Introduction

KnowledgeBase Systems (KBS), along with object-oriented systems, have been much discussed in the literature. This chapter attempts to explain exactly what is meant by a knowledgebase system and makes some suggestions as to the place of knowledgebase systems within information systems development.

The easiest way to approach the problem of defining a KBS is to contrast it with a database system, particularly a relational database system as discussed in chapter 6 (Beynon-Davies, 1991). In this chapter we introduce the concept of a semantic data model and the related concept of an object-oriented database. This is used to illustrate the important concepts of facts, rules and inference.

9.2 Information and Knowledge

Standard relational databases store facts about the properties of objects in some domain and some primitive information about the relationships between objects. For instance, the insurance database in chapter 6 represents two objects: policies and policy-holders. The tables store facts about the properties of the objects such as the renewal date of a particular policy. The tables also store facts about the relationships between particular policies and particular holders.

However, facts can be said to come in five major forms, many of which cannot be handled conveniently in a relational database:

1. Relationships between objects and object classes, sometimes referred to as ISA relationships. ISA is similar to set membership. When we state that Paul Beynon-Davies ISA PolicyHolder we are defining a particular object as being a member of the set of policy holders.
2. Relationships between classes and other more general object classes, sometimes referred to as AKO (A Kind Of) relationships. AKO is similar to the idea of a subset. When we state that PolicyHolder AKO Customer we are defining the set of policy holders to be a subset of the set of customers.
3. Relationships between object classes at the same level of generalisation, sometimes said to be relationships of association. When we state that Policy-Holder Holds Policy, we are stating there is an inherent link between policy holders and policies.

4. Relationships between an object and a property or attribute (HASA relationships). When we state that Policy HASA RenewalDate we are specifying that members of the class of policies have a renewal date attribute.
5. PARTOF relationships compose an object out of an assembly of other objects. When we state that railwayStation PARTOF railway and railwayLine PARTOF railway we are specifying a railway as being made up of an aggregation of stations and lines.

9.3 Semantic Data Models

The relational data model is fundamentally only designed to handle HASA relationships and ASSOC relationships. The various other relationships can be represented in the relational data model, but not in a natural manner. In other words, the relational data model does not offer a sufficiently rich set of constructs for modelling the 'real world'. The past decade has therefore seen the emergence of a large number of alternative data models. This collection of data models can be loosely categorised as 'semantic' since their one unifying characteristic is that they attempt to provide more meaningful content than the relational model.

Semantic data models are conceptual models. That is, they are primarily models expressed in abstract or theoretical terms, much in the sense that the original relational model was expressed. However, just like the relational model, a number of semantic models have achieved a practical realisation. In recent years many of these systems have characterised themselves as object-oriented database systems because they embody many of the concepts discussed in chapter 5.

In the next section we illustrate some of the advantages of a database built using a data model known as the binary relational data model. This data model can encapsulate all of the relationships discussed in section 9.2.

9.4 Binary Relations

The binary-relational (BR) approach regards a universe of discourse as consisting of entities with binary-relationships between them. An entity is any thing of interest in this universe. A binary-relationship is an association between two entities. The first entity in a relationship is called the subject and the second entity in a relationship is called the object. A relationship is specified by identifying the subject, the type of the relationship, and the object. We shall write relationships as subject-type-object triples, such as Customer HASA Name.

Binary relations can be used to store both intensional and extensional information. Intensional information defines the structure of information in the knowledgebase. Extensional information comprises the actual occurrences of relationships.

Intensional information is defined through use of four predefined relationship types — ISA, AKO, HASA and PARTOF.

The binary relational store (BRS) is a data structure into which BR triples can be inserted and from which triples may be deleted or retrieved. Triples are inserted singly and retrieved or deleted in sets. Intensional information specified in the manner described above is used to define the allowable structure for the extension of a given BR database. That is, any insertion, amendment or deletion activity made on the BRS is checked against the intensional specification of AKO, ISA, PARTOF and HASA triples.

The BRS may hence be thought of as a black box into which both intensional and extensional information is written and from which both intensional and extensional information is retrieved.

Three basic operations can thus be performed with this store:

1. A triple can be inserted into the store.
2. A triple or set of triples can be deleted from the store.
3. A triple or set of triples can be retrieved from the store.

9.5 An Example Semantic Database

Suppose we wish to build a semantic database to store information on building society customers and the accounts they hold. We first need to create the object classes in the domain. This we do by inserting the following triples into the BRS:

> Customer HASA Name
> Customer HASA Branch
> Customer HASA TelNo
> BuildingAccount HASA StartDate
> BuildingAccount HASA CurrentBalance
> OrdinaryShare ISA BuildingAccount

The first few triples merely build the properties of objects. The last triple declares ordinary share accounts to be a subclass of building society accounts. In a true database system we would also probably need to provide a data type for each of the properties of an object. For example:

> Name TYPE CHAR(20)
> StartDate TYPE DATE

Data can then be recorded against each object:

> 4324 ISA OrdinaryShare
> 4324 StartDate 12/02/92
> 4324 CurrentBalance 50

Note that to create an object we first have to declare an identifier for an object and assign it to a given object class. The system can then prompt for the relevant properties of the assigned class.

In its present form, the example could be implemented in a relational database, excepting the need to introduce primary keys. Suppose, however, we add the following triples to the BRS:

> BuildingAccount HASA InterestRate
> OrdinaryShare InterestRate 12

Here we have established a fact, an interest rate of 12%, relevant to all ordinary share accounts. Establishing this fact allows us to infer the following triple:

> 4324 InterestRate 12

9.6 Inference

The word inference is derived from the Latin words *in* and *ferre*, meaning to carry or bring forward. Inference is therefore the process of bringing forward new knowledge from existing knowledge. In the example above, the existing knowledge represented by the collection of triples in the BRS is turned into new knowledge, a new fact, by the application of inference. In our case, this is via the application of the following inference rule:

> IF Object ISA ObjectClass
> AND ObjectClass Property Value
> THEN Object Property Value

Similar inference rules apply to AKO and PARTOF relations.

We can generalise the concept of a rule to include rules specific to the application domain - domain-specific rules. For instance, we might write the following rule into our building society system:

> IF Object1 ISA Customer
> THEN Object1 Holds Object2
> AND Object2 ISA BuildingAccount

This statement is basically specifying the fact that all customers of the building society can be assumed to hold building society accounts. A rule such as this can be used in a number of ways. Probably the most relevant would be for the system to request details of a building society account after completion of customer entry, or to request details of a customer after entry of account details. This example is actually an instance of an integrity constraint, similar in nature to the entity and referential integrity constraints of the relational model (see chapter 6).

Domain-specific rules can also be used in a more proactive sense to propagate changes to the BRS. Proactive rules are referred to as transition constraints in the sense that they specify valid transitions between states of a database system. Consider the rule below:

> IF Object ISA Employee
> AND Employee Location B
> THEN Object ISA Customer
> AND Customer Branch B

Here we are stating that if someone is an employee, he or she is also a customer (i.e., holds a building society account) and his or her branch should be set to the location of employment. In other words, if we entered the triples:

> PDJames ISA Employee
> PDJames Location Pontypridd

into our knowledgebase, the rule above would cause the following triples also to be inserted:

> PDJames ISA Customer
> PDJames Branch Pontypridd

9.7 Semantic Nets, Frames and Objects

A set of binary relations can be conceived of as a representation of a semantic net — a knowledge representation formalism popular in AI and Cognitive Psychology (Rousopoulos and Mylopoulos, 1989). Many of the concepts embodied in semantic nets, particularly generalisation hierarchies, have influenced developments in the areas of frame-based systems (Minsky, 1975), semantic data modelling (King and Mcleod, 1985) and object-oriented databases (Brown, 1991). The characterisation of semantic nets in terms of binary relations is evident in the work of Sowa (1984).

The discussion of rules in section 9.5 has much in common with the idea of production rules in expert systems. Indeed, the type of system described above can be seen as an amalgam of expert system and database system concepts (Beynon-Davies, 1991).

9.8   An Expert System Application

An expert system might be defined as a computer system which uses a representation of human expertise in some domain. Consider a simple system designed to help customers select from among a number of investment accounts offered by a building society. Suppose we conduct an investigation and find that the following factors help

us to distinguish between types of account:
1. The minimum investment required.
2. The amount of access needed to the money invested.
3. Whether a regular income is required from the investment.

The following rules might constitute an expert system for investment selection:

> IF Account Investment I
> AND I >= 5
> AND Account Access instant
> AND Account income none
> THEN Account ISA OrdinaryShare

> IF Account Investment I
> AND I >= 500
> AND Account Access instant
> AND Account income none
> THEN Account ISA InstantXtra

> IF Account Investment I
> AND I >= 500
> AND Account access 90days
> AND Account income none
> THEN Account ISA 90DaysXtra

> IF Account Investment I
> AND I >= 1000
> AND Account Access 90days
> AND Account Income monthly
> THEN Account ISA MonthlyIncome

> IF Account Investment I
> AND I > 1000
> AND Account Access 90days
> AND Account Income monthly
> THEN Account ISA GoldOption

The inference mechanism in our system is known as backward or goal-directed chaining. This means that the system is first given a goal to solve. In the simple example above there is only one goal — to find a value for account. To find a value for account the inference mechanism works out that it needs a value for investment, access and income. The system first asks the user for an investment amount. The user replies 550. The system asks for a value for access. The user replies 'instant'. Finally, the expert system asks for a value for income. The user replies none. The system then fires rule two and returns with a recommendation of an instant Xtra account.

9.9 Conclusion

The term knowledge has been the subject of debate for centuries. Knowledge in the computational perspective might be defined as being the symbolic representation of aspects of some named universe of discourse (Winston, 1984). Note the two assumptions of this definition:

1. We can symbolise knowledge. That is, it can be represented in some way. Hence, AI has often seen itself as being a discipline concerned with symbolic processing (Simon, 1969).
2. We understand that an area of knowledge, often referred to as a knowledge domain, can be named or referenced in some way.

A more pragmatic definition of knowledge is to say that knowledge is made up of three component parts: facts, rules and inference.

Knowledge engineering is the discipline devoted to building knowledgebase systems. Knowledge engineering is normally defined in terms of two major types of activity:

1. Knowledge elicitation (sometimes referred to as knowledge acquisition). The process of extracting knowledge from one or more experts in a particular domain.
2. Knowledge representation. Where knowledge is stored in a knowledgebase in a form most appropriate for the given application.

Knowledge elicitation is a methodological issue. In the large, it concerns the whole process of interacting with people and documenting the results of this interaction. In contrast, knowledge representation is an implementation issue. It concerns the means of implementing the 'intelligence' involved in some particular domain in a computational medium.

The term knowledge representation is conventionally used purely in the domain of Artificial Intelligence. However, this is a narrow usage of the term. Most of what we mean by computing, particularly commercial computing, is knowledge representation. Knowledge representation is not simply the domain of the AI worker, it is of profound concern to the information systems professional.

9.10 Keywords

AKO
Artificial Intelligence
Binary Relation

Frame
HASA
ISA
Knowledge
Knowledge Elicitation
Knowledge Engineering
Knowledge Representation
KnowledgeBase System
PARTOF
Semantic Data Model
Semantic Net

9.11 References

Beynon-Davies P. (1991). *Expert Database Systems: A Gentle Introduction*. McGraw-Hill, Maidenhead.

King R. and Mcleod D. Semantic Data Models. (1985). In Bing Yao S. (Ed.) *Principles of Database Design*, Vol. 1: Logical Organisations. Prentice-Hall, Englewood Cliffs, N.J.

Minsky M. (1975). A Framework for Representing Knowledge. In *The Psychology of Computer Vision*. Winston P. (ed.). McGraw-Hill, New York. 211-277.

Roussopoulos N. and Mylopoulos J. (1989). Using Semantic Networks for Database Management. In Mylopoulos J. and Brodie M. *Readings in Artificial Intelligence and Databases*. Morgan Kaufmann, New York.

Sowa J.F. (1984). *Conceptual Structures: Information Processing in Mind and Machine*. Addison-Wesley, Reading, Mass.

Winston P.H. (1984). *Artificial Intelligence*. Addison-Wesley, Reading, Mass.

9.12 Exercises

1. Write BR triples to represent the relational database in section 5.7.1.
2. Suppose you are given the brief of building a knowledgebase to represent the planets of the solar system. Specify the planets and their properties as a series of BR triples.
3. Assume we create the following knowledgebase:

   Zeus ISA Male
   Ares ISA Male
   Hera ISA Female
   Hephaestos ISA Male
   Zeus ParentOf Ares

      Hera ParentOf Ares
      Zeus ParentOf Hephaestos
      Hera ParentOf Hephaestos

4. Write a rule for defining that some object is the brother of some other object, and generate the appropriate inference from the knowledgebase above.
5. Discuss some of the advantages that knowledgebases may have over conventional databases.
6. Express the idea that an investment portfolio is made up of a collection of different types of investments using the syntax discussed in section 9.2.
7. Philosophers define knowledge as 'justified true belief'. Contrast this with the computational definition of knowledge given in section 9.8.

10 Hypermedia Systems

10.1 Introduction

Hypermedia is the approach to building information systems made up of nodes of various media connected together by a collection of associative links. A subset of this discipline known as hypertext concentrates on the construction of loosely connected textual systems. The term multimedia is frequently used as a synonym for hypermedia.

This chapter discusses the general concepts underlying hypermedia systems and particularly seeks to identify the place of hypermedia in current and future information systems.

10.2 History

Hypermedia systems were envisaged in the 1940s by Vannevar Bush (1945). Bush discussed the concept of a memex (memory extender), a device capable of storing and retrieving information on the basis of content.

In 1968, Douglas Englebart demonstrated the Augment system. Augment is an on-line working environment designed to augment the human intellect. It could be used to store memos, research notes and documentation. It also had facilities for computer conferencing and collaborative working.

Ted Nelson extended Bush's original concepts in the Xanadu project. Xanadu is designed to be an ever-expanding environment that can be used to create and interconnect documents containing text, video, audio and graphics. Nelson actually coined the term hypertext and defined it as being "non-linear reading or writing".

A number of prominent hypermedia prototypes were developed in the 1980s. Amongst these are NoteCards, InterMedia and Zog.

However, probably the single most important factor which has contributed to the rise of interest in hypermedia is HyperCard, a software tool packaged with the Apple Macintosh.

10.3 Hypertext

Hypertext is normally discussed in terms of three models of organisation for text: linear text; hierarchical text and network text (see figure 10.1):

91

1. Linear text. Linear text is exemplified in the format of a conventional novel. A novel is linear text in the sense that the reader is expected to start at the beginning and progress to the conclusion via sequential reading of chapters.
2. Hierarchical text. Many textbooks or reports are organised hierarchically in terms of chapters, sections, sub-sections, etc. The reader can now access the material at a number of different points in the hierarchy.
3. Network text. Network text is exemplified by the dictionary or encyclopedia. In a dictionary each entry has an independent existence but is linked to a number of other entries via references.

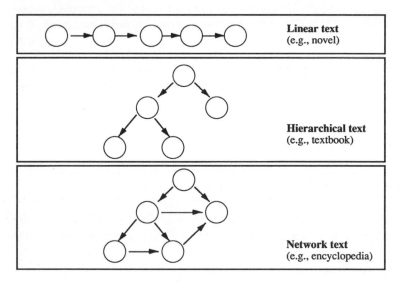

Figure 10.1   Types of Hypertext

Although examples of linear text and hierarchical text are discussed in the literature on hypertext, it is the network model that most hypertext systems attempt to emulate. A hypertext system might be regarded as an on-line implementation of network text (Conklin, 1987).

Rada (1991) also makes the distinction between small-volume hypertext, large-volume hypertext, collaborative hypertext and intelligent hypertext. Most existing commercial systems have been small-volume, standalone systems. Multi-user, large-volume hypertexts with intelligent access are still very much a research endeavour.

Contemporary hypertext systems would not be possible without the development of direct manipulation, WYSIWYG (What-You-See-Is-What-You-Get) (see chapter 19) interfaces with high volume storage devices such as CD-ROM.

The present application of hypertext systems lie in the area of on-line dictionaries, encyclopedias and medical textbooks. It is likely that the commercial world will see an explosion of products in this area in the next decade ranging from interactive catalogues, technical documentation, help systems and computer-aided instruction.

10.4 Hypermedia

Hypermedia expands the concept of hypertext with various other media:

1. Data — as held in databases and spreadsheets
2. Graphics — icons, photographs, images, diagrams
3. Sound — commentary, sound-effects
4. Video — film, animation

Some companies such as Walt Disney are already investigating the use of techniques that affect our kinaesthetic, tactile and olfactory senses. The term virtual reality is becoming associated with systems that offer a multi-sensory interface to computers.

10.5 Hypercard

In this section, we examine one sample hypermedia authoring tool available on the Apple Macintosh, Hypercard (APPLE, 1987).

Hypercard is both an authoring tool and and a presentation system for information. As a presentation system, the user navigates through a series of non-linear connections between pieces of information. As an authoring tool, Hypercard can be used to create a hypermedia database.

The central unit of information in a Hypercard system is the card, which is a screenful of information. It may be a map, a data entry screen or any other screen of information. Cards are normally made up of entities known as fields and buttons. A field is a display area and may correspond to the conventional data processing notion of the term. A button is a navigating mechanism. Buttons are used to provide the necessary inter-connections between cards stored together in units called stacks. A stack in Hypercard is therefore a hypermedia database (see figure 10.2).

The simplest use of Hypercard is in browsing mode. Here, the user navigates through a given stack by using a mouse device to click on a button. Every button may have an associated script, a piece of code written in the Hypercard authoring language, Hypertalk. It is this script which tells the system where to go next. Below, we have one of the simplest forms of script:

```
on mouseUp
        go to next card
end mouseUp
```

It simply tells the system to display the next associated card in the stack when the mouse button is released.

Hypercard is built upon object-oriented principles (chapter 5). While Hypercard is running, the system sends messages to objects in the stack about the current state of the system. For instance, when the mouse button is pressed, a mouseDown message is sent. The receiver of the message depends upon where the browse pointer is located at the time the message is sent. If the object under the pointer contains a message handler — an associated script for the message — then the actions specified in the handler are executed. If there is no such message handler then the message is passed upwards through the Hypercard hierarchy (see figure 10.2) to the stack level, and so on.

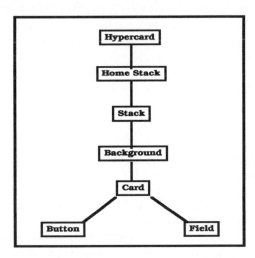

Figure 10.2   Apple Macintosh Hypercard

10.6 A Sample of Contemporary Systems

In this section we outline three sample applications of hypermedia to give a flavour of the technology. It should be emphasised that many commercial organisations such as banks and travel agencies are beginning to experiment with the technology.

10.6.1 The Oxford English Dictionary

Darrel and Tampa (1988) report how the Oxford University Press have investigated a hypertext version of its world-famous Oxford English Dictionary (OED). The OED is the largest and most scholarly dictionary of written English in existence. In its standard form, the OED consists of 12 volumes containing 41 million words. The main reason for considering hypertext and the use of CD-ROM is to support browsing of a large text database.

10.6.2 The Dynamic Medical Handbook

Frisse (1988) describes a project which attempts to demonstrate the feasibility of hypermedia systems for medical information. The idea is to support the various cognitive needs of medical staff in locating diverse types of information (text, pictures, case histories) on specific medical conditions quickly and efficiently. The project is particularly interested in allowing the system to adapt to the needs of its users over a period of time.

10.6.3 The National Gallery System

One of the most significant hypermedia developments in the UK made its debut with the opening of the Sainsbury wing of the National Gallery in 1991. Called the micro gallery it is the culmination of three years of intensive development in C and Hypercard 2.0. Designed to aid the adult visitor wanting more information on any of the gallery's paintings it allows one to access via touch screens over 4,000 pages of text and thumbnail reproductions. The user can access the information via a number of routes: e.g., by artist's name, by historical period or area, and by artistic period.

10.7 Hypermedia Systems and Commercial Information Systems Development

The major short-term impact of hypermedia systems in commerce is likely to be in the area of user interfaces or in rich database applications.

For instance, Hypercard can be used in association with a conventional RDBMS such as ORACLE. This allows application-builders the attractive possibility of creating visual interfaces to data contained in relational databases. One example known to the author, for instance, simulates a distributed database system for hotel administration. On startup the user can gain an overview of the hotels owned by the company by clicking on the overview button. A map of the United States is then displayed with icons for the four hotels run by the company located over major cities. To book a reservation at one of these hotels we click on the reservations button. We then select the hotel that we are interested in and fill in the relevant details of our stay on the card displayed. Assuming the details entered pass the validation rules established for the application, a series of entries are made to the underlying ORACLE database.

Many high street banks and building societies are now placing hypermedia systems in each of their major branches which publicise the range of financial services on offer.

10.8 Graphical User Interfaces

Graphics systems and hypermedia systems are closely interlinked. The idea of a graphical user interface (GUI) looks set to dominate business software over the next decade. A GUI is made up of a number of component parts:

1. Windows that display what a computer is doing graphically.
2. Icons that represent files, directories and services.
3. Menus that pull-down or pop-up under the control of pointing devices.
4. An array of 'Wimps' such as sliders, dialogue boxes, and buttons.

These component parts are built using a set of tools and commands embodied in a so-called windowing system. The windowing system is the mechanism by which a system's windows, dialogue boxes and menus are constructed. GUIs also contain an imaging model. This is a definition of how fonts and graphics are created on-screen. A third element is the application programming interface (API). This is used to attach interface objects to underlying application code.

Microsoft's Windows and the Apple Macintosh operating system constitute GUIs. IBM's Presentation Manager is primarily an API.

10.9 Conclusion

In this chapter we have provided a brief overview of a technology which is certain to dominate the interfaces of the near future. In chapter 19 we outline how direct manipulation interfaces popular in hypermedia systems are beginning to dominate the issues surrounding user interface development. In chapter 30 we discuss how hypermedia will form part of the hybrid architecture of future information systems.

10.10 References

Apple (1987). *Hypercard User's Guide*. Cupertino, California.

Bush V. (1945). As We May Think. *Atlantic Monthly*. 176(1). July. 101-103.

Conklin E.J. (1987). Hypertext: An Introduction and Survey. *IEEE Computer*. 2(9). Sept. 17-41.

Darrel R.R and Tampa F.W.M (1988). Hypertext and the Oxford English Dictionary. *CACM*. 31(7). July. 871-879.

Frisse M.E. (1988). Searching for Information in a Hypertext Medical Handbook. *CACM*. 31(7). 880-886.

Rada R. (1991). *Hypertext: from text to expertext*. McGraw-Hill, London.

10.11 Keywords

Hypermedia
Hypertext
Multimedia

10.12 Exercises

1. In what way is a hypermedia system different from a database system?
2. How much hype do you think is in hypermedia?
3. What sort of media might be important to an insurance company handling motor accident claims over and above conventional data?
4. Why do you think object-oriented systems have been seen as good vehicles for implementing hypermedia?
5. What sort of hypermedia systems might be of use to an organisation such as an University?
6. In what area might hypermedia be applicable to the Goronwy Galvanising application?

Part Three
Techniques

Technique
Method of achieving one's purpose. (*Oxford English Dictionary*)
Manner, style, mode, line, procedure, process, way of doing. (*Roget's Thesaurus*)

In this part we introduce a number of the major techniques in the armoury of the information systems engineer. The techniques are divided into three groups: data analysis, process analysis and related techniques. The first two groups relate to the dynamic/static divide discussed in section 3.5. The last group contains a series of tecniques which either fall outside of classic systems analysis and design, or attempt to bridge across process and data analysis.

Part Three
Section 1
Data Analysis

In this section we discuss the central process of contemporary database development - a process known as data analysis or data modelling. In the next section we discuss a number of process analysis techniques. Figure S1.1 illustrates how the products of data analysis and process analysis relate.

The intention of data analysis is to develop stable foundations for application systems. The end-result of data analysis is a set of data structures designed to suit some application. This set is generally called a data model: a set of business rules embodied in some architectural principles such as those described for relational databases in chapter 6.

There are normally held to be two complementary approaches to conducting data analysis: top-down and bottom-up (see figure S1.2).

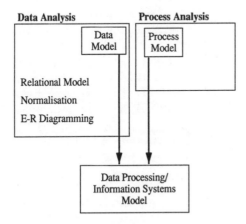

Figure S1.1   Data Analysis

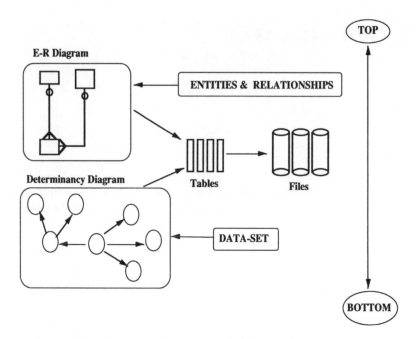

Figure S1.2   Top-Down and Bottom-up Data Analysis

Conducting data analysis top-down means that we use a diagramming technique such as entity-relationship diagramming to map what we believe to be the things of interest to the enterprise and the relationships between these things of interest. Top-down data analysis is frequently referred to as conceptual modelling because we remain at a high-level or on a fairly abstract plane. The product of such a modelling exercise is usually an entity-relationship diagram. This diagram can be transformed into a set of table-structures - a relational schema — via a straightforward process of translation or accommodation.

Rather than dealing with abstract concepts, bottom-up data analysis deals with concrete data. To do bottom-up data analysis we must have a pool of data items, extracted probably from an examination of existing enterprise documentation. To this pool of data items we apply a series of transformation rules. Bottom-up data analysis is also called normalisation.

We consider normalisation first as this approach directly relates to the principles of the relational data model. We then consider entity modelling, a technique on which most database development is based.

100

11 Normalisation

11.1 Introduction

In his seminal paper on the relational data model, E.F. Codd formulated a number of design principles for a relational database (Codd, 1970). These principles were formalised in terms of three normal forms: first normal form, second normal form and third normal form. The process of transforming a database design through these three normal forms is known as normalisation. By the mid-1970s third normal form was shown to have certain inadequacies and a stronger normal form, known as Boyce-Codd normal form was introduced (Codd, 1974). Subsequently Fagin introduced fourth normal form and indeed fifth normal form (Fagin 1977, 1979).

11.2 Why Normalise?

Suppose we are given the brief of designing a database to maintain information about the infant immunisation programme run by a district health authority (Beynon-Davies, 1992). An analysis of the documentation used by the programme staff gives us the following sample data set with which to work. If we pool all the data together in one table as below, a number of problems would arise in maintaining this data set.

Immunisations

practice name	doctor name	infant nhsNo	infant name	parent nhsNo	vacc. code	vaccine name
Ystrad	J Thomas	12456	Jenkins	14534	1523	Mumps
Ystrad	J Thomas	25643	Thomas	22223	1524	Mumps
Ystrad	D Evans	43256	Jenkins	14534	1525	Mumps
Ystrad	D Evans	43256	Jenkins	14534	1425	Polio
Pentre	P Davies	33445	Evans	38976	1626	Polio
Pentre	P Davies	42389	Davies	22447	1627	Polio
Pentre	P Davies	42389	Davies	22447	1342	Rubella
Pentre	I Jones	33129	Howells	35612	1324	Rubella
Treorci	F Evans	32445	Evans	30976	1726	Polio

1. What if we wish to delete patient 32445? The result is that we lose some valuable information. We lose information about a doctor and practice. This is called a deletion side-effect.

101

2. What if we change the doctor of patient 12456 from J. Thomas to D. Evans? We need to update not only the doctor name but also the name of the practice. This is called an update side-effect.
3. What if we admit a new patient on to the programme, say 7777,Vaughn? We need to know more information, namely about the patient's doctor, practice, and parent. We also cannot enter a patient record until a patient has had at least one vaccination. These are known as insertion side-effects.

The size of our sample file is small. One can imagine the seriousness of the file-maintenance anomalies mentioned above multiplying as the size of the file grows. The above organisation is therefore clearly not a good one for the data of this enterprise. Normalisation is a formal process whose aim is to eliminate file maintenance anomalies.

11.3 Stages of Normalisation

Normalisation is carried out in the following steps:

1. Represent the data as an unnormalised table.
2. Transform the unnormalised table to first normal form.
3. Transform first normal form tables to second normal form.
4. Transform second normal form tables to third normal form.

Occasionally, the data may still be subject to anomalies in third normal form. In this case, we may have to perform further steps:

5. Transform third normal form to fourth normal form.
6. Transform fourth normal form to fifth normal form.

In this chapter we shall concentrate on normalisation to third normal form. Those interested in fourth and fifth normal forms are referred to Beynon-Davies (1992).

The process of transforming an unnormalised database into a fully normalised database is frequently referred to as a process of non-loss decomposition (see figure 11.1). This is because we continually fragment our data structure into more and more tables (through relational projects, see section 6.7.2) without losing the fundamental relationships between data-items.

11.4 Representing the Data as an Unnormalised Table

Suppose we are given the task of designing a database for a small tiling supplies company. An analysis of this business leads us to suspect that the following data are the most relevant to the order processing section of the company: orderNo, orderDate, customerNo, customerName, productNo, productName, qty, unitPrice.

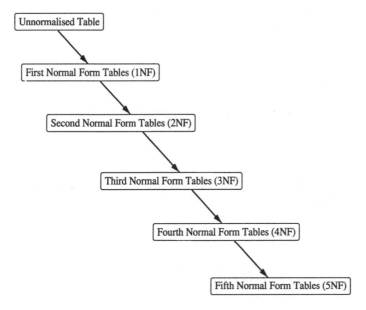

Figure 11.1   Stages of Normalisation

Our first task is to build a sample data-set for this business in the form of an unnormalised table. This table is illustrated below:

Orders

order no.	order date	cust. no.	cust. name	product no.	name	qty	unit price
0/23	01/02/91	2235	Davies	487	tiles (blue)	200	0.25
0/24	08/02/91	3444	Jones	488	tiles (white)	300	0.20
0/25	10/02/91	3444	Jones	489	tiles (red)	150	0.25
0/23	01/02/91	2235	Davies	340	grout (1kg)	10	1.25
0/24	08/02/91	3444	Jones	340	grout (1kg)	30	1.25
0/24	08/02/91	3444	Jones	342	cement (1kg)	30	1.50
0/26	01/02/91	2237	Evans	488	tiles (white)	400	0.20

11.5 Unnormalised Table to First Normal Form

We transform an unnormalised table to first normal form by identifying repeating groups and turning such repeating groups into separate tables. We first choose a key for this data-set. Let us suppose that we choose the data-item orderNo.

Having chosen a key for the unnormalised table we look for a group of data-items that has multiple values for a single value of the key. Examining the table above we see that productNo, productName, qty and unitPrice all repeat with respect to orderNo. We therefore form a separate table of all the repeating data-items, called orderLines and transfer orderNo across as a foreign key.

Orders

order no.	order date	customer no.	name
0/23	01/02/91	2235	Davies
0/24	08/02/91	3444	Jones
0/25	10/02/91	3444	Jones
0/23	01/02/91	2235	Davies
0/24	08/02/91	3444	Jones
0/24	08/02/91	3444	Jones
0/26	01/02/91	2237	Evans

OrderLines

order no.	product no.	name	qty	unit price
0/23	487	tiles (blue)	200	0.25
0/24	488	tiles (white)	300	0.20
0/25	489	tiles (red)	150	0.25
0/23	340	grout (1kg)	10	1.25
0/24	340	grout (1kg)	30	1.25
0/24	342	cement (1kg)	30	1.50
0/26	488	tiles (white)	400	0.20

11.6 First Normal Form to Second Normal Form

To move from first normal form to second normal form we remove part-key dependencies. This involves examining those tables that have a compound key and for each non-key data-item in the table asking the question: can the data-item be uniquely identified by part of the compound key?

Take, for instance, the table named OrderLines. Here we have a 2-part compound key. We ask the question above for the data-items productName, qty and unitPrice. Clearly we need both the orderNo and the productNo to tell us what the qty is likely to be. OrderNo however has no influence on the productName or the unitPrice. This leads to a decomposition of the tables as follows:

Orders

order no.	order date	customer no.	name
0/23	01/02/91	2235	Davies
0/24	08/02/91	3444	Jones
0/25	10/02/91	3444	Jones
0/23	01/02/91	2235	Davies
0/24	08/02/91	3444	Jones
0/24	08/02/91	3444	Jones
0/26	01/02/91	2237	Evans

OrderLines

order no.	product no.	qty
0/23	487	200
0/24	488	300
0/25	489	150
0/23	340	10
0/24	340	30
0/24	342	30
0/26	488	400

Products

product no.	name	unit price
487	tiles (blue)	0.25
488	tiles (white)	0.20
489	tiles (red)	0.25
340	grout (1kg)	1.25
342	cement (1kg)	1.50

11.7 Second Normal Form to Third Normal Form

To move from second normal form to third normal form we remove inter-data dependencies. To do this we examine every table and ask of each pair of non-key data-items: is the value of field A dependent on the value of field B, or vice versa? If the answer is yes we split off the relevant data-items into a separate table.

The only place where this is relevant to our present example is in the table called Orders. Here, customerNo determines customerName. We therefore create a separate table to be called Customers with customerNo as the key. This is illustrated below:

Orders

order no.	order date	customer no.
0/23	01/02/91	2235
0/24	08/02/91	3444
0/25	10/02/91	3444
0/23	01/02/91	2235
0/24	08/02/91	3444
0/24	08/02/91	3444
0/26	01/02/91	2237

OrderLines

order no.	product no.	qty
0/23	487	200
0/24	488	300
0/25	489	150
0/23	340	10
0/24	340	30
0/24	342	30
0/26	488	400

Products

product no.	name	unit price
487	tiles (blue)	0.25
488	tiles (white)	0.20
489	tiles (red)	0.25
340	grout (1kg)	1.25
342	cement (1kg)	1.50

Customers

customer no.	name
2235	Davies
3444	Jones
2237	Evans

11.8 The Bracketing Notation

To represent the relational schema in an implementation-independent form we use a notation sometimes known as the bracketing notation. We list a suitable mnemonic name for the table first. This is followed by a list of data-items or column names delimited by commas. It is conventional to list the primary key for the table first and underline this data item. If the primary key is made up of two or more attributes, we underline all the component data items. For instance, the third normal form tables for our order processing example would look as follows:

Orders(<u>orderNo</u>, orderDate, customerNo)
OrderLines(<u>orderNo, productNo</u>, qty)
Products(<u>productNo</u>, productName, unitPrice)
Customers(<u>customerNo</u>, customerName)

11.9 The Normalisation Oath

A useful mnemonic for remembering the rationale for normalisation is the distortion of the legal oath presented below:

1. No Repeating,
2. The Fields Depend Upon The Key,
3. The Whole Key,
4. And Nothing But The Key,
5. So Help Me Codd.

Line 5 simply reminds us that the techniques were originally developed by E.F.Codd in the 1970s. Line 2 states that all data items in a table must depend solely upon the key. Line 1 indicates that there should be no repeating groups of data in a table. Line 3 indicates that there should be no part-key dependencies in a table. Finally, line 4 reminds us that there should be no inter-data dependencies in a table. The only dependency should be between the key and other data-items in a table.

Classic normalisation is described as a process of non-loss decomposition. The decomposition approach starts with one (universal) relation. File maintenance anomalies such as insertion, deletion and update anomalies are gradually removed by a series of projections. Non-loss decomposition is therefore a design process guaranteed to produce a data-set free from file-maintenance problems. It does however suffer from a number of disadvantages, particularly as a practicable database design technique:

1. It requires all of the data-set to be in place before the process can begin.
2. For any reasonably large data-set the process is:
   a. extremely time-consuming.
   b. difficult to apply.
   c. prone to human error.

This chapter will therefore concentrate on describing a contrasting approach to normalisation which uses a graphical notation. This makes the technique easier to use and less prone to error.

11.10 Determinancy and Dependency

Normalisation is the process of identifying the logical associations between data-items and designing a database which will represent such associations but without suffering the file maintenance anomalies discussed in section 11.2. The logical associations between data-items that point the database designer in the direction of a good database design are referred to as determinant or dependent relationships. Two data-items, A and B, are said to be in a determinant or dependent relationship if certain values of data-item B always appear with certain values of data-item A.

Determinancy/dependency also implies some direction in the association. If data-item A is the determinant data-item and B the dependent data-item then the direction of the association is from A to B and not vice versa.

There are two major types of determinancy or its opposite dependency: functional (single-valued) determinancy, and non-functional (multi-valued) determinancy. Most normalisation can be conducted satisfactorarily using functional dependencies. We therefore concentrate on functional dependencies in this chapter. Readers interested in non-functional dependencies are referred to Beynon-Davies (1992).

Data-item B is said to be functionally dependent on data-item A if for every value of A there is one, unambiguous value for B. In such a relationship data-item A is referred to as the determinant data-item, while data-item B is referred to as the dependent data-item. Functional determinancy is so-called because it is modelled on the idea of a mathematical function. A function is a directed one-to-one mapping between the elements of one set and the elements of another set.

For example, in a personnel database, employeeNo and employeeName would be in a functional determinant relationship. EmployeeNo is the determinant and employeeName is the dependent data-item. This is because for every employee number there is only one associated value of employee name. For example, 7369 may be associated with the value J.Smith. This does not mean to say that we cannot have more than one employee named J.Smith in our organisation. It simply means that each J.Smith will have a different employee number. Hence, although there is a functional determinancy from employee number to employee name the same is not true in the opposite direction — employee name does not functionally determine employee number.

11.11 Determinancy Diagrams

A diagram which documents the determinancy or dependency between data-items we shall refer to as a determinancy or dependency diagram. Data-items are drawn on a determinancy diagram as labelled ovals, circles or bubbles. Functional dependency is represented between two data-items by drawing a single-headed arrow from the determinant data-item to the dependent data-item. For example, figure 11.2 represents a number of functional dependencies as diagrams.

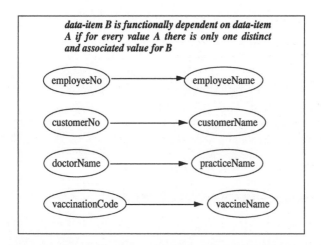

Figure 11.2   Functional Dependency Diagrams

11.12 Transitive and Compound Determinancy

Figure 11.3a documents a transitive dependency. A functional dependency exists from *manager* to *department*, from *department* to *location*, and from *manager* to *location*. Any situation in which A determines B, B determines C and A also

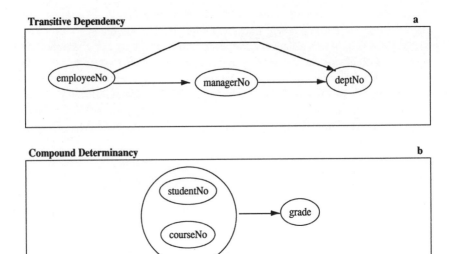

Figure 11.3   Transitive and Compound Determinancy

determines C can usually be simplified into the chain A to B and B to C. Identifying transitive determinancies can frequently simplify complex determinancy diagrams and indeed is an important part of the process of normalisation.

Frequently, one data-item is insufficient to fully determine the values of some other data-item. However, the combination of two or more data-items gives us a dependent relationship. In such situations we call the group of determinants a compound determinant. A compound determinant is drawn as an enclosing bubble around two or more data-item bubbles. Hence, in figure 11.3b we need both *studentNo* and *courseNo* to functionally determine *grade*. The functional dependency is drawn from the outermost bubble.

11.13 Accommodating Functional Dependencies

In this and the following section we examine the process of transforming a determinancy diagram into a set of table structures or relational schema — a process frequently known as accommodation.

Suppose we are given the determinancy diagram in figure 11.4. This diagram documents the dependencies between data-items in the unnormalised table described in section 11.5. We transform the diagram into a set of table structures by applying the rule:

Every functional determinant becomes the primary key of a table. All immediate dependent data-items become non-key attributes of the table.

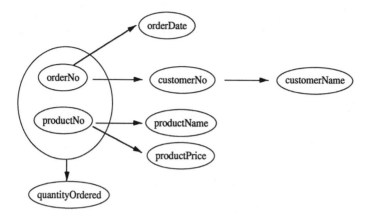

Figure 11.4   A Complete Determinancy Diagram

This is a simplification of what is known as the Boyce-Codd rule after its inventors.

A straightforward way of conducting accommodation with a determinancy diagram is to draw enclosing boundaries around what will fundamentally be table-structures. Figure 11.5 indicates the boundaries that will result from the problem discussed in section 11.8.

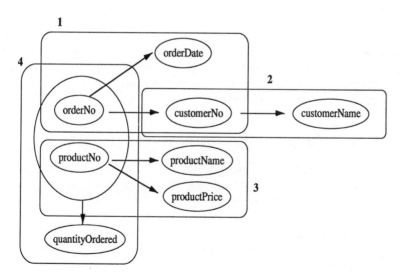

Figure 11.5   Drawing Boundaries for Accommodation

11.14 De-Normalisation

Few data analysts would treat the file organisation proposed by third normal form as gospel. In real-life, the organisation proposed by third normal form usually represents too many files to be managed practically within the context of a given information system. Many sites would therefore regard first normal form to be good enough, particularly if data volumes are small, or transaction rates are low. Other sites may consider second normal form tables to be sufficiently flexible to meet the demands of higher volumes of data and transactions. Yet other sites may merge bits of third normal form relations together to optimise processing requirements.

11.15 Goronwy Galvanising Case Study

Figure11.6 represents a determinancy diagram drawn from an analysis of manual documentation such as the document displayed in figure 3.4. Figure 11.7 represents a determinancy diagram drawn from an analysis of the form displayed in figure 3.5. Note the compound determinant in figure 11.7. There are a number of points of communality between the two diagrams. We therefore draw a combined diagram as in figure 11.8.

This diagram can then be transformed to the relational schema below by application of the rule discussed in section 11.10. A schema expressed in the bracketing notation is given below:

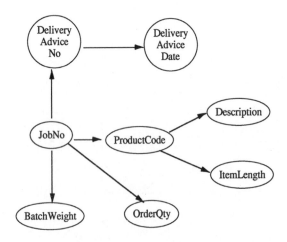

Figure 11.6   Determinancy diagram for a Delivery Advice

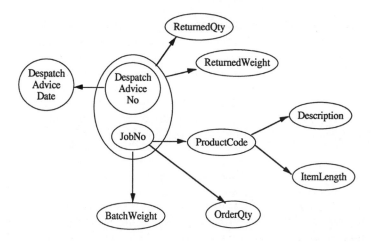

Figure 11.7   Determinancy Diagram for Despatch Advice

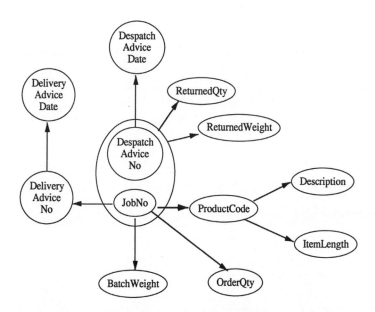

Figure 11.8   Combined Determinancy Diagram for Goronwy

DespatchAdvices(<u>despatchAdviceNo</u>, despatchAdviceDate)
DeliveryAdvices(<u>deliveryAdviceNo</u>, deliveryAdviceDate)
Jobs(<u>jobNo</u>, deliveryAdviceNo, totalWeight, orderQty, productCode)
Despatches(<u>despatchAdviceNo</u>, <u>jobNo</u>, returnedQty, returnedWeight)
Products(<u>productCode</u>, description, itemLength)

11.16 Conclusion

This chapter has considered two distinct approaches to conducting normalisation. The approach, known as non-loss decomposition, is the one mainly discussed in the literature. However, the main advantage of the determinancy diagramming technique is that it provides a mechanism for designing a database incrementally. One does not need a complete data-set in hand to begin the process of design. The data analyst can begin his work with a small collection of central data-items and continuously add to this core until the dependencies are fully documented.

11.17 References

Beynon-Davies P. (1992). *Relational Database Design*. Blackwell Scientific, Oxford.

Codd E.F. (1970). A Relational Model for Large Shared Data Banks. *CACM*. 13 (1). 377-387.

Codd E.F. (1974). Recent Investigations into Relational Database Systems. *Proc. IFIP Congress*.

Fagin R. (1977). Multi-Valued Dependencies and a New Normal Form for Relational Databases. *ACM Trans. on Database Systems*. 2(1).

Fagin R. (1979). Normal Forms and Relational Database Operators. *ACM SIGMOD Int. Symposium on the Management of Data*. 153-160.

11.18 Keywords

Accommodation
Bracketing notation
De-normalisation
Dependent data-item
Determinant data-item
First Normal Form
Functional determinancy
Non-functional determinancy
Non-loss decomposition
Normalisation
Second normal form
Third normal form

11.19 Exercises

1. Draw a determinancy diagram for each of the following types of marriage:
   a. monogamy — one man marries one woman;
   b. polygamy — one man can marry many women, but every woman marries single man;
   c. polyandry— one woman can marry many men, but every man marries a single woman;
   d. group marriage—one man can marry many women, one woman can marry many men.
2. Accommodate each dependency diagram in 1 above into a relational schema.
3. Produce third normal form table-structures from the table below:

Cinemas

film No.	film Name	cinema Code	cinema Name	town	population	man. No.	man. Name	takings
25	Star Wars	BX	Rex	Cardiff	300000	01	Jones	900
25	Star Wars	KT	Rialto	Swansea	200000	03	Thomas	350
25	Star Wars	DJ	Odeon	Newport	250000	01	Jones	800
50	Jaws	BX	Rex	Cardiff	300000	01	Jones	1200
50	Jaws	DJ	Odeon	Newport	250000	01	Jones	400
50	Jaws	TL	Rex	Bridgend	150000	02	Davies	300
50	Jaws	RP	Grand	Bristol	350000	04	Smith	1500
50	Jaws	HF	State	Bristol	350000	04	Smith	1000
30	Star Trek	BX	Rex	Cardiff	300000	01	Jones	850
30	Star Trek	TL	Rex	Bridgend	150000	02	Davies	500
40	ET	KT	Rialto	Swansea	200000	03	Davies	1200
40	ET	RP	Grand	Bristol	350000	04	Smith	2000

4. Take any receipt produced by a major supermarket chain and conduct a normalisation exercise.
5. The Boyce-Codd rule should actually be phrased as, every functional determinant becomes a candidate key for a relation. In what way does this revision affect the accommodation process?
6. Generate a set of fully normalised tables from the following unnormalised table:

Operating Schedule

doctor	doctor	operation	opDate	opTime	patient	pName	admission
18654	Smith	AA1234	04/02/92	08:30	2468	Davies M.	20/01/92
18654	Smith	BA1598	04/02/92	10:30	3542	Jones D.	11/01/92
18654	Smith	FG1965	04/02/92	16:00	1287	Evans I.	25/12/91
18654	Smith	AA1235	13/02/92	14:00	2468	Davies M.	20/01/92
13855	Evans	LP1564	13/02/92	14:00	4443	Beynon P.	05/01/92
18592	Jones	PP9900	15/02/92	14:00	2222	Scott I.	04/01/92
18592	Jones	BA1598	04/02/92	10:30	3542	Jones D.	11/01/92
18592	Jones	FG1965	04/02/92	16:00	1287	Evans I.	25/12/91

7. Goronwy Galvanising employ 30 shift workers. Each employee is identified by a national insurance number. This number identifies an employee card on which is written the employee's name, home address, telephone number, date of birth and current weekly salary.

   Each employee works a given shift. Each shift is identified by a unique shift number which documents the start and ending hour of each shift. The current shift number relevant to a given worker is updated on his card each week.

   Produce a determinancy diagram for this system. Produce a set of table structures from the determinancy diagram.

12 Entity-Relationship Diagramming

12.1 Semantic Data Models

Database design is fundamentally a task in data modelling. A data model is an architecture for data (chapter 6). Brodie has made a distinction between three generations of data model (Brodie, 1984):

1. Primitive Data Models. In this approach objects are represented by record-structures grouped in file-structures. The main operations available are read and write operations over records.
2. Classic Data Models. These are the hierarchical, network and relational data models. The hierarchical data model is an extension of the primitive data model discussed above. The network is an extension of the hierarchical approach. The relational data model is a fundamental departure from the hierarchical and network approaches.
3. Semantic Data Models. The main problem with classic data models like the relational data model is that they maintain a fundamental record-orientation. In other words, the meaning of the information in the database — its semantics – – is not readily apparent from the database itself. Semantic information must be consciously applied by the user of databases using the classic approach. For this reason, a number of so-called semantic data models have been proposed (King and Mcleod, 1985). Semantic data models (SDMs) attempt to provide a more expressive means of representing the meaning of information than is available in the classic models.

Probably the most frequently cited of the SDMs is the Entity-Relationship data model (E-R model) (Chen, 1976). In the E-R model the 'real world' is represented in terms of entities, the relationships between entities and the attributes associated with entities. Entities represent objects of interest in the real world such as employees, departments and projects. Relationships represent named associations between entities. A department employs many employees. An employee is assigned to a number of projects. Employs and is assigned to are both relationships in the Entity-Relationship approach. Attributes are properties of an entity or relationship. Name is an attribute of the employee entity. Duration of employment is an attribute of the employ's relationship.

12.2 Entity Models

An entity model is a model of the entities, relationships and attributes in some domain of discourse. An entity may be defined as "a thing which the enterprise recognises as being capable of an independent existence and which can be uniquely identified" (Howe, 1986). A relationship can be defined as "an association between entities" (Beynon-Davies, 1992). An attribute is a property of some entity.

12.2.1 Entities

An entity may be a physical object such as a house or a car, an event such as a house sale or a car service, or a concept such as a transaction or order. Although the term entity is the one most commonly used following Chen (1976) we should really distinguish between an entity and an entity-type. An entity-type is a category. An entity, strictly speaking, is an instance of a given entity-type. There are usually many instances of entity-types.

Because the term entity-type is somewhat cumbersome, most people tend to use the term entity as a synonym. We shall conform to this practice. It must be remembered however that whenever we refer to an entity we mean an entity-type.

12.2.2 Relationships

More than one relationship can exist between any two entities. For instance, the entities house and person can be related by ownership and/or by occupation. In theory, having identified a set of say 6 entities, up to 15 relationships could exist betwen these entities. In practice, it will usually be quite obvious that many entities are quite unrelated. Furthermore, the object of entity modelling is to document only so-called direct relationships. For instance, direct relationships exist between the entities Parent and Child and between Child and School. The relationship between Parent and School is indirect; it exists only by virtue of the child entity (Shave, 1981).

12.2.3 Attributes

An entity is an aggregation of attributes. Values assigned to attributes are used to distinguish one entity from another. Hence, deptNo, deptName, and location are all attributes which characterise the Department entity. One or more of the attributes of an entity are normally chosen as an entity identifier. The attribute deptNo is a suitable identifier for the entity Department.

12.3 Semantic Modelling

The data needed to support a given information system do not usually fall irrevocably into one of the three categories: entity, relationship and attribute. A classic example is the data needed to be stored on marriages. Marriage could be regarded as an entity with attributes such as date, place, and names of bride and groom. It could similarly be regarded as the attribute marital status associated with the entity Person. Finally, it could be represented as a relationship between the entities Man and Woman.

One of the tasks of the entity modeller is to decide which of these viewpoints is the most important for the information system under consideration. Hence, data analysis is frequently referred to as semantic modelling (Date, 1990). The aim is to represent data as it is perceived in the organisation under consideration (Klein and Hirscheim, 1987).

12.4 Notation

Entity models are usually mapped out as entity-relationship diagrams (E-R diagrams). The end-product of entity-relationship diagramming is a model of the entities and relationships in a particular domain of discourse.

An entity is represented on the diagram by a rectangular box in which is written a meaningful name for the entity (figure 12.1a). A relationship between entities is represented by drawing a line (sometimes labelled) between the relevant boxes on the diagram (figure 12.1b). An attribute is represented by a circle or oval attached by a line to the appropriate entity. The entity identifier is underlined (figure 12.1c).

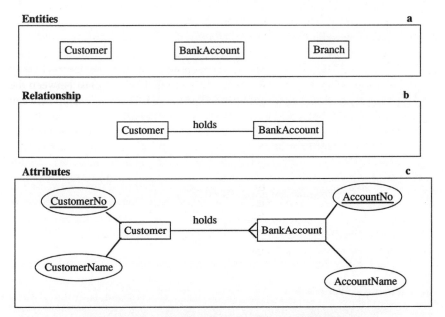

Figure 12.1   Entities, Relationships and Attributes

12.4.1 Properties of a Relationship

There are two properties of the concept of a relationship which are usually considered important: we shall refer to them as cardinality and participation.

Cardinality (or degree) concerns the number of instances involved in a relationship. A relationship can be said to be either a 1:1 (one-to-one) relationship, a 1:M (one-to-many) relationship, or a M:N (many-to-many) relationship.

For instance, the relationship between bankaccounts and customers can be said to be one-to-one (1:1) if it can be defined in the following way:

> A bankaccount is held by at most one customer.
> A customer may hold at most, one bankaccount.

In contrast, the relationship between bankaccounts and customers is one-to-many (1:M) if it is defined as:

> A customer holds many bankaccounts.
> A bankaccount is held by at most one customer.

Finally, we are approaching a realistic representation of the relationship when we describe it as being many-to-many (M:N). That is:

> A customer holds many bankaccounts.
> A bankaccount may be held by many customers.

There are a number of competing notational devices available for portraying the cardinality of a relationship. We choose to represent cardinality by drawing a crow's foot on the many end of a relationship (see figure 12.2a).

Participation (or optionality) concerns the involvement of entities in a relationship. An entity's participation is optional if there is at least one instance of an entity which does not participate in the relationship. An entity's participation is mandatory if all instances of an entity must participate in the relationship. The default participation is mandatory. If the participation is optional we add a circle (an 'O' for optional) alongside the relevant entity (see 12.2b).

12.5 Abstraction Mechanisms

The original Entity-Relationship model has been extended in a number of ways (Teorey *et al.*, 1986). One of the most important extensions is the support for generalisation hierarchies (Smith and Smith, 1977). This allows us to declare certain entities as subtypes of other entities. For instance, Manager, Secretary and Techni-

Degree / Cardinality

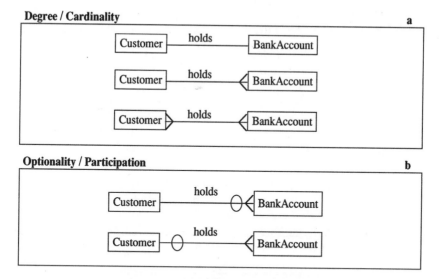

Optionality / Participation

Figure 12.2   Properties of a Relationship

cian might all be declared subtypes of an Employee entity. Likewise, SalesManager, ProductionManager, etc., would all be declared subtypes of the Manager entity. The important consequence of this facility is that entities lower down in the generalisation hierarchy inherit the attributes and relationships of entities higher up in the hierarchy. Hence, a sales manager would inherit properties of managers in general, and indeed of employees in general. Likewise, a sales manager would inherit the relationship of an employee to a department.

In relatively simple cases it is convenient to indicate generalisation on an E-R diagram by drawing disjoint or overlapping boxes (see figure 12.3a) (Harel, 1988). As the size of a diagram increases it is more practical to use a notation built on relationship lines. In figure 12.3b we have represented generalisation by an empty triangle (Rumbaugh *et al.*, 1991).

The Abstraction mechanisms of aggregation and association can also be represented on E-R diagrams.

Aggregation is the process by which a higher-level object is used to group together a number of lower-level objects. For instance, iSBN, title, author, publisher and dateOfPublication may all be aggregated together to form a Book entity. In the Entity-Relationship model, therefore, aggregation is implicit in assigning attributes to an entity. Aggregation of entities can also appear on an entity model. Hence, for instance, a Car entity might be built up of an assembly of wheels, chassis, engine, etc. Assemblies of this kind can be represented by a forked link from the aggregate entity to the part entities and a semi-circle at the junction of relationship lines (see figure 12.4).

Association is a form of abstraction in which instances of one entity are associated

Generalisation

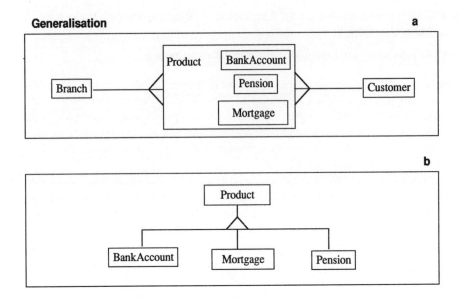

Figure 12.3   Generalisation

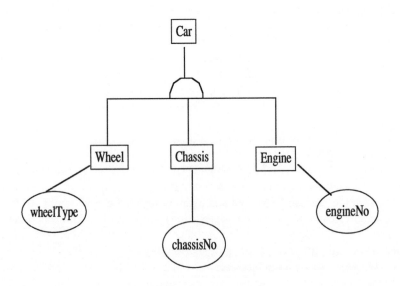

Figure 12.4   Aggregation

with instances of another entity. Association is, of course, implicit in the way we define relationships on entity models.

12.6 Validating an Entity Model against Requirements

A first-pass E-R diagram represents the basic structure of data needed in a given information system. Most of the adherents of the technique recommend that an entity model should be validated against some definition of processing requirements. This definition will identify which entities and relationships must be accessed, in what order, by what means, and for what purpose. A detailed discussion of this topic is given in Beynon-Davies (1992).

Suppose we have the following extract from an E-R diagram representing an educational application (figure 12.5) (Shave, 1981). We wish to validate this entity model against a requirement to produce the staff/student ratio for a given department. To perform this processing we need to access:

1. All staff of a department.
2. Each course taught by a member of staff.
3. Each student registered for a course.

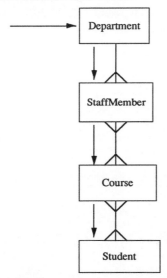

Figure 12.5   Validating an Entity Model

This is indicated on the E-R diagram in figure 12.5 as a series of arrows.

12.7 Producing a Relational Schema

E-R diagrams are generally drawn as a means of designing relational schema. The process of transforming an E-R diagram into a relational database design we refer to as accommodation. The process of accommodating E-R diagrams involves the following steps:

1. Break down each many-to-many relationship into two one-to-many relationships. This is done by interposing a link entity between the two previous entities and drawing crow's-feet to the link entity. The entity identifiers for the two previous entities then become a compound entity identifier for the link entity.
2. For each entity on our diagram we form a table, usually by making the entity names plural.
3. The identifying attribute of each entity becomes the primary key of the table.
3. All other attributes of the entity become non-key attributes of the table.
4. For each one-to-many relationship post the primary key from the one end of the relationship into the table on the many end of the relationship.
5. Optionality on the many end of a relationship tells us whether a foreign key can be null or not. If the many end is mandatory the foreign key is not null. If the many end is optional the foreign key can be null.

Taking the educational application we transform all many-to-many relationships to give us figure 12.6. Note, we have added some sample attributes to the diagram. A skeleton relational schema expressed in the bracketing notation is given below:

> Departments(<u>deptNo</u>, deptName, ...)
> StaffMembers(<u>StaffNo</u>, staffName, deptNo, ...)
> Courses(<u>courseNo</u>, courseName, ...)
> Students(<u>studentNo</u>, studentName, ...)
> Allocation(<u>staffNo</u>, <u>courseNo</u>, ...)
> Registration(<u>studentNo</u>, <u>courseNo</u>, ...)

12.8 Case Study: A General Hospital Appointments and Operations System

Suppose we are given the brief of designing an appropriate information system for the patients' appointments and operations activities of a large general hospital. Our initial analysis work provides us with the following brief description of the existing manual system:

1. Patients must make an appointment at a given clinic session held at one of the hospital's clinics.
2. Doctors are allocated one or more appointments within a clinic session, but only one doctor will be present at each appointment.
3. Operations are scheduled and allocated to one of a number of theatre sessions held in the hospital's operating theatres. Each doctor may perform a number of given operations on patients. A given operation is done on only one patient, but there may be more than one doctor in attendance.

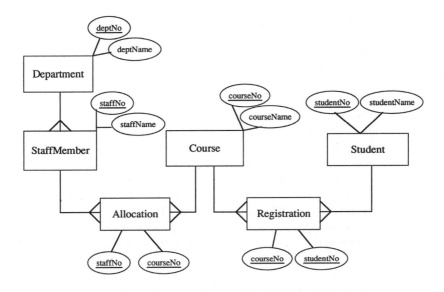

Figure 12.6   Educational E-R Model

From such a description, we get some initial idea of the important entities involved in this system:

> Clinic
> ClinicSession
> Appointment
> Patient
> Doctor
> Operation
> OperatingTheatre
> TheatreSession

Note that we might have been tempted to add the entity Hospital to this list. However, in this system there is only one instance of a hospital. Entities should normally have many instances associated with them.

The text also gives some idea of relationships. A possible list is given below:

> Patient — Operation
> Doctor — Operation
> Doctor — Appointment
> Patient — Appointment
> ClinicSession — Appointment

          Clinic — ClinicSession
          TheatreSession — Operation
          Theatre — TheatreSession

Each of these relationships then needs to be characterised in terms of cardinality and participation. For some relationships the text above does not provide enough information. We therefore make a number of assumptions which would have to be confirmed or otherwise by users. A possible diagram is given in figure 12.7.

From this E-R diagram we arrive at the following relational schema by applying the guidelines discussed in section 12.6.

          Clinics(<u>clinicName</u>, ...)
          ClinicSessions(<u>clinicName, sessionNo</u>, ...)
          Appointments(<u>clinicName, sessionNo, patientNo</u>, doctorNo, ...)
          Patients(<u>patientNo</u>, ...)
          Doctors(<u>doctorNo</u>, ...)
          Operations(<u>theatreName, theatreSession, operationNo</u>, patientNo, ...)
          Schedule(<u>doctorNo, operationNo</u>, ...)
          Theatres(<u>theatreName</u>, ...)
          TheatreSessions(<u>theatreName, theatreSession</u>, ...)

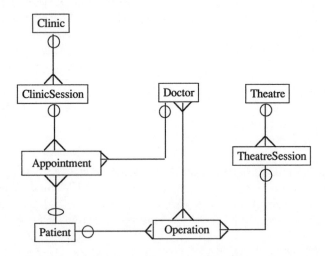

Figure 12.7   Appointments and Operations System

Note how we have formed compound keys in a number of tables, where the foreign keys form part of the primary key. Note also how the table schedule constitutes a link entity between doctors and operations.

12.9 Goronwy Galvanising Case Study

Figure 12.8 illustrates an E-R diagram drawn for the case of the Goronwy Galvanising system. Note how we have distinguished between delivery advice notes and despatch advice notes. The entity despatch is a break-down of the many-to-many relationship between Job and DespatchAdvice. In other words, a given job can be recorded on more than one despatch advice note.

Applying the rules of accommodation as described in section 12.6 would mean that we arrive at the following set of skeleton table structures:

> DespatchAdvices(<u>despatchAdviceNo</u>, ...)
> DeliveryAdvices(<u>deliveryAdviceNo</u>, ...)
> Jobs(<u>jobNo</u>, despatchAdviceNo, productCode, ...)
> Products(<u>productCode</u>, ...)
> Despatches(<u>despatchAdviceNo, jobNo</u>, ...)

Fortunately, this relational schema matches closely with the one generated from the determinancy diagrams in chapter 10. In many circumstances this will not be the case. The analyst frequently has to reconcile the results from top-down data analysis with the results from bottom-up data analysis. See Beynon-Davies (1992) for a more detailed discussion of reconciliation. Figure 12.9 indicates how we might modify the

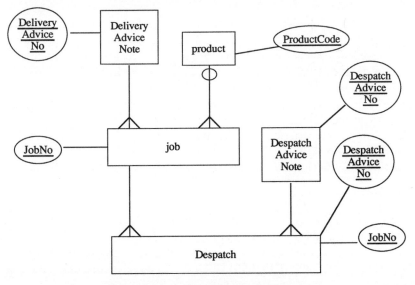

Figure 12.8   Goronwy E-R Diagram

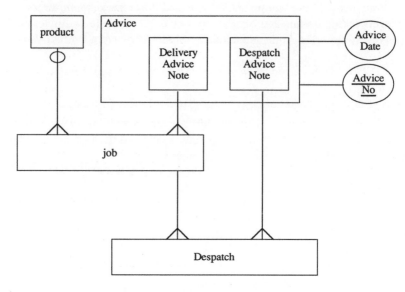

Figure 12.9   Generalisation Applied to Goronwy

E-R diagram in figure 12.8 to exploit generalisation. Here we have made delivery advices and despatch advices both subtypes of an advice class. We continue discussing this example in chapter 25.

12.10 Conclusion

Entity modelling as represented by the technique of E-R diagramming is primarily a database design technique. An E-R diagram is conventionally referred to as a conceptual model of a database system. From this conceptual model we derive a logical model expressed usually as a series of table structures in third normal form. The final step in database development is to produce a physical model. That is, a series of record structures expressed in the syntax of some programming language or DBMS. If the DBMS is relational this step is relatively straightforward. If physical structures are COBOL files then the process is a little more convoluted but not difficult (Howe, 1986).

12.11 References

Beynon-Davies P. (1992). *Relational Database Design*. Blackwell Scientific, Oxford.

Brodie M.L. (1984) On the Development of Data Models. In Brodie M.L., Mylopoulos J. and Schmidt T.W. (eds) (1984) *On Conceptual Modelling: Perspec-*

tives from Artificial Intelligence, Databases and Programming Languages. Springer-Verlag, Berlin.

Chen P.P.S. (1976). The Entity-Relationship Model - Toward a Unified View of Data. *ACM Trans. on Database Systems.* 1. 9-36.

Date C.J. (1990) *An Introduction to Database Systems. Vol. 1.* 5th ed. Addison-Wesley, Reading, Mass.

Harel D. (1986) On Visual Formalisms. *CACM.* 31(5) May 514-529.

Howe D.R. (1986). *Data Analysis for Database Design.* (2nd Edn.). Edward Arnold, London.

King R. and McCleod D. (1985) *Semantic Data Models.* In Bing Yao S. (ed.). Principles of Database Design. Vol 1: Logical Organisations. Prentice-Hall, Englewood Cliffs. N.J.

Klein H.K. and Hirschheim R.A. (1989). Four Paradigms of Information Systems Development. *CACM.* 32(10) October 1199-1216.

Shave M.J.R. (1981). Entities, Functions and Binary Relations: steps to a conceptual schema. *The Computer Journal.* 24(1).

Smith J.M. and Smith D.C.P. (1977) Database Abstractions: Aggregation and Generalisation. *ACM Trans. Database Sys.* 2(2) 105-133.

Teorey T.J. Yang D., and Fry J.P. (1986). A Logical Design Methodology for Relational Databases Using the Extended Entity-Relationship Model. *ACM Computing Surveys.* 18 197-222.

12.12 Keywords

Attribute
Cardinality
Entity
Entity Type
Optionality
Relationship

12.13 Exercises

1. Produce an E-R diagram which represents the following information describing a horses breeding register: A racing horse is identified by a unique name. The date of birth of the horse and its sex are also recorded. Each horse has a father and mother. The system must be able to produce a genealogy for each horse.
2. Produce a set of table structures from the E-R diagram produced for 1.
3. Draw an extended E-R diagram to represent the following classification problem: Lions and Tigers are big cats; BigCats are Mammals; Mammals are Animals.

4. Draw an E-R diagram to represent the following assertions: An Employee uses a CompanyCar; a given CompanyCar will be used by a number of different employees; some employees do not use any company car; all company cars are used by at least one employee.
5. Why do you think the accommodation process to COBOL file structures is more involved than that for relational systems?
6. Produce and E-R diagram for the system described in chapter 11, exercise 8.
7. Produce an E-R diagram to handle the data on the supermarket bill illustrated in figure 12.10.
8. Produce an E-R diagram to handle the data on the gas bill illustrated in figure 12.11.

|||||||||||||||||||||||||||||||||||||||||||||||||||||||||||

FRESCO

|||||||||||||||||||||||||||||||||||||||||||||||||||||||||||

Item	Amt	£
Corned Beef	1	0.75
Instant Coffee	1	1.69
Raspberries	1	0.75
Catfood	1	0.36
Apple Juice	2	0.83
Yoghurt	6	0.29
Total		**6.95**

12 items

|||||||||||||||||||||||||||||||||||||||||||||||||||||||||||

Thank You for shopping at Fresco
Newbridge Branch
27/3/93 13:02   003 1114 6467

Figure 12.10   A Supermarket Bill

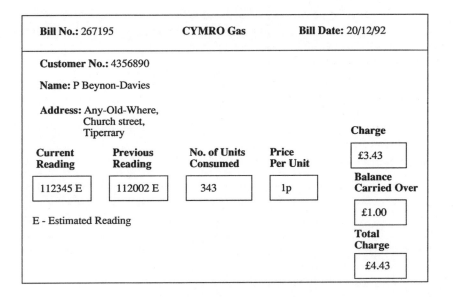

Figure 12.11   A Gas Bill

Part Three
Section 2
Process Analysis

Process analysis takes a dynamic view of information systems. Process analysis techniques concentrate on the movement of data through systems and the transformation of data within systems. Process analysis and data analysis are necessarily inter-linked. The structure of data determines the functions that can be performed with data, and vice versa. An information system made up solely of data structures is inconceivable. Most information systems are built to provide the means for data manipulation, particularly information retrieval.

Figure S2.1 illustrates one way of conceiving the relationship between process analysis and data analysis. Process analysis is seen here as the mechanism by which the various processes which feed off a common bed of data structures are derived.

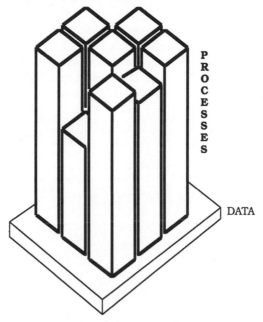

Figure S2.1   The Place of Process Analysis and Data Analysis

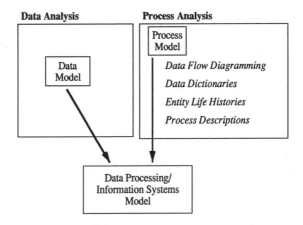

Figure S2.2   Process Analysis

Figure S2.2 illustrates how process analysis can be considered as the mechanism which produces a process model. Whereas a data model is an abstract representation of the data structures required of some application, a process model is an abstract representation of the activities associated with some application. To this end a number of techniques have been devised of which the most influential is data flow diagramming. This technique is normally supported by two others: data dictionaries and process descriptions. Entity life histories are a useful process-oriented adjunct to entity modelling, and it for this reason that we include them in this part of the book.

13 Data Flow Diagramming

13.1 Introduction

A data flow diagram (DFD) is a representation of a system or subsystem in terms of how data moves through the system.

A number of people have been involved in developing the data flow diagram as an analysis and design tool. Among the earliest exponents of the method were Tom DeMarco and Edward Yourdon (DeMarco, 1979). Gane and Sarson have modified and extended the technique to approach something like the technique discussed in this chapter (Gane and Sarson, 1977). The major difference of the technique used here is in the notation. We shall be using the notation recommended within the British methodology SSADM (Structured Systems Analysis and Design Method) (Cutts, 1991).

13.2 The Plumbing Analogy

Probably the easiest way to understand the rationale behind a data flow diagram is to make the analogy between an information system and a household plumbing system. Plumbing systems are designed to handle flows of water. Information systems are designed to handle flows of data. A plumbing system receives its water from external sources such as the public water supply, and deposits its used water in external entities such as drains. An information system receives its data from external sources such as customers, banks, retailers, etc., and communicates the results of its processing to other entities, perhaps other information systems. Household plumbing systems are usually designed to process water in some way. For instance, a boiler engages in the process of heating the water to a given temperature. In information systems far more various forms of processing occur; data is transformed by some process and then passed on to another process, and so on. Finally, in a plumbing system there are usually repositories of water, eg., sinks, cisterns etc. In information systems, such repositories are referred to as data stores.

13.3 Elements

DFDs are hence made up of four basic elements: processes, data flows, data stores and external entities (sometimes called sources or sinks).

13.3.1 Processes

A process is a transformation of incoming data flow(s) into outgoing data flow(s). A process is represented on a DFD by a labelled square or rectangle, as in figure 13.1a.

13.3.2 Data Flows

A data flow is a pipeline through which packets of data of known composition flow. Data flow is represented on a DFD by a labelled directed arrow, as in figure 13.1b.

13.3.3 Data Stores

A data store is a repository of data. For example, a waste-paper basket, a register, a card index, an indexed-sequential file. A data store is represented on a DFD by an open rectangle or box with an appropriate label, as in figure 13.1c.

13.3.4 External Entities

An external entity (also called a source or sink) is something (usually a person, department or organisation), lying outside the context of the system, that is a net originator or receiver of system data. It is represented on a DFD by some form of rounded shape — circle or oval — with an appropriate name, as in figure 13.1d. Note, external entities on DFDs should not be confused with entities on E-R diagrams.

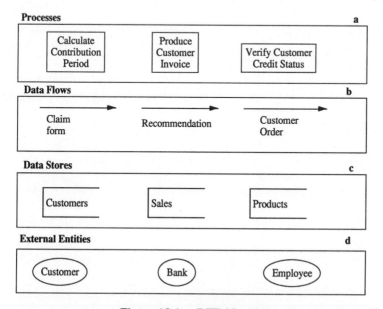

Figure 13.1   DFD Notation

13.4 Conventions

A number of conventions are normally applied to each of these constructs:

13.4.1 Processes

1. No two processes should have the same name. This is really to enable processes to form unique elements in a data dictionary (see chapter 14).
2. Each process should precisely state a transformation. Labels for processes hence usually include some form of verb such as verify, store, record, etc.
3. A process is subject to the 'conservation of data' principle — a process cannot create new data. New data can only come from external entities. A process may only take its input data and transform it in some way to make output data.

13.4.2 Data Flow

1. A data flow is not a representation of the flow of control (see figure 13.2a).
2. Every data flow should have an associated meaningful label (figure 13.2b).
3. No two flows should have the same name. Input data from a process should not appear as output data from that process. If it does, then it has not been transformed (see figure 13.2c).

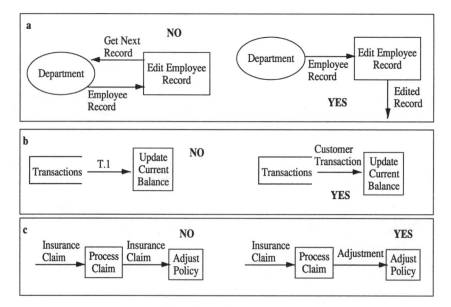

Figure 13.2   Data Flow Conventions

4. If data flows pass through processes to get to other processes then we redraw that part of the diagram so that data is shown as direct input to the processes that use it (see figure 13.3a).

13.4.3 Data Stores

1. A data store can be read, written to, or read and written to (see figure 13.3b).
2. Data stores are conventionally labelled with plural nouns to emphasise the multiple instances of information contained within the data store. A consistent naming convention is normally applied. In other words, we do not name a store customers on one diagram and customer details on another diagram.
3. A data store is subject to the 'conservation of data' principle. What comes out of a data store must first go into the data store. It is not possible for a data store to create new data.

13.4.4 External Entities

1. An external entity lies outside the context of an information system. Hence, this construct is used primarily to define system boundaries — a system's interface to the external world (see figure 13.3c).
2. It is conventional to label external entities with a singular noun. We talk of a bank, not of banks, of an employee, not of employees.

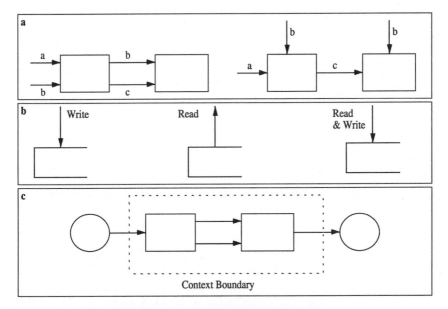

Figure 13.3   More DFD Conventions

13.5 Additions to the Basic Notation

When conducting the analysis of information systems it has been found useful to add the following constructs to the basic DFD notation:

1. Materials or Goods Flow. In looking for a place to start, systems analysts often concentrate initially on the physical movement of materials through systems. Such movement can be documented on a DFD as a broad, labelled arrow (see figure 13.4a). It is conventional to draw such materials flow as coming from an entity or process, and going to an entity or process. No connection is made to data stores.
2. Documents Flow. One of the most important requirements of early analysis is to make sure that all relevant documents such as invoices and order forms that apply in a manual information system are collected, examined and analysed. It is therefore useful to record such documents by name on a DFD. This is done by drawing a traditional document symbol on a data flow (figure 13.4b).
3. Boolean Constucts. Sometimes it is useful to specify the operators AND and OR on DFDs. Two flows with a '+' between them are inextricably linked in the sense that both must be input to a process or output from a process at the same time. A '*' between flows means that either one flow occurs or another flow, but not both (see figure 13.4c).

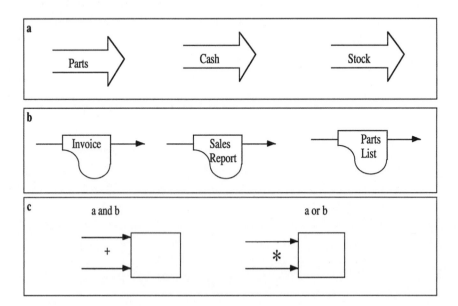

Figure 13.4   Additions to the Basic Notation

13.6 Levelling

Most real-life systems are too involved to represent as a DFD on one single sheet of paper. In representing systems, analysts therefore usually approach the problem in a top-down manner. They attempt to level the problem beginning with an overview diagram of the entire system. As a minimum this might be made up of one process with associated flows, stores and entities. They then take the process or processes represented on the overview DFD and break them down into their own DFDs. They may continue this decomposition process for a number of levels until they can represent the entire system in sufficient detail. A rough guideline is that an appropriately partitioned system is one in which no individual diagram has more than nine processes represented upon it (Miller, 1967).

Given that our system of DFDs represents a hierarchically organised documentation system, a number of conventions are normally applied to the construction of such a system (see figure 13.5).

First, each DFD is headed with the name of its parent process. In the case of the overview diagram this will of course represent the title of the system. For all other DFD's it will refer to the master process which is exploded in the present DFD.

Second, all inputs and outputs between parent and child diagrams are balanced. If flows A and B input to process 1 and flow C outputs, then the child diagram should also detail flows A, B and C.

Third, to indicate the position in the DFD hierarchy of any particular process it is found useful to number each process uniquely within a documentation system.

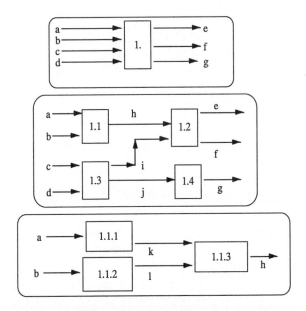

Figure 13.5   Levelling

13.7 Constructing a DFD

Some suggested guidelines for constructing a DFD hierarchy are given below. We illustrate the production of a DFD set to describe a simple manual information system:

1. Start with a name which adequately describes the information system, for example, Video Shop System.
2. Identify the main external entities that will be used to define the boundaries of the information system, for example, member, supplier, etc. Place a single process box with a label for the system in the centre of a page and arrange the external entities around it. Consider the major flows from the external entities to the central process. This context diagram (illustrated in figure 13.6) should provide an accurate picture of the essence of the information system.
3. Identify the major activities of the information system. For example: Creating a Member; Issuing a Video; Returning a Video; Reserving a Video; Customer Enquiries; Acquiring New Videos. Draw an overview diagram to represent the interaction of the major activities of the system. Represent each activity as a process box. Transfer the external entities and flows on the context diagram on to the overview diagram. Consider the internal flows between processes (figure 13.7).
4. Take each of the major activities on the overview diagram and identify the sub-activities. For example:

Creating a Member
       Requesting Identification
       Recording Membership Details
       Producing a Membership Card
Issuing a Video
       Recording Hire Details
       Retrieving the Video
       Requesting Payment
       Handing Over the Video
Returning a Video
       Receiving the Video
       Checking for Reserved Status
       Checking for Overdue Status
       Erasing Hire Details
Reserving a Video
       Extracting Video Details
       Making a Reservation Mark

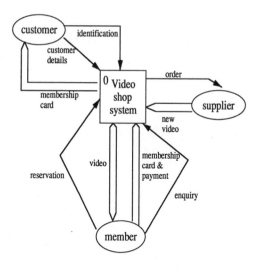

Figure 13.6   Video Shop Context Diagram

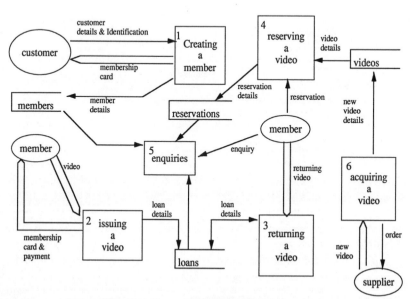

Figure 13.7   Overview Diagram

Customer Enquiries
>   Identifying Purpose of Query
>   Answering Query

Acquiring New Videos
>   Ordering a New Video
>   Receiving a New Video

Take each of the main activities and draw a DFD to represent it. Ensure that any relevant flows, entities and stores on the overview diagram are duly represented on the first level diagram. Figure 13.8 illustrates a first-level DFD drawn from the creating a member process.

4. Iterate up and down between the various levels of the DFD. If we add extra process boxes and flows at lower levels, consider the effect on higher levels and vice versa.

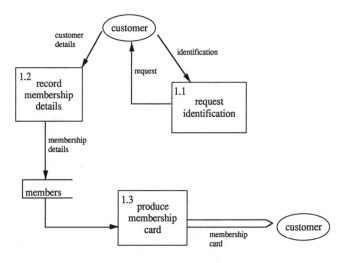

Figure 13.8   First-Level DFD

13.8 Case Study: the Fast Foods System

Fast foods is a business serving small retailers. Such retailers order canned foods and packaged items such as sugar, tea and rice from the company in bulk quantities. Fast foods holds no stock, but orders in bulk from wholesalers at correspondingly discounted prices. When the bulk supplies arrive, the retailer's orders are filled and despatched.

Before orders are processed, retailers are checked for credit status. If such credit status is unacceptable, the retailer is requested to send cash with the order. This usually means that Fast Foods puts the order on hold while the customer is requested to make prepayment.

Fast Foods operate a discount policy. Such discounts are determined by the total value of the order and the status of the retailer, particularly whether or not they pay their bills promptly.

Retailers order goods by detailing manufacturer and product name or by specifying a standard product code, which identifies the manufacturer as well as the product. Such information is written on a standard sales order by the retailer and sent to Fast Foods. The company distributes a catalogue of their products to retailers, together with a set of order forms on a regular basis.

The main documents used in the system are:

1. A sales order from the retailer
2. A purchase order to the wholesaler
3. A delivery note to the wholesaler
4. A shipping note to the retailer
5. Invoices to the retailer and wholesaler
6. Remittance advices from the retailer to the wholesaler

An overview DFD representing this manual system is illustrated in figure 13.9. A number of assumptions have been made in drawing this DFD. These are necessary in the sense that the narrative description detailed above does not provide enough information to produce a sensible solution to the problem. Most of the assumptions made incorporate background knowledge or commonsensical reasoning. For instance, there is nothing in the text to indicate how a purchase order is produced from

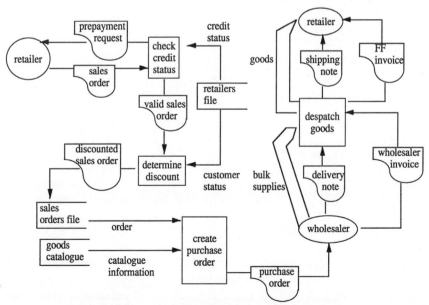

Figure 13.9   Fast Foods—Current Physical DFD

sales orders. It seems sensible therefore to indicate that some form of batching activity occurs. Sales orders are accumulated until a satisfactory bulk order for a particular product is produced.

Drawing a DFD before all the information is known is a perfectly valid exercise. In this sense, we are using the DFD as an analysis tool. We are making a first attempt at understanding the problem by constructing an initial description. This exercise will generate many questions that we will need to ask our users. The diagram is then redrawn, taken back to the users, and the whole process repeated until we are happy that our diagrams accurately specify the workings of the current system.

13.9 Logical and Physical Systems

The diagram in figure 13.9 is usually referred to as a model of the current physical system. It is a high-level description of how the current manual system at Fast Foods works. In contrast, figure 13.10 is a model of the current logical system. In this figure we have abstracted out as much of the implementation detail as possible. In particular, we have removed references to goods and documents flow. We are left with a description of abstract data flow.

DFDs are therefore normally used in at least four different ways in structured systems analysis and design:

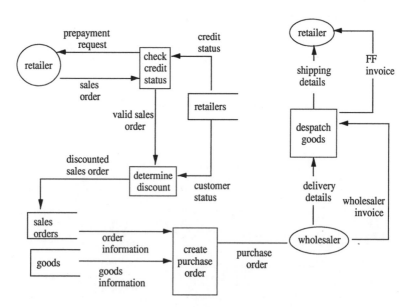

Figure 13.10   Fast Foods—Current Logical DFD

1. To represent the current physical system.
2. To represent the current logical system.
3. To represent the proposed logical system - the current logical system plus new requirements.
4. The proposed physical system — a detailed representation of the workings of the proposed system.

13.10 Goronwy Galvanising Case Study

Figure 13.11 illustrates how we might draw a context DFD for the existing Goronwy system. Note how we have included materials flow to help the reader see at-a-glance the primary function of the information system — to manage the flow of goods.

Figure 13.12 represents an overview diagram for the manual system. We identify four major processes: delivery, job-sheet creation, updating job-sheets, and despatch. Note that galvanising is really a physical process. For the sake of brevity we have included both materials and data flow into and from this process.

13.11 Conclusion

Data flow diagramming as a technique might be summarised as follows:

1. A DFD is composed of processes, flows, external entities and data stores.
2. A DFD forms part of a levelled set of diagrams.
3. A DFD is supported by a data dictionary.

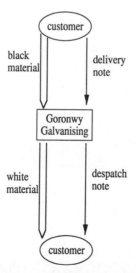

Figure 13.11   Context DFD—Goronwy

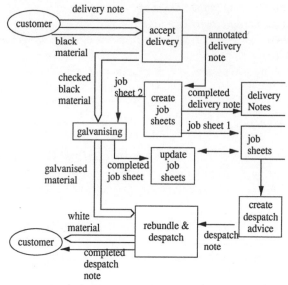

Figure 13.12   Overview DFD—Goronwy

Most contemporary information systems development methodologies (see chapter 21) exploit this technique in some form. This is because it is an extremely effective process analysis technique applicable in various ways to a number of different stages in the standard project life-cycle.

13.12 References

Cutts G. (1991). (2nd Ed.). *SSADM: Structured Systems Anlaysis and Design Methodology*. Blackwell Scientific, Oxford.

DeMarco T. (1979). *Structured Analysis and System Specification*. Prentice-Hall, Englewood-Cliffs, NJ.

Gane C. and Sarson T. (1977). *Structured Systems Analysis: tools and techniques*. Prentice-Hall, Englewood-Cliffs, NJ.

Miller G. (1967). The Magic Number Seven, Plus or Minus Two: Some Limits on Our Capacity for Processing Information. In *The Psychology of Communication: Seven Essays*. Penguin. Harmondsworth.

13.13 Keywords

Context Diagram
Data flow
Data store

External entity
Levelling
Overview Diagram
Process

13.14 Exercises

1. Draw a context diagram for the Fast Foods system.
2. What are the main advantages of using a DFD as opposed to a narrative description of some problem?
3. What is wrong with the DFD extracts in figure 13.13A?
4. What is wrong with the DFD hierarchy in figure 13.14B?
5. Why is an external entity different from an entity as defined in chapter 12?
6. In a house removals system how would you distinguish between the contents being moved and an inventory of the contents on a DFD?
7. Why is the idea of levelling so important in the documentation of large-scale systems?
8. Why do you think we refer to data flow and not information flow?
9. Draw a level 1 DFD for the accept delivery process on figure 13.12.

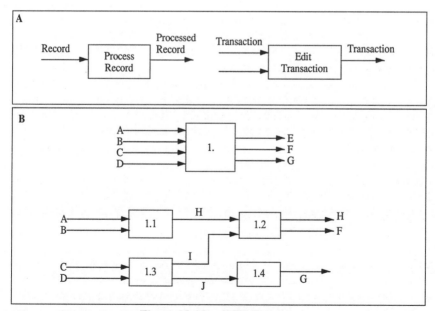

Figure 13.13   DFD Extracts

14 Data Dictionaries

14.1 Introduction

A data dictionary is a means for recording the metadata of some organisation. That is, data about data. Data dictionaries have been used in two ways within information systems development:

1. Logical data dictionaries are used to record process and data requirements independently of how these requirements are to be met.
2. Physical data dictionaries are used to record design decisions. In terms of data, physical dictionaries store details of actual database or file structures. In terms of process, physical dictionaries will store details of programs and program libraries.

In terms of metadata therefore we conventionally mean both resources and requirements. A data dictionary is a mechanism for recording the data resources, process resources, data requirements and process requirements of some organisation. This means that a data dictionary cannot be considered solely as a technique for the analysis and design of information systems. It is also emerging as an important implementation tool (chapter 8) and an important part of what we might call the corporate information architecture (chapter 23).

Note that the term data dictionary is normally stretched to accommodate process detail. Perhaps a data dictionary should really be called something like a project directory, or information systems encyclopedia. Many integrated CAISE tools (chapter 8) use such encyclopedias to drive development projects. However, the term data dictionary is the one in common use, so we shall continue to use it in this chapter.

In this chapter we concentrate on the role of a data dictionary as an analysis and design technique.

14.2 The Need for a Logical Data Dictionary

Logical data dictionaries have traditionally been associated with DFDs. DFDs cannot provide all the necessary information needed to specify an information system. For example, a DFD gives us very little idea of the composition of flows, processes and stores. Data dictionaries are used to overcome this deficiency. They record additional facts about each of the elements of DFDs.

Logical data dictionaries have also been used as an alternative technique for representing entity models. A diagrammatic technique for representing entity models was presented in chapter 12. When E-R diagrams become sufficiently detailed however, the information represented on the diagram is more conveniently held in a data dictionary.

Given that we can represent both process and data information in a logical data dictionary, data dictionaries are also a useful means of connecting up the elements on a set of DFDs with the elements on a set of E-R diagrams.

14.3 Data Structures and Data Elements

Gane and Sarson (1977) define data flows as being data structures in motion, while data stores are data structures at rest. Data flows and data stores are both made up of data structures. A data flow represents the way in which a data structure moves between processes. A data store represents some repository for data structures. To this we might add that a process is a mechanism for transforming data structures into other data structures.

Gane and Sarson define a data structure as being a set of data elements that are related to one another and which collectively describe some component in an information system. An invoice is a classic example of a data structure. An invoice is made up of a number of data elements such as invoice number, invoice date and amount due. A data element, sometimes known as a data item, is hence the smallest and most fundamental unit in an information system.

14.4 Contents of a Logical Data Dictionary

There is no readily acknowledged standard for the contents of a logical data dictionary. As a minimum, we might limit ourselves to some description of the data structures used by an information system. This is the technique employed in this section.

Analysts often use a notation to limit the amount of narrative needed to describe relationships between data structures and data elements. The one used here is an adaptation of BNF (Backus-Naur Form), a notation primarily used to specify the syntax of programming languages. The notation is made up of the following symbols:

1. An equals sign, =, means that the data structure to the left of the sign consists of whatever is to the right.
2. A plus sign, +, is equivalent to the word 'and'. We use it to aggregate items together into a data structure.
3. Square brackets, [..], mean that the structure being defined consists of one, and only one, of the elements in brackets. This is equivalent to the idea of selection. Each contained item is separated by a semi-colon.

4. Curly braces, {..}, means that the defined item contains from zero to an infinite number of occurrences of the item contained within braces. This expresses the concept of iteration.
5. Information contained in parentheses, (..), is optional. That is, zero, or one occurrence may appear.
6. Information contained in asterisks, *..*, is regarded as a comment. It hence does not usually form part of the definition.

Hence, we might describe an order in the following terms:

order = orderNo + orderDate + customerNo + salesmanNo + {productNo + productName + price + qty + orderValue} + (totalOrderValue)

Or alternatively:

order = orderNo + orderDate + customerNo + salesmanNo + {lineItem}+ (total_order_value)

lineItem = productNo + productName + price + qty + orderValue

The second alternative is an example of how we might express a normalised schema for data structures using BNF (chapter 11).

14.5 The Gane and Sarson Approach

For many purposes, the type of data dictionary described above is insufficient. A mechanism for representing a more complete set of information system requirements is required. What follows is a description of the type of data dictionary advocated by Gane and Sarson (1977) in their book *Structured Systems Analysis*.

In this approach, each data flow, data store or process in a set of DFDs is given a unique, meaningful name which is applied consistently throughout the DFD hierarchy. The first part of the data dictionary lists such names suitably nested to reflect the levelling in a set of DFDs. This comprises the table of contents.

Each item in the table of contents then has a template description of its own describing the element in more detail:

1. The template for data flows details the name, a description of the flow, from what process the flow is coming, and to what process the flow is going, followed by a list of the data structures used by the flow.
2. The template for processes details a name and description followed by a list of inbound and outbound data flows. When we have reached a sufficient level of detail, we might even include a process description in something like Structured English (chapter 15).

3. Data stores are described by items such as the name of the store, a description, data flows, and a list of the data structures stored. At the design stage we might even include some indication of the volume of data and the type of access required to data.
4. When we reach a sufficient level of detail we may seek to document the data structures and elements used by the constructs above.

14.6 Case Study: An Order Processing System

Suppose we have to document a simple order processing system. Extracts from the table of contents might look as follows:

Data Stores

CustomerAccountsReceivable
    customerName
    customerAddress
    dateBilled
    amountBilled
    interestCharges
    currentBalance
Invoice
    invoiceNo
    customerName
    productNo
    qty
    totalCharge

Data Flows

acknowledgement
    customerName
    customerAddress
    acknowledgementBody
order
    customerName
    customerAddress
    productNumber
    qty
statement
    customerName
    customerAddress
    currentBalance

Processes

Enter Order
    Acknowledge Order
    Verify Order
    Approve Order
    File Order
Produce Invoice
    Prepare Invoice
    Send Invoice
    File Invoice
    ..
    ..

Each of the elements listed in the table of contents can be expanded as in figure 14.1.

```
DATA FLOW NAME:  invoice
DESCRIPTION:  Details of the order for which the customer is billed
FROM PROCESSES:  4.1 Prepare Invoice
TO PROCESSES:  4.2 Assign Invoice Number
DATA STRUCTURES: invoice
```

```
PROCESS NAME:  1.0 Enter Order
DESCRIPTION: Customer order received and approved for further processing.
INBOUND FLOWS: Approved Order
OUTBOUND FLOWS: Order Details
```

```
DATA STORE:  Approved Invoices
DESCRIPTION: Itemises merchandise received, cost of each and contains signature of
             receiving employee
INBOUND FLOWS:  Invoice
OUTBOUND FLOWS:  BatchedInvoiceDetails
DESCRIPTION:  approvedInvoice = invoice + signature
VOLUME:  200 daily
ACCESS:  Accessed in batches. Sequentially processed from within batch
```

Figure 14.1   Sample Templates

14.7 Data Dictionaries for Entity Models

Representing an entity model in a data dictionary has a number of advantages over its diagrammatic representation. Perhaps the most important is that large entity models are more easily maintained in the form of a data dictionary than in the form of a diagram.

We consider here a simple scheme for representing entity models based upon the template approach of Gane and Sarson. Each entity in our system is given a template detailing the name and attributes of an entity. Each relationship is also given a template in which we detail the names of participating entities and the properties of the relationship (see figure 14.2)

```
ENTITY NAME: Customer
IDENTIFIER: customerNo
ATTRIBUTES: customerName, address, telNo
```

```
RELATIONSHIP NAME: makesOrder
ENTITY NAME: Customer
DEGREE: 1
MEMBERSHIP: optional
ENTITY NAME: Order
DEGREE: N
MEMBERSHIP: mandatory
```

Figure 14.2   Data Dictionary Entries for an Entity Model

14.8 Entity Models and DFDs via Data Dictionaries

A data dictionary may act as a useful means of connecting up the static information provided by entity models with the dynamic information represented on data flow diagrams. The easiest way to achieve this integration is to recognise the communality between these two forms of representation in terms of the concept of a data structure. Both data stores and entities are mechanisms for clustering data elements into data structures. Data flows are data structures in motion. Processes are mechanisms for transforming data structures.

Data structure references can hence be transferred between data and process models in a data dictionary. In this way, a data dictionary frequently acts as the centralised repository for many computer aided information systems engineering (CAISE) tools (chapter 8).

14.9 Conclusion

Besides its use as an addendum to a set of DFDs, and/or entity models, a data dictionary has a number of other uses in information systems development:

1. As a means of enforcing a standard set of data representations for a team undertaking a software project.
2. As a means for checking the consistency and completeness of a representation of some information system.
3. If the dictionary is sufficiently comprehensive and rigorous, generation of machine-readable data definitions and even programs becomes possible.

14. 10 Goronwy Galvanising Case Study

The major data structures at Goronwy are delivery advices and despatch advices. These can be formally specified using our modified BNF as below:

deliveryAdvice = deliveryNo + deliveryDate + {jobNo + productCode+ description + itemLength + orderQty + batchWeight}

deliveryNo = [blackheadsNo; otherNo]

jobNo = [blackheadsNo; otherNo + lineNo]

despatchAdvice = despatchNo + despatchDate + {jobNo + productCode+ description + itemLength + orderQty + batchWeight + returnedQty + returnedWeight}

Note how we have specified a deliveryNo as having two possible definitions: a Blackheads number and another manufacturer number.

The Gane and Sarson approach would involve us in documenting each of the flows, processes and stores in the Goronwy system. A sample template for one of the data stores given on the overview DFD discussed in chapter 13 is illustrated in figure 14.3.

14.11 References

Gane C. and Sarson T. (1977). *Structured Systems Analysis: Tools and Techniques*. Prentice-Hall, Englewood-Cliffs, NJ.

DATA STORE:	JobSheets
DESCRIPTION:	record of incoming black material and processed white material
INBOUND DATA FLOWS:	jobSheet1
OUTBOUND DATA FLOWS:	jobSheet1
DATA DESCRIPTION:	jobSheet = jobNo + productCode + itemLength + orderQty + batchWeight

Figure 14.3   Data Store Template — Goronwy

Gane C. and Sarson T. (1977). *Structured Systems Analysis: Tools and Techniques*. Prentice-Hall, Englewood-Cliffs, NJ.

14.12 Keywords

Attribute
BNF
Data Element
Data Flow
Data Store
Data Structure
Entity
Process
Relationship

14.13 Exercises

1. Write a BNF description of a textbook.
2. Write a BNF description of a data dictionary.
3. What is wrong with the following BNF description: totalItemPrice = unitPrice + vat ?

6. A clerk within Fast Foods describes an invoice in the following way: Each invoice is given a unique number. The customer's name and address are written at the top of the invoice and the date of despatch may be written on by the despatch handler. Underneath the customer information we list for each product ordered the product number, product description, quantity ordered, unit price and value of order. At the bottom of the invoice we write the total value of the order. Write a modified BNF description for this type of invoice.

7. In what way do you think modified BNF can be used to aid the process of normalisation?

8. At what size of entity model do you think a data dictionary representation becomes more convenient than a diagrammatic form?

15 Process Descriptions

15.1 Introduction

Information systems are generally described in terms of three major components: data flows, data structures and processes. Data flows have been the subject of the chapters on DFDs (chapter 13) and data dictionaries (chapter 14). Data structures have been discussed using the techniques of normalisation (chapter 11) and E-R diagramming (chapter 12). The third component, processes, are the subject of this chapter.

One of the major reasons for using structured approaches to systems development is the need to remove ambiguity from system descriptions. Such ambiguity frequently arises in the natural language description of processes. For this reason, structured systems development has exploited a number of techniques for describing processes which are less subject to ambiguity:

1. Structured English/pseudo-code.
2. Formatted charts/diagrams (Warnier-Orr diagrams, Nassi-Schneiderman charts, Action diagrams).
3. Decision Tables/ trees.

15.2 Structured English and Pseudo-Code

The constructs of structured English (sometimes referred to as program description language (PDL) or program specification language (PSL)) are a direct emulation of the constructs of structured programming. Descriptions written in structured English look very similar to programs written in block-structured languages such as Pascal (see chapter 4). Structured English puts verbal descriptions in a form which removes much ambiguity without losing the benefits of English narrative.

Some people make a distinction between structured English and pseudo-code. A Structured English description is an attempt at logical description. As such, it should remain as high-level, or as implementation-independent, as possible. When implementation details become important, such descriptions are said to be written in pseudo-code. Pseudo-code descriptions are physical descriptions. It is a very small step from a pseudo-code description to a program.

Another way of looking at it is that structured English is primarily a technique used in the analysis of information systems. Pseudo-code, in contrast, is a technique to be used in the design of information systems.

157

15.3 The Components of Structured English

A structured English description of any process is likely to be made up of blocks of imperative sentences embedded within suitable control structures.

15.3.1 Imperative Sentences

An imperative sentence is usually made up of a verb followed by a number of data items. For example:

> READ salesRecord FROM Sales

The data items in this sentence usually reference the data flows and data stores on a DFD, or other items held in a data dictionary. Hence, in the example above, salesRecord is a data flow, while Sales is a data store.

It is conventional to group a collection of imperative sentences into a block, delineated by the keywords BEGIN and END. For example, the description below represents the process of handling sale-slips.

> **HandleSales**
>
> BEGIN
> > receive salesSlip
> > READ customerRecord FROM Customers
> > READ productRecord FROM Products
> > totalSaleValue = qtySold * unitPrice
> > customerCredit = customerCredit + totalSaleValue
> > UPDATE customerCredit ON customerRecord
> > create salesRecord
> > create adviceNote
> > WRITE customerRecord TO Customers
> > WRITE salesRecord TO Sales
> > send adviceNote to customer
> END

Note that we provide a name for each process description. Such names will usually refer to templates within a data dictionary (chapter 14). Note also that it may prove useful for a given organisation to standardise on the use of certain keywords such as READ, UPDATE and WRITE.

15.3.2 Control Structures

According to the advocates of structured programming (chapter 4) (Dahl *et al.*, 1972), only three control structures are needed to describe any process: the sequence, the condition and the loop.

The Sequence

This is the simplest control structure, in which each statement is executed in turn. For example:

HandleOrders

```
BEGIN
  READ stockRecord FROM Stock
  qtyInStock = qtyInStock − orderQty
  update stockRecord
  WRITE stockRecord TO Stock
END
```

The Condition

This is the control structure which allows us to deal with a number of different situations in different ways. Without the condition, a different description would be needed to handle every minor variation in the specification of a problem. Conditions can be subdivided into three types:

1. Single-Branched

IF <condition> THEN <action> ENDIF. For example:

HandleOrders

```
BEGIN
  receive order
  READ customerRecord FROM Customers
  IF creditRating is 'good' THEN
    BEGIN
      READ stockRecord FROM stock
      qtyInStock = qtyInStock − orderQty; update stockRecord
      WRITE stockRecord TO stock
    END
  ENDIF
  create invoice
  send stock and invoice to customer
END
```

2. Double-Branched

IF <condition> THEN <action> ELSE <action> ENDIF. For example:

HandleOrders

```
BEGIN
  receive order
  READ customerRecord FROM Customers
  IF creditRating is 'good' THEN
   BEGIN
     READ stockRecord FROM stock
     qtyInStock = qtyInStock − orderQty
     update stockRecord
     WRITE stockRecord TO stock
   END
  ELSE
   BEGIN
     create requestForPayment
     send requestForPayment to customer
   END
  ENDIF
  create invoice
  send stock and invoice to customer
END
```

3. Multi-Branched

CASE <condition> <action> CASE <condition> <action> ENDCASE:

HandleOrders

```
BEGIN
  receive order
  READ customerRecord FROM Customers
  CASE creditRating is 'good'
     Do update stock record
  CASE creditRating is 'average'
     Do request for payment
  CASE creditRating is 'bad'
     Do settlement request
   ENDCASE
END
```

The Loop

The loop is an important control structure in that it permits the analyst to repeat a series of sentences without a need to duplicate the necessary descriptions. There are three types of looping structure popular in languages such as Pascal: while loops, repeat loops and for loops (see chapter 4). For example:

```
WHILE there are more orders
 BEGIN
  DO handleOrders
 END
ENDWHILE

REPEAT
 BEGIN
  DO handleOrders
 END
UNTIL there are no more orders

FOR 100 orders
 BEGIN
  DO handleOrders
 END
NEXT order
```

15.4 Formatted Diagrams

The principles of structured development are also used in a number of other techniques such a Warnier-Orr diagrams, Nassi-Schneidermann charts and action diagrams. These techniques differ from structured English in providing a diagrammatic layout for process structures. Warnier-Orr diagrams use large curly brackets and symbols; Nassi-Schneiderman charts include statements within a segmented box structure. Action diagrams use nested, square brackets. We shall illustrate this approach here by considering action diagrams (Martin and McClure, 1985).

Figure 15.1 illustrates the basic constructs of action diagrams. Sequences are represented by statements enclosed in a large square bracket. This replaces the BEGIN and END statements of structured English. Conditions are represented by one or more forks in the bracket structure. Loops are represented by a double bar at the top of the enclosing bracket.

Martin and McClure maintain that the addition of the graphic element improves their understandability and application. Action diagrams are much used in the information engineering approach to information systems development (chapter 21).

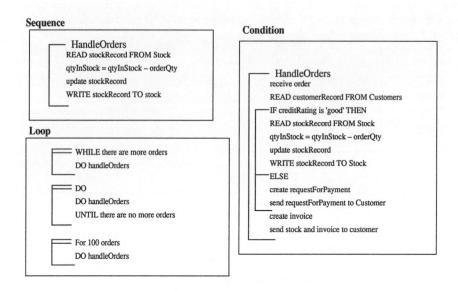

Figure 15.1   Action Diagramming

15.5 Decision Tables and Decision Trees

Processes that involve many nested conditions are difficult to describe using Structured English. For this class of problems, two other techniques, namely decision tables and decision trees, are more appropriate.

Let us assume, for instance, that the process of admitting people to a zoological garden can be described in everyday terms as follows:

> A child under 3 years of age is not to be charged an admission fee. A person under 18 is to be charged half full admission. If a child under 12 is accompanied by an adult however, then that person is to be charged quarter full admission. For persons over 18 full admission is to be charged, except for students who are to be charged half admission and senior citizens (women over 60; men over 65) who are to be charged quarter full admission. A discount of 10% is to apply to all persons subject to full admission who are members of a party of 10 or more. Finally, there are no student concessions on the weekend.

15.5.1 Decision Table

A decision table for this problem is given in figure 15.2. It is made up of four parts:

1. A conditions stub. This is the top-left section of the table. It indicates the questions to be asked.

2. A conditions entry. This is the top-right section. It indicates the particular combinations of conditions that apply.
3. An actions stub. This is the bottom-left section. It indicates the appropriate actions to be taken.
4. An actions entry. This is the bottom-right section. It indicates the appropriate action that applies given the combination of conditions.

The decision table in figure 15.2 is an example of an extended decision table. The simpler form of decision table merely has yes (Y) or no (N) values in the condition entry section. In the admissions problem above however, age is a crucial factor. Age must use some continuous scale of values.

Condition Stub:	Condition Entry:									
Age	<3	3-12	3-12	12-18	>18	>18	>18	>18	>18	SC
Accompanied		Y	N							
Student					Y	Y	Y	N	N	
Weekend					N	Y	Y			
Party Member					Y	N	Y	N		

Action Stub:	Action Entry:									
Free	X									
Quarter		X								
Half			X	X	X					X
90%						X		X		
Full							X		X	

Figure 15.2   Decision Table — Zoological Garden

15.5.2 Decision Trees

Figure 15.3 represents a decision tree for the same admissions problem. A decision tree represents conditions as a series of left to right tests. We first ask the age of the person, as this is the most discriminatory attribute. If the person is between 3 years and 12 years of age, we ask if the child is accompanied. If the child is accompanied he is charged quarter admission. Each node of the tree is therefore a question. Each branch of the tree constitutes an action. A conclusion is reached at a terminal node of the tree.

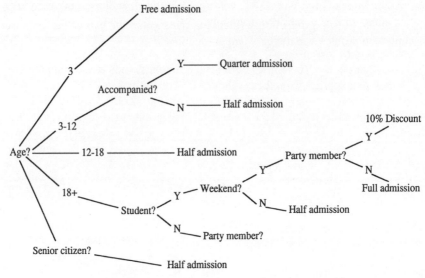

Figure 15.3   Decision Tree — Zoological Garden

15.6 Goronwy Galvanising Case Study

Below we illustrate how structured English can be used to specify in greater detail the processes represented on a DFD. This process description is an attempt to represent the logic employed in the present manual system when job sheets are created:

Create Job Sheets

```
DO WHILE there are jobs still left on the annotatedDeliveryNote
  Get blank jobSheet
  Enter deliveryAdviceNo, deliveryAdviceDate
  Enter jobNo, productCode and itemLength
  IF jobEntry is annotated
    CASE count discrepancy
      amend orderQty and batchWeight
      enter discrepancyIndicator
    CASE nonConforming material
      enter nonConforming indicator and nonConforming amount
    ENDCASE
  ENDIF
  enter batchWeight on jobSheet; send jobSheet1 to shop floor
  file jobSheet2 in jobSheets
ENDDO
file deliveryNote in deliveryNotes
```

Figure 15.4 illustrates a simple application of decision trees to Goronwy. This tree is meant to help production staff fill out the appropriate part of the job sheet dealing with problems in delivery and production.

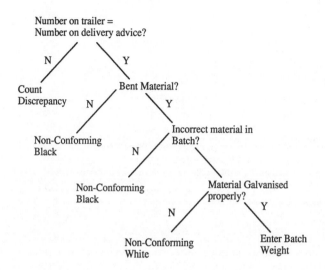

Figure 15.4   Decision Tree — Non-Conforming Material

15.7 Conclusion

In this chapter we have considered four techniques for documenting processes. Most of the techniques are equally applicable to design as they are to analysis. This is evident in the hazy distinction between Structured English and Pseudo-Code.

Structured English, or a variant such as Action Diagramming, is normally the preferred method of documenting processes. Decision tables and decision trees are preferred when one of a large number of actions is to be selected, or where a large number of conditions contribute to the actions undertaken.

15.8 References

Dahl O.J., Djikstra E.W. , Hoare C.A.R. (1972). *Structured Programming*. Academic Press, New York.

Martin J. and McClureT. (1985). *Diagramming Techniques for Analysts and Programmers*. Prentice-Hall. Englewood-Cliffs, NJ.

15.9 Keywords

Condition
Decision tree
Decision table
Loop
Psuedo-code
Sequence
Stuctured English

15.10 Exercises

1. Identify the ambiguities in the following sentence:

   All customers with more than £1000 in their deposit account who have an average monthly balance in their current account of £100 or who have been customers of the bank for more than five years are entitled to free banking services.

2. Write a structured English sentence for each of the possible meanings in question 1.
3. Draw a decision table or decision tree for the following application:

   Shady sellers operate a graded commission policy for their salesmen. The company makes a distinction between products selling at more than £10,000, and items selling under £10,000. Items above £10,000 are subject to a commission of 16% if more than 500 items are sold and the salesman's salary is below £12,000. Salaries in the region £12-20,000 gain 14% commission, and salaries above £20,000 gain 12%. If less than 500 items are sold then the commission is 8%, 7% and 6% for the same classification of salesmen. For items having a value under £10,000, sales over 1000 items gain a 12% commission for staff on salaries under £12,000. Those on £12-20,000 gain 11%, and those on £20,000 plus get 8%. Under 1000 items gain a 6%, 5% and 4% commission respectively.

4. Represent the rules for transforming an E-R diagram into a relational schema as an action diagram.

5. The current production controller at Goronwy describes how he produces a despatch advice as follows:

"I look through my jobs file for completed jobs — those jobs where the completion indicator is set to 'Y'. If there are enough of these to fill a trailer I'll simply despatch these. I have to do a rough calculation on the job weights as the maximum loading on a trailer is 20 tonnes.
If there are not enough completed jobs I'll look through the file for jobs that have been partially completed I'll then part-despatch some or all of these jobs up to the loading limit".

Produce a structured English specification of this process.

16 Entity Life Histories

16.1 Introduction

The entity life history (ELH) technique was originally designed to extend the available database design techniques such as E-R diagramming (chapter 12) and normalisation (chapter 11) (Robinson, 1979). Such data analysis techniques concentrate almost exclusively on a static view of the information system being modelled. ELHs, in contrast, were developed as a technique for the explicit modelling of system dynamics (Rosenquist, 1982). In this sense, the ELH may be seen as a competitor of the DFD (chapter 13) and associated process specification techniques (chapter 15). However, the ELH is more closely linked to the logical modelling ideas underlying data analysis.

Recently, a number of methodologies, such as SSADM (chapter 21), have cast the ELH in a more integrative role, mediating between such techniques as E-R diagrams and DFDs (Cutts, 1991). Jackson (1984) has even used a similar representation to one of the notations discussed in this chapter as the basis of his structured programming methodology (chapter 18).

16.2 Definition and Objectives

From a traditional data modelling point of view, the entities that we have considered in our discussion of E-R diagramming are usually thought of as static or structural concepts. An entity model represents a time-independent slice of reality.

An entity may however be considered from a contrasting point of view. An entity is realistically in a state of flux. It is the subject of a large number of processes or events which change its state. In a library, for instance, the entity Book may proceed through a number of different states: it is first acquired, then it is catalogued, it is lent to borrowers, and perhaps finally it is sold off.

An ELH is a diagrammatic technique for charting the usage of a particular entity by the processes or events making up an information system. Its primary objective is therefore to offer a means to connect up the entities detailed on E-R diagrams, with the processes present on a set of DFDs.

As a result, ELHs are useful in two senses. First, developing an ELH helps analysts to understand entities better. Second, they are the first step in documenting the detailed outline of processes. As such, they are an extremely useful technique for validating DFDs.

16.3 Technique

There are at least three different conventions used for drawing an ELH:

1. A notation based on the theory of Petri nets or state transition diagrams.
2. A network-like notation derived from PERT scheduling.
3. A hierarchical convention similar to the symbols used in JSP (Jackson Structured Programming) which we shall discuss in chapter 18.

Each of these conventions incorporates the basic characteristics of the ELH as an analysis and design tool. Therefore, primarily for the sake of brevity, we choose to concentrate on describing the hierarchical notation. We also briefly discuss the notation of state transition diagrams. Those interested in more detail on the Petri net and network-like notation are referred to Martin and McClure (1985). We further assume that ELHs are to be used in conjunction with other techniques such as DFDs and E-R diagrams. The production of any set of ELHs is a four-step process:

1. List entities from E-R diagrams.
2. List events from DFDs.
3. Construct an ELH matrix.
4. Produce an ELH for each entity.

16.3.1 List Entities

The entities used in a set of ELHs are usually taken directly from an E-R diagram or set of E-R diagrams. In a simple library system we might have the following entities: Book, Borrower, Reservation, Loan.

16.3.2 List Events

Events are usually taken from the set of DFDs documenting an information system. An event can be thought of as a real-world transaction, such as the arrival of a sales order or the receipt of goods. The net effect of an event is to change the state of an entity. Hence, we might say that a catalogue event changes the state of a book entity from acquired to catalogued. However, events can be categorised in a more abstract sense in terms of the effect that they have on the life of an entity. Four such primary events are possible: create events (C), read events (R), amend events (A) and delete (D) events. A list of possible events for our simple library system might be:

1. Creating a borrower — a C event for Borrower.
2. Acquiring a book — a C event for Book.
3. Cataloguing a book — an A event for Book.
4. Loaning a book — an A event for Borrower and Book. A D event for Reservation and a C event for Loan.
5. Selling a book — a D event for Book.

16.3.3 Constructing an ELH Matrix

A 2-dimensional matrix can be produced in which each cell represents the action of an event on an entity.

	Book	Borrower	Reservation	Loan
Create a Borrower		C		
Acquire a Book	C			
Catalogue a Book	A			
Loan a Book	A	A	D	C
Reserve a Book	R		C	A
Sell a Book	D			

16.3.4 Constructing an ELH

An ELH matrix suffers in its ability to document the sequence of events which impact on an entity. It also fails to document the effect of abnormal or exceptional events. ELHs are drawn to overcome these inadequacies. An ELH charts the sequence of events in the life of an entity. They also chart the effect of abnormal events.

In our notation an ELH constitutes a hierarchical system of boxes. The root box in the hierarchy indicates the name of the entity under consideration. The lower-level boxes represent the events that act upon the entity. ELH diagrams use three basic constructs (figure 16.1):

1. Sequence. Represented by a horizontal row of boxes read from left to right.
2. Selection. Represented by boxes at the same level in the hierarchy with an 'o' for optional within each box.
3. Iteration. Represented by boxes with an asterisk, '*', within the box.

16.4 Creation of ELHs

The easiest way to construct an ELH is to start with a simple entity life first and add complexities later. Many entities have simple lives in which an entity is created, read and/or modified a number of times, and eventually deleted. In our library system, for instance, a book is first created by an acquisitions process, then it is modified by a cataloguing and lending process, and finally deleted by a process which sells off old books (see figure 16.2).

A complexity arises when we consider that a book is likely to be loaned a number of times throughout its life. We therefore demote the loan box to a position underneath a box which we now label library life. We also designate a loan to involve iteration. Similarly, we break down the acquisition process into the sub-processes order, receive and payment.

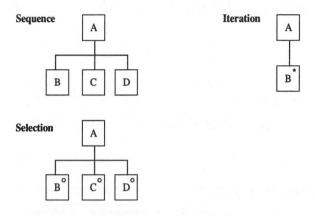

Figure 16.1   ELH Notation

Further complexities occur if we consider a loan event in greater detail. The loan of a book actually involves two separate processes which we label issues and returns. The issuing process is relatively straightforward. We record details of the borrower and the book, we stamp the book with a return date, and we issue the book to the borrower. Most returns will, we hope, take place before or on the return date, but inevitably some books will run overdue. In this case we issue as many return requests as it takes to get the book returned (see figure 16.4).

16.5 Goronwy Galvanising Case Study

Consider one of the fundamental entities appropriate to the information system at Goronwy, Job. Figure 16.5 illustrates how we might begin drawing a life history for this entity. A Job has a standard life composed of creation at the time of delivery, modification while at the plant and deletion at time of despatch. Delivery is made up of unbundling and checking batches. If a batch has some discrepancy then an annotation is made to the delivery note. The plant life of the job consists of creating a job sheet, processing the job and marking completion. The despatch either directly emulates the original batch delivered, in which case it is a full despatch, or it goes back on separate trailers, in which case it is made up of a series of partial despatches.

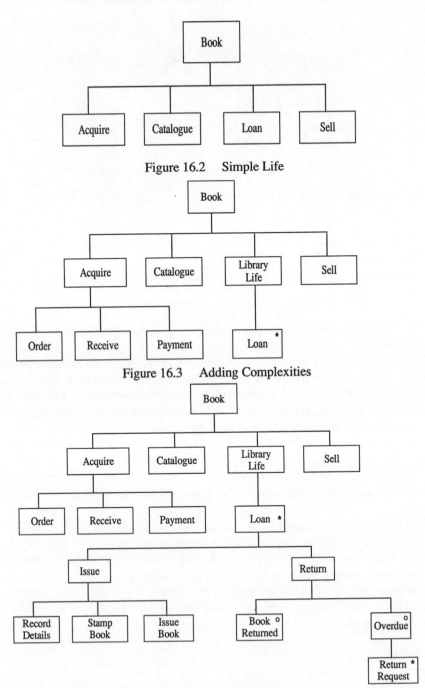

Figure 16.2   Simple Life

Figure 16.3   Adding Complexities

Figure 16.4   Complete Life

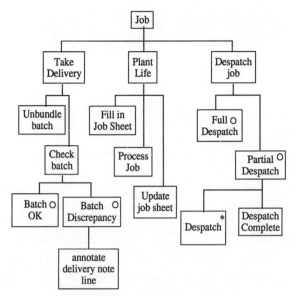

Figure 16.5   ELH for Job Entity

16.6 State Transition Diagrams

An alternative notation for entity life histories is considered briefly in this section. This notation is based on the idea of a finite state machine. A finite state machine is a hypothetical mechanism which can be in one of a finite number of discrete states at one time. Events cause changes to the machine's state. A given process can therefore be represented as a series of finite state machines.

Suppose we are interested in recording the process of people registering for attendance on a technical seminar. A given registration can be in one of the following number of states: submitted, accepted, rejected, withdrawn, or attended. The relationships between states and events can be represented on a diagram as in figure 16.6. The states are represented here as bubbles, the events as directed arrows between bubbles. An incoming arrow without an associated starting state initialises the process. A double-bubble indicates the terminating state. Note also how the transfer registration event cycles on the same state.

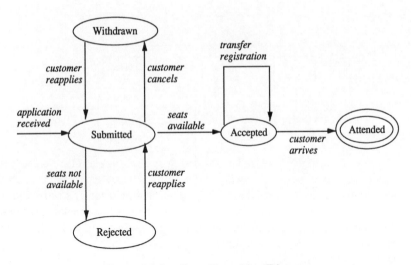

Figure 16.6   State Transition Diagram

16.7 Conclusion

A sequence of steps for the generation of ELHs might be summarised as follows:

1. Select from the ELH matrix an entity and the events that affect it.
2. Order the events in sequence.
3. Include selections and iterations.
4. Rework the ELH if the iterations and selections alter the sequence.

As an aid to E-R diagramming and perhaps data flow diagramming, ELHs can be used at the feasibility study, analysis and design stages of the standard project life-cycle. Jackson has used a similar technique as a tool for deriving program structures (chapter 18). In this respect, ELHs can be seen as relevant to the implementation phase.

16.8 References

Jackson M.A. (1984). *Principles of Program Design*. Academic Press. New York.

Robinson K.A. (1979). An Entity/Event Data Modelling Method. *The Computer Journal*. 22. 270-281.

Rosenquist C.J. (1982). Entity Life Cycle Models and their Applicability to Information System Development. *The Computer Journal*. 25. 307-315.

16.9 Keywords

Entity
Entity Life History
ELH Matrix
Event

16.10 Exercises

1. Consider a customer in an order-processing system such as Fast Foods. The event that makes the system aware of this entity is when an account is opened and details are first taken of the customer. During the Customer's active life he or she might place orders, take deliveries, be invoiced and make payments. Assume that the only reason the warehouse may lose a customer is if he or she goes out of business. Draw a simple life for this system.
2. Draw an entity life history for an order within the Fast Foods system. An order is first produced by an order entry process, then modified by a process which produces a delivery note and invoice, and finally deleted by a process which receives the payment of invoice.
3. Combine the ELH produced for question 1 with the ELH for question 2.
4. A new customer opening an account with Fast Foods may negotiate a discount. The discount rate offered to a customer is dependent on the delivery distance. Occasionally, customers will move to new premises. In this case, a new discount rate needs to be renegotiated. Incorporate this analysis into the ELH produced from 3.
5. Redraw the ELH of question 1 as a state transition diagram.
6. Redraw the ELH of question 2 as a state transition diagram.
7. Discuss the relative merits of the hierarchical and state transition notations for ELH.
8. Draw a state transition diagram for the states of unmarried, married, divorced, widowed, and separated.
9. Redraw the ELH from Goronwy Galvanising in figure 6.6 as a state transition diagram.

Part Three
Section 3
Related Techniques

In this section we include three techniques which do not logically find themselves either in the data analysis or process analysis camp. Formal specification can be applied both to the definition of data or process and relates to the use of the tools of mathematics. Structured programming techniques are fundamentally about taking the results of process and data analysis and building designs for programs. User Interface development is a growing area whose product, a model of the user interface, may eventually achieve an equal place with a process model and a data model in an information systems model.

17 Formal Specification

17.1 Introduction

There is some confusion over the word formal. In a sense, techniques such as entity-relationship diagramming and data flow diagramming are formal in that they use a notation founded in the use of some systematic rules for the specification of user requirements and information systems design. Because they lack the rigour of true formal languages however, such techniques are more accurately defined as being 'formalised'. The word formal is normally reserved for the application of mathematics to system specification.

The literature uses the term formal methods to describe a set of techniques for the specification and proof of information systems. Some approaches have well-developed rules for moving from specification to program code. However, formal methods generally restrict themselves to the design stage of the standard project life-cycle discussed in section 2.5. It is for this reason that we site this discussion in our techniques section.

In this chapter we use a number of simple examples of formal specification to illustrate the principles of this approach. We concentrate on the specification of some simple systems and ignore the related question of proof. Readers interested in pursuing this topic are referred to (Woodcock and Loomes, 1988).

17.2 VDM and Z

Much of the practical work in formal methods has been stimulated by the development of abstraction mechanisms in modern programming languages. The primary mechanism is that of an abstract data type - a module consisting of a data structure and the operations associated with the data structure. The objective is to treat these modules in much the same way as the programmer treats ordinary data types such integers and reals. The idea of an abstract data type therefore effectively extends the set of types available to a program (Shaw, 1984). Abstract data types are very similar to the concept of an object as discussed in chapter 5 (see also chapter 25).

Although there are a number of different approaches, the two main formal methods currently being used on real-life development projects are VDM and Z.

VDM stands for Vienna Development Method because it was developed at the Vienna research labs of IBM. Originally designed as a mechanism for specifying the structure and meaning of programming languages it has now achieved a more over-arching purpose.

Using VDM the developer first identifies the objects and operations that occur in the application area. For instance, in an air traffic control system typical objects would be planes and radar. Typical operations might be the creation of an aircraft when it came within radar range and the deletion of an aircraft from the system when it landed. Specification in VDM consists of defining the objects using a branch of mathematics known as discrete mathematics which includes such constructs as sets, relations, etc. Operations are specified in terms of pre and post-conditions. A pre-condition defines what must be true before an operation is legally applied. A post-condition specifies what must be true of the relationship between input and output if an operation is to be regarded as being successful. Both these expressions are expressed using logic.

Z was originally developed by the French computer scientist Jean Abrial. It has now been considerably expanded by the programming research group at Oxford (Ince, 1989). A specification in Z consists of mathematics enclosed in boxes known as schemas (Spivey, 1989). Each such schema describes some stored data and the effect of operations on that data. Its main advantage is that it provides a more modular description of systems than VDM. Z has however been applied to fewer actual projects than VDM.

In this chapter we illustrate the principles of formal specification using VDM. Some of the syntax of this particular specification language has been simplified for the purposes of exposition. Those wishing more detail are referred to Andrews and Ince (1991).

17.3 Set Theory

Formal specification involves modelling the components of an information system using mathematical structures. In this chapter we shall concentrate on using two mathematical structures: sets and propositions. A realistic specification will also need to exploit structures such as functions, sequences, bags, etc. Much of the art of formal specification is in finding the most appropriate mathematical structure to model the parts of an application system.

Most of the basic mathematics used for formal specification is derived from set theory. A set is simply a collection of objects with no duplicates. We have already seen in chapter 6 that the relations of relational databases are modelled on sets. Sets, however, have many other uses.

Suppose we wish to model the directory and file structures of an operating system such as UNIX and MSDOS (Ince, 1988). In particular, we wish define a number of different sets for users of the file system. SystemUsers represents the set of users currently allowed to access all files in the system. NormalUsers is the set of users who can access only their own directories. AllUsers represents the set of all users.

Also suppose we wish to specify the following aspects for this file system:

1. The number of users who have special privileges should always be less than the number of users who have normal privileges.
2. There will be a user called SuperUser who will have special privileges.
3. No user may have both special and normal privileges.
4. Apart from users with special and normal privileges there are no other users of the file system.

These four statements can be translated into statements in set theory:

1. CARDINALITY SystemUsers < CARDINALITY NormalUsers.
2. SuperUser ∈ SystemUsers.
3. SystemUsers ∩ NormalUsers = { }.
4. SystemUsers ∪ NormalUsers = AllUsers.

Intersect and union are the standard operators of set theory. Intersect or intersection returns the members common to both sets. Union returns the member of both SystemUsers and NormalUsers. { } represents the null set - the set with no members. Cardinality returns the number of members in a set. ∈ returns a true or false value depending on whether the object on its left hand side is a member of the set on its right hand side.

These four statements are actually known as invariants. They state what must be true for this particular application throughout the life of the application.

17.4 Pre and Post Conditions

If we assume that a given information system can be characterised at least from one viewpoint as a set of processes, then formal logic can be used to specify the behaviour of such processes. A given process or operation can be described in terms of a kind of logical statement known as an assertion or condition. An assertion states the condition that holds before or after a process has been executed. An assertion specifies what should be the case, without describing how the condition should be brought about.

There are two types of assertions: pre and post assertions. A pre-assertion describes a condition that is expected to hold before a process is executed. A post-assertion describes a condition that is intended to hold between the input and output of an operation.

Assertions are normally written as propositions using the syntax of predicate logic.

17.5 The Basic Building Blocks of Predicate Logic

Let us suppose that we want to represent the following two assertions:

Evans manages the sales department
Jones works for the sales department

In predicate logic we represent such assertions as:

manages (evans, sales)
works-for (jones, sales)

Within predicate logic the terms 'manages' and 'worksFor' are called predicates, while the terms 'evans', 'jones' and 'sales', are called arguments. Predicates and arguments are collected under the general title of a proposition, and each proposition may take only one of two possible values, namely, true or false. Hence, each of the following propositions has a truth-value.

isA (davies, manager)
isA (davies, salesMan)
isA (davies, clerk)

Each argument in a proposition can be bound to either a constant or a variable. A constant indicates a particular individual or class of individuals. A variable is a place-holder in the sense that it indicates that such an individual or class of individuals remains unspecified. Hence, one interpretation of the following proposition might be, 'there is some entity X that is a salesMan'.

isA (X, salesMan)

Individual propositions are often referred to as being 'atomic'. By this is meant that the internal structure and meaning of such propositions are not determined by the logic. They are in a sense the primitive material from which we build. Such atomic propositions may however be combined by the use of logical connectives. These include:

$\wedge$ (AND), $\vee$ (OR), $\neg$(NOT) and $\Rightarrow$ IMPLIES

Thus we might have the following compound proposition :

worksFor (evans, marketingDivision) $\wedge$ manages (evans, sales)

which reads, 'evans works for the marketing division and manages the sales department'. The IMPLIES connective is particularly important in the sense that it allows us to construct rules of the form:

reportsTo (smith, jones) $\Rightarrow$ manages (jones, smith)

That is, 'if smith reports to jones then this implies that jones manages smith'. This is similar to the IF THEN construct described in chapter 9.

For predicate logic to handle variables satisfactorily, we need an additional structure called a quantifier. Quantifiers are used to indicate how many of a variables instantiations need to be true for the whole of the proposition to be true. There are two types of quantifier:

1. The 'universal quantifier', symbolised as ∀.
2. The 'existential quantifier', symbolised as ∃.

With universal quantification, all instantiations of a variable within some domain of interest must be true for the proposition to be true. With existential quantification, only some of the instantiations need to be true for the proposition to be true. For instance, an example of universal quantification might be:

$$\forall (X) \ (\text{salesMan} \ (X) \ \Rightarrow \text{employee} \ (X))$$

which reads, 'for all X, if X is a salesMan, then X is an employee'. In contrast, an example of existential quantification might be:

$$\exists (X) \ (\text{isA}(X,\text{employee}) \wedge \text{aged}(X, 40))$$

which reads, 'there is some X where X is an employee and X is aged 40'.

We may also combine these two forms of quantification in any one proposition. For instance:

$$\forall (X) \ \exists(Y) \ (\text{employee}(X) \Rightarrow \text{manager} \ (Y, X))$$

which reads, 'for all X and for some Y if X is an employee then there is some Y who is the manager of X'.

Variables are normally said to range over sets. Hence we might write:

$$\forall (X,Y) \in \text{NaturalNumbers} \ (X <> Y \ \Rightarrow X > Y \ \vee \ X < Y)$$

That is, the set of natural numbers are discrete and ordered.

17.6 Specifying a Simple Library System

A VDM specification comes in five major parts: types, values, functions, states and operations. Suppose we have a simple library system in which we wish to record details of which books have been borrowed from the system. We might write the first part of a specification in VDM as follows:

TYPES

Books = BookId-SET

STATE Library OF
    LibraryBooks :Books
    ShelfBooks : Books
    BorrowedBooks : Books
INVARIANT ShelfBooks $\cup$ BorrowedBooks = LibraryBooks $\wedge$ ShelfBooks $\cap$
        BorrowedBooks = { }
END

The first line of the specification indicates that the data type to be used in the system which we have named Books is defined on the superset of book identifiers. Suppose we have four book identifiers b1, b2, b3, and b4. The superset of these IDs is made up of the following combinations: {{ },{b1}, {b2}, {b3}, {b4}, {b1,b2}, {b3, b4}, etc.}.

Stored data is known in VDM as a state. In this case, the name of the state is Library. ShelfBooks BorrowedBooks and LibraryBooks are declared on the Books domain. The data invariant merely states that the state of the library at any time is made up of the union of the set of books on the shelves with the set of books out on loan. We also specify that a book cannot be on the shelf and borrowed at the same time.

A number of operations can be specified on this state, corresponding to some of the discussion of chapter 16. We illustrate below how we might define an operation that registers a book as being borrowed:

    borrowBook (bk: BookId)
    EXTERNAL WR shelfBooks, borrowedBooks : Books
    PRE-ASSERTION bk $\in$ shelfBooks
    POST-ASSERTION shelfBooks = shelfBooks' - bk $\wedge$ borrowedBooks =
    borrowedBooks' $\cup$ bk

The first line states that the operation is to be named borrowBook and that it has one argument bk defined on the domain of book identifiers. The next line states that write and read access is required to the set of borrowed books and shelf books. The pre-condition states that for the operation to work, the book to be borrowed must be on the shelves — i.e., contained in the set shelfBooks. The post-assertion states that the effect of the operation is to remove bk from the set shelfBooks and insert bk into the set borrowedBooks. The symbol ' here is used to distinguish the sets before the operation takes place from those after an operation takes place.

In a similar manner, the operation returnBook can be defined as below:

returnBook (bk: BookId)
EXTERNAL WR shelfBooks, borrowedBooks : Books
PRE-ASSERTION bk ∈ borrowedBooks
POST-ASSERTION borrowedBooks = borrowedBooks' - bk ∧ shelfBooks
= shelfBooks' ∪ bk

17.7 DFDs and E-R Diagrams

Formal specification need not be a standalone technique. It can be combined with other techniques such as data flow diagrams and entity-relationship diagrams. Consider figure 17.1 which documents as a DFD the two operations considered in section 17.6. In this sense, a formal specification can be used to add greater rigour to a diagrammatic technique such as DFDs.

Assertions viewed in the context of data models equate to integrity constraints. An integrity constraint specifies the allowable state of a database. Many of the constraints on an E-R diagram can be modelled formally by the mathematical idea of a map. A map is used to define objects relating to two sets. Consider the E-R diagram in figure 17.2. We assume that the entities customer and account can be modelled as two sets. Figure 17.3 represents these sets as two Venn diagrams. The oval on the left represents the set of customers: {Davies, Jones, Rees, Evans}. The oval on the right represents the set of bankaccount identifiers: {4324, 2689, 5492, 6633}. The arrows between the members of each set constitute the map. The set on the left is referred to as the domain of the map. The set on the right is referred to as the range of the map.

A map is written as D → R, which can be read as type T will take values from all the possible maps that can be constructed that have their domain a subset of D and their range a subset of R. Hence, the statement:

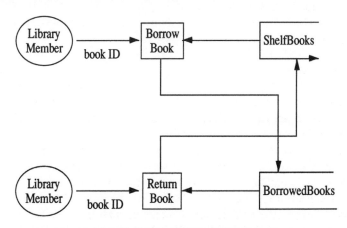

Figure 17.1   A Simple DFD

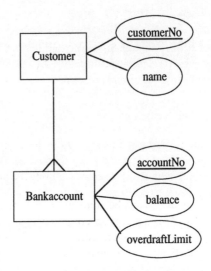

Figure 17.2   A Simple E-R Diagram

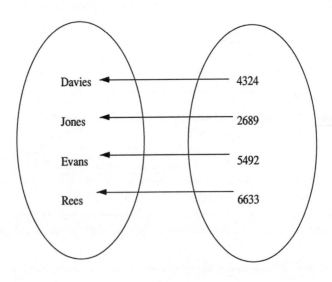

Figure 17.3   A Map

BankSystem = {1000, ..., 9000} → Customers

formalises much of the relationship expressed in diagram 17.2. Note however that this map represents a 1:1 relationship. A 1:M relationship can be modelled by relating a customer to a set of bankaccounts:

Banksystem = {1000, ..., 9000} → Customers-SET

17.8 Advantages of Formal Methods

Two important advantages arise from the application of formal methods:

1. Formal specifications can be studied mathematically, while informal specifications cannot. This has further consequences:
   a. A correct program can be proven to meet its specification.
   b. Formal specifications can be processed by computer.
2. This means that formal methods are particularly appropriate in systems where safety is critical and fault-tolerance is paramount. Hence, military and scientific applications have been particularly resonant in the literature on formal methods.

One of the most publicised successes in the formal methods domain is IBM's use of Z to specify a major rewrite of its systems software CICS.

17.9 Problems with Formal Methods

Formal methods have however still proven slow to take off, particularly in the commercial sector. Some probable reasons for this situation are:

1. The main bottleneck in information systems development is capturing user requirements. Formal methods have little to say in this area.
2. It can be argued that some areas of information systems development, such as user-interface development, are unsuitable for formal specification.
3. Only a relatively small proportion of information systems people have the skills required for formal specification. The practice of finding the most appropriate mathematical structures to model realistic information system requirements is still very much an esoteric art-form. As the body of practical examples increases this is less likely to be the case.

17.10 Goronwy Galvanising Case Study

We illustrate here how we might apply a formal specification approach to the task of defining aspects of the Goronwy Galvanising system. We deliberately ignore

some of the complications involved in the system and concentrate on formally
defining the jobs in the system as follows:

TYPES

Jobs = JobNo-SET

STATE Production OF
    DeliveryJobs : Jobs
    DespatchJobs : Jobs
INVARIANT Production = DeliveryJobs $\cup$ DespatchJobs
END

AddJob (jb : JobNo)
EXTERNAL WR DeliveryJobs : Jobs
PRE-ASSERTION jb $\notin$ DeliveryJobs
POST-ASSERTION DeliveryJobs = DeliveryJobs' $\cup$ jb

17.11 Conclusion

The application of formal methods was recently given a boost by the adoption of a
software development standard which makes formal methods a mandatory part of
any UK defence system specification (Barrie, 1989). Interestingly, the UK government methodology SSADM (chapter 21) was omitted from the standard because of
its stated lack of a formal basis. This means a divergence between civil and military
software development. This is disappointing given the fact that an adoption of
formal approaches by CAISE tools (chapter 8) would be likely to be very fruitful.

17.12 References

Andrews D. and Ince D. (1991). *Practical Formal Methods with VDM*. Mcgraw-
    Hill, Maidenhead.
Barrie D. (1989). Might is Right. *Datalink*. January.
Gehani N. and McGettrick A.D. (1986). *Software Specification Techniques*.
    Addison-Wesley. Reading, Mass.
Ince D. (1988). *An Introduction to Discrete Mathematics and Formal System
    Specification*. Clarendon Press, Oxford.
Ince D. (1989). Set Piece. *Datalink*. January.
Shaw M. (1984). The Impact of Modelling and Abstraction Concerns on Modern
    Programming Languages. In Brodie M.L. Mylopoulos J., Schmidt J.W. *On
    Conceptual Modelling: perspectives from Artificial Intelligence, Databases and
    Programming Languages*. Springer-Verlag, Berlin.

Spivey J.M. (1989). *The Z Handbook*. Prentice-Hall, Englewood-Cliffs, NJ.
Woodcock J. and Loomes M. (1988). *Software Engineering Mathematics*. Pitman, London.

17.13 Keywords

Assertion
Constraint
Existential Quantifier
Invariant
Formal Methods
Pre-Assertion
Post-Assertion
Quantifier
Set
Universal Quantifier
VDM
Z

17.14 Exercises

1. Write the following as assertions in predicate logic:
   a. Every life policy is an insurance policy
   b. Every insurance policy is either a life policy or a vehicle policy
2. Discuss whether formal methods will ever find a place in commercial development.
3. Model the E-R diagram in figure 12.8 as a series of maps.
4. Write a VDM operation for despatch job in the Goronwy system.
5. What role do you think CAISE might play in formal specification?

18 Structured Program Design

18.1 Introduction

In previous chapters we have concentrated on a range of techniques applicable to the analysis and design of information systems. In this chapter we begin to concentrate on implementation. We discuss a number of techniques applicable to the process of program design.

Program design can be described as the process whereby the requirements defined in the documentation of some system are turned into a representation the purpose of which is to direct actual coding. Since the essential role of requirements is to show how for each process in a system input is transformed into output, the program design process may be represented schematically as in figure 18.1.

From this diagram three basic alternatives to program design are possible. Two are structured approaches, one is founded in the principles of object-orientation.

One approach based on the idea of functional decomposition has been promulgated by Yourdon and Constantine (1979). The other, data-oriented approach, is due to Jackson (1975) and Warnier (1981).

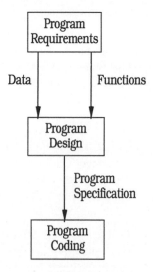

Figure 18.1   Program Design

188

An object-oriented approach to program development attempts to encapsulate both data and functions. It is exemplified by the likes of Booch (1990). This topic is covered in chapter 25.

In this chapter we present an overview of the structured approaches to program design. Readers wishing to learn more of the various approaches are referred to the works cited above.

18.2 The Functional Approach

In the late 1970s, Edward Yourdon and Larry Constantine published an influential book entitled *Structured Design: Fundamentals of a Discipline of Computer Program and System Design* (1979). The major theme of this work was that the fundamental problem with software is complexity. Yourdon and Constantine introduced a number of principles for managing such complexity which they bundled together under the term structured design. Structured design seeks to conquer the complexity of large information systems in three ways:

1. By partitioning systems into black boxes.
2. By organising these black boxes hierarchically.
3. By ensuring that each black box demonstrates the properties of high cohesion and low coupling.

18.2.1 Partitioning the System into Black Boxes

A black box is a software module in which:

1. The inputs to the module can be clearly specified.
2. The outputs from the module can be clearly specified.
3. The function of the module can be clearly specified. That is, what it does to the inputs to produce the outputs.
4. One does not need to know how the module carries out its function in order to use it.

An example of a black box would be a module which produces a list of customers in sorted order of name. This is a specification of its function. Its inputs constitute a customers file. Its outputs constitute an ordered listing of customers. We do not need to know how the module is implemented in order to use it.

The principles of the black-box approach are as follows:

1. Each black box should solve one well-defined piece of the problem. This normally means that each module should perform at most one function.
2. The system should be suitably partitioned so that the function of each black box is easy to understand. Division along 'natural' boundaries is hence preferred to

division along the lines of pure efficiency.

3. Partitioning should be such that any connection between modules is introduced only because of a connection between pieces of a problem.
4. Partitioning should aim to achieve the simplest connection between modules.

18.2.2 Organising Black Boxes into Hierarchies

It is useful to make the analogy between the structure of a computer system and the structure of a business organisation. This helps us to suggest some general guidelines for the design of information systems:

1. Work and management should be seperated in a system. Work should be done by subordinates with no managerial duties. Managers should be restricted to coordinating the work of subordinates.
2. A manager should not have more than seven immeadiate subordinates (Miller, 1967).
3. Every department should have a well-defined function:
   a. Every job should be allocated to the proper department.
   b. Messages between functions should be clear and meaningful.
   c. Managers should give only as much information to a subordinate as that person needs to do his job.

This analogy is useful in emphasising that most viable information systems are subject to some form of restricted hierarchy. Control in the system is vested in manager modules in the upper regions of the hierarchy. Work in the system is done at the lowest levels in worker modules. Communication between modules is through well-defined channels using simple messages. This is similar to the model of technical information systems presented in chapter 3.

18.3 Cohesion and Coupling

As well as black-boxedness and hierarchy, Yourdon and Constantine provide two other concepts which they use to assess the quality (chapter 26) of any software design: coupling and cohesion.

18.3.1 Coupling

Coupling is a measure of the degree of interdependence between modules. The objective of good systems design is to minimise coupling; i.e., to make modules as independent as possible. Low coupling indicates a well-partitioned system:

1. The fewer connections there are between two modules, the less chance there is of a bug in one module appearing as a symptom in another.
2. We want to be able to change one module with the minimum risk of having to change another module. We also want each change to affect as few modules as possible.
3. While maintaining one module, we do not want to worry about the internal working of another module.

Low coupling can be attained in three ways:

1. By eliminating unnecessary relationships between modules.
2. By reducing the number of necessary relationships.
3. By easing the 'tightness' of necessary relationships.

Low coupling occurs if two modules communicate solely by parameters, each parameter being an item of data. Data coupling constitutes the necessary communication between modules. High coupling occurs when, for instance, two modules refer to the same common data area. Common coupling is dangerous, particularly for its tendency to propagate software errors.

18.3.2 Cohesion

Cohesion is a function of how closely elements within a single module are related together. The objective is strong, highly cohesive, modules - modules in which all the elements are genuinely related together.

High cohesion is functional cohesion. A functionally cohesive module is one in which all the elements contribute to the execution of one, and only one, task. Read transaction, determine customer mortgage repayment, calculate net employee salary, are all probably functionally cohesive modules.

Low cohesion is temporal cohesion. A temporally cohesive module is one in which the elements are related together in time. The classic example of a temporally cohesive module is an initialisation module. The problem with such a module is that it is difficult to reuse. If the module involves such activities as clearing matrices and setting pointers to the start of sequential files, it is impossible to initialise any one file without resetting the entire system.

Coupling and cohesion are clearly interrelated. The greater the cohesion within individual modules of a system, the lower the coupling between modules.

18.4 DFDs and Design

Data flow diagrams can be used as the first stage of the program design process. Yourdon and Constantine demonstrate a technique of moving from DFDs to structured programs via a notation called structure charts. A structure chart is a graphic representation of the hierarchical decomposition of a system in terms of black boxes. A structure chart is made up of three elements (see figure 18.2):

1. The module. A named, bounded, contiguous set of statements, represented by a labelled, rectangular box.
2. The connection. Any reference from one module to another. A connection normally means that one module has called another. It is represented by a directed arrow or line between two modules.
3. The couple. An item that moves from one module to another. It is represented by a short arrow with a circular tail. A dotted circle means that an element of control is involved. An open circle means that an element of data is being passed between two modules.

Figure 18.2 illustrates a schematic structure chart.

A DFD is a statement of requirement. It declares what has to be accomplished. A structure chart is a statement of design. Design must be derived from requirement. An appropriate structure chart must be derived from a corresponding DFD. Yourdon and Constantine specify two methods for such derivation: transform analysis and transaction analysis. These two approaches deal with two different types of DFD. The main objective of transform analysis is to identify the primary processing functions in a system. In contrast, transaction analysis applies to those cases where a process splits an input data stream into several discrete output streams. Transform

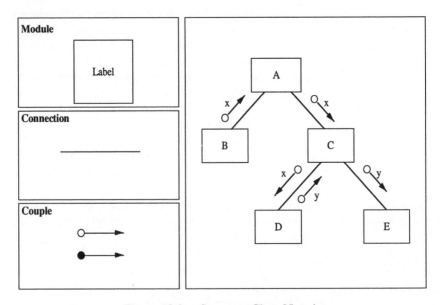

Figure 18.2   Structure Chart Notation

analysis is undoubtedly the technique applicable to more systems than transaction analysis. We will therefore concentrate on this technique in the present chapter.

18.5 Transform Analysis

Transform analysis involves the following steps:

1. State the problem as a DFD. Figure 18.3 represents a schematic DFD from which we wish to derive a structure chart.
2. Identify high-level inputs and high-level outputs. High-level inputs are those elements of data that are furthest removed from physical input, yet still constitute inputs to the system. To identify high-level inputs we start at the extreme physical inputs to the system and move inward along the flows of the DFD until we identify a set of data flows that can no longer be considered as incoming. We perform this for each input stream. High-level outputs are those data elements that are furthest removed from physical outputs but which still may be regarded as outgoing. To identify high-level outputs, we start at physical outputs and perform the same process as for inputs. These steps usually leave a set of processes (transforms) which are neither high-level inputs nor outputs. These are designated the central transforms of the system. They constitute the main work of the system in that they transform major inputs into major outputs. Process 2 has been designated the central transform on figure 18.3.
3. First Level Factoring. Having identified the central transform, we then begin the process of constructing the structure chart. All such charts begin with a top-level control module called the executive. Underneath this executive we need three modules: one module to get the data flow B; one module to transform B into C; and one module to output C. Figure 18.4 represents this first level factoring of the DFD in figure 18.3.

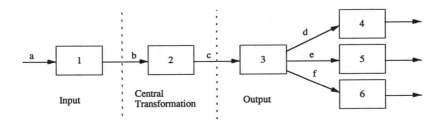

Figure 18.3   Transform Analysis

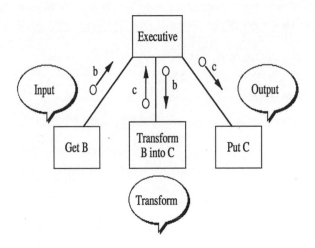

Figure 18.4   First-Level Factoring

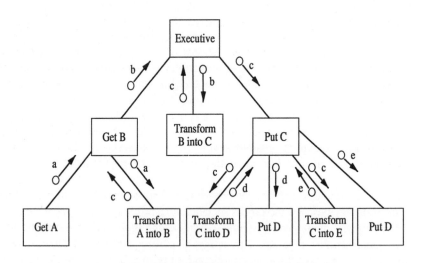

Figure 18.5   First-Level Factoring

4. Lower-level Factoring. We continue this factoring process until we are sure that we have adequately represented the problem. Figure 18.5 represents the factoring of the get B module, and put C module.

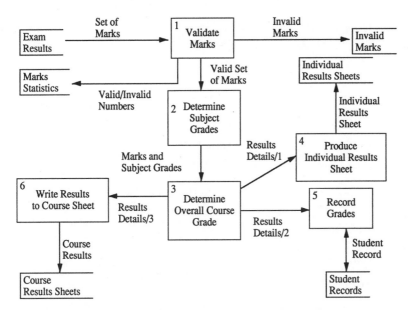

Figure 18.6   Examinations Systems DFD

18.6 Case Study: an examinations system

The diagram in figure 18.6 describes the data flow through a system for handling student examination results. Sets of examination results are first read from a file and validated. Invalid marks are written to another file, and statistics of the number of valid and invalid marks are kept.

The valid marks are then processed to determine the relevant student grades in each subject, and the overall grade for the course. Marks and grades for each student are recorded in a student records file. An individual results sheet is also produced for each student, and an entry is made in the overall course results sheet.

The task is to convert this network representation into a hierarchical representation. The first step is to identify the central transform or transforms of the system. In our example, these are the processes labelled *determine subject grades* and *determine overall course grade*. In more complex, and probably more realistic situations, identification of the central transform usually requires considerable analysis. Indeed, different analysts, working independently, might identify different processes as being the central transform.

The next step is to identify those data flows which input data to the main processes, and distribute data from the main processes. In our example, the data flow named *valid sets of marks* inputs to the transform and the data flows named *valid set of marks*, *subject grades* and *overall course grade* outputs from the central transform as a data package called *results detail*.

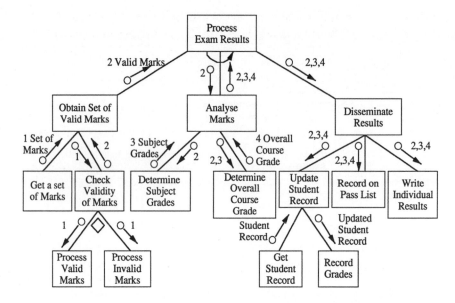

Figure 18.7   Examinations System Structure Chart

The structure chart is then produced by defining the executive module. This we have chosen to call *process exam results*. Underneath the executive we construct a data collection module (*obtain set of valid results*), a processing module (*analyse marks*), and an output module (*disseminate results*) (figure 18.7).

These modules in turn control further modules at lower levels in the hierarchy which perform subordinate processes. The sequence of execution of the various modules making up the structure chart is from left to right. Iteration is shown on the chart by a circular arrow. In our example this circular arrow indicates that the top-level modules are to be repeated. Selection can also be indicated by the use of a diamond between the appropriate connections. On our structure chart, the module *check validity of marks* has the choice of performing either the *process valid marks* module or the *process invalid marks* module.

It remains to annotate the structure chart with the data couples that are passed between modules. The emphasis in structured design is on the use of data couples as opposed to control couples. It is possible, for instance, to incorporate the process valid marks and process invalid marks into one module. However, a control couple would then be needed to indicate the appropriate function to be carried out. The existence of control couples results in a high degree of coupling between modules which, in turn, leads to increased amendment problems.

The resulting structure chart is thus an example of good software design. It is characterised by low coupling between modules and high cohesion within modules. Each module comprises a black box in that it is a simple module which performs one function well. The only communication between modules is through data couples. Control is exercised at appropriate points in the hierarchy via the simple calling of appropriate modules. All these characteristics lead to systems that are easy to understand, construct and maintain.

18.7 Data-Oriented Program Design

The basic premise of data-oriented program design is that the structure of the data detemines the structure of the program. Probably the best known, and certainly the best documented, program design technique was developed by M. Jackson in the early to mid-1970s (Jackson, 1975). Jackson Structured Programming (JSP) was subsequently chosen as a standard for all UK government installations as Structured Design Methodology (SDM).

18.8 Structure Diagrams

In order to design programs from data, Jackson needs a notation to represent both data structures and process structures. Jackson uses a hierarchical diagram, known as a structure diagram, to represent both.

For any programming problem, structure diagrams may be constructed from the three basic constructs of sequence, selection and iteration. The notation used is identical to that described in the chapter on entity life histories (chapter 16).

18.9 Stages of JSP

JSP comprises five distinct stages performed in strict sequence:

1. Draw a structure diagram for each input and output in the problem.
2. Identify correspondences between data structures.
3. Use correspondences to combine separate data structures into a single program structure.
4. List the executable operations and allocate them to appropriate places within the program structure.
5. Write schematic logic for the program.

18.10 Case Study: A Simple Banking Program

Let us assume that we are given the following simple problem:

A program is required to process a file containing a series of transactions in account number sequence to produce a printed summary report for a manager. In addition to the account number, each transaction record contains the amount of the transaction and an indicator to type the transaction as credit or debit. The

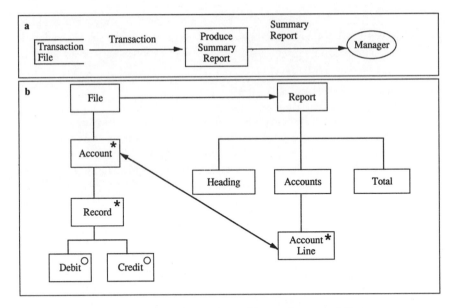

Figure 18.8   Banking System DFD and Structure Diagrams

summary report is to be headed 'account summary' and is to have one line per account showing the total value of transactions for each account.

A context DFD for this simple system might be drawn as in figure 18.8a. Our input data flow is the file of transactions; our output data flow is the summary report. The first step is to draw structure diagrams for both these flows. Two such diagrams are presented in figure 18.8b.

The second step is to identify correspondences between these data structures. For correspondences to exist, the following conditions must be satisfied.

1. Each item in the data structures must occur the same number of times.
2. The items must be in the same sequence.

In our example, File corresponds with Report, since there is only one of each for each program execution. Similarly there is a correspondence between Account and Account Line. Having identified correspondences, we indicate them by drawing a double-headed arrow between corresponding components as in figure 18.8b.

The third step in JSP involves taking the corresponding component data structures and combining them into a single box in the program structure. Then the non-corresponding boxes are taken from each data structure and added to the program structure in turn whilst preserving the original hierarchy. This is illustrated in figure 18.9.

The fourth step is to list program operations such as terminating the program,

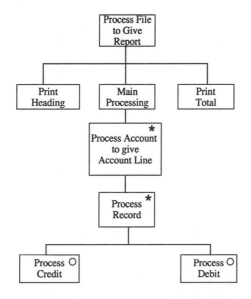

Figure 18.9   Banking Program Structure

opening and closing files, performing calculations, reading records, etc. Having listed the operations, the next step is to allocate them to appropriate points in the program structure. Strictly speaking, operations can only be allocated to sequences. Therefore, this may entail adding dummy boxes to the program structure. Two questions must be asked for each operation in turn:

1. With which component box or boxes is the operation associated?
2. Whereabouts in the sequence does it belong - beginning, end, or elsewhere?

Hence, we might allocate the various operations in the following way:

A) 1)   stop

B) 2)   open FILE, REPORT
    3)   close FILE, REPORT

C) 4)   print title
    5)   print account line
    6)   print total

D) 7)   ACCOUNT = ACCOUNT + CREDIT
    8)   ACCOUNT = ACCOUNT − DEBIT
    9)   TOTAL = TOTAL + ACCOUNT

E) 10)   read FILE record

F)   11)   ACCOUNT = 0
     12)   TOTAL = 0
     13)   store account number

The fifth step is to write the schematic logic or structured text. The syntax for each of the structured concepts is illustrated in figure 18.10. Schematic logic is a language-independent pseudo-code designed to translate the program structure diagram into a form more amenable to coding. The schematic logic for the banking application is given below:

```
A - SEQUENCE
  open FILE, REPORT
  read FILE record
  TOTAL = 0
  B1 - print title
  B2 - ITER until end of file (FILE)
    C - SEQUENCE
      D1 - ACCOUNT = 0
      store account number
      D2 - ITER until account number <> stored account number or end
      of  file (FILE)
        F1 - SELECT credit record
              G1 - ACCOUNT = ACCOUNT + CREDIT
        F1 - OR debit record
              G2 - ACCOUNT = ACCOUNT – DEBIT
        F1 - END
        F2 - SEQUENCE
              read FILE record
              TOTAL = TOTAL + ACCOUNT
        F2 - END
      D2 - END
      D3 - print account line
    C - END
  B2 - END
  B3 - print total
  close FILE, REPORT; stop
A-END
```

18.11 Goronwy Galvanising Case Study

Figure 18.11 represents a structure diagram for a key process in the new computer-

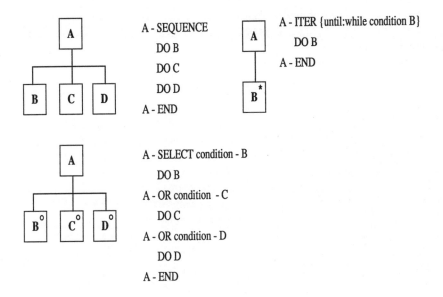

Figure 18.10   Schematic Logic

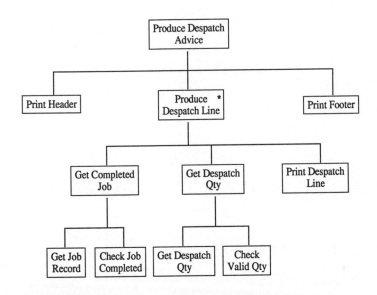

Figure 18.11   Structure Diagram — Produce Despatch Advice

ised system to be built for Goronwy — the production of a despatch advice. This process is built from a sequence of print header, produce despatch line and print footer. Note that the produce despatch line iterates for each completed job. The production of pseudo-code from this diagram is left as an exercise for the reader.

18.12 Conclusion

In this chapter we have considered two contrasting methods for structured program design: Yourdon and Constantine's functional design and Jackson's data-oriented design. Functional design works from other techniques such as DFDs and data dictionaries. Jackson's technique is less easy to place within a standard systems development methodology. Probably for this reason Jackson has created his own.

However, clearly to use JSP effectively the information systems engineer must have a clear idea of data structures. This suggests that techniques such as E-R diagramming and normalisation have a useful role in preparing for data-oriented program design.

18.13 References

Booch G. (1990). *Object-Oriented Design with Applications*. Benjamin-Cummings. Redwood City, Calif.

Jackson M.A. (1984). *Principles of Program Design*. Academic Press, New York.

Yourdon E. and Constantine L.L. (1979). *Structured Design: Fundamentals of a Discipline of Computer Program and System Design*. Prentice-Hall, Englewood-Cliffs, NJ.

18.14 Keywords

Central Transform
Cohesion
Connection
Couple

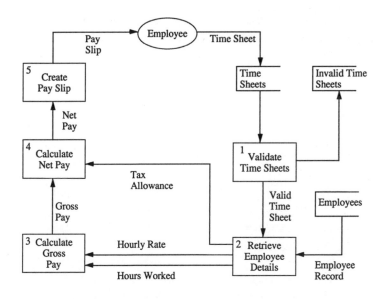

Figure 18.12   Structure Chart Problem

Coupling
Module
Schematic Logic
Structure Chart
Structure Diagram

18.15 Exercises

1. Distinguish between a structure chart and a structure diagram.
2. Compare ELHs and JSP. What do you think are the major similarities and differences?
3. Compare the syntax of structured English as discussed in chapter 15 with the syntax of schematic logic.
4. Create a structure chart from the DFD in figure 18.12.
5. Discuss whether functional and data-oriented program design are suitable for an object-oriented approach to programming.

19 *User Interface Development*

19.1 Introduction

What is the user interface? In one sense, we might define the user interface as everything concerning the human side of information systems, an area sometimes referred to as human factors. Hence, all the topics related to the social dimension of information systems development (see chapter 29) might be seen as having a bearing on the user interface.

In another, more limited sense, the user interface is usually defined in terms of screen-based interfaces to information systems. It is using this latter sense that we discuss the user interface in this chapter. One of the important facts to recognise is that as much as 50% of the application code devoted to a standard commercial information system is taken up by the user interface. With newer, more complex, approaches to user interface development, this percentage is likely to increase.

In this chapter we shall discuss three approaches to user interface development: character-based approaches, windows-based approaches and multi-media approaches. The discussion is meant to illustrate a rough historical development. Character-based approaches have been, and still are used in many information systems, particularly large, multi-user applications. Windows-based approaches are beginning to have a large impact, particularly at the PC end of the market. Multi-media interfaces are likely to form a significant part of the short-term future for interface development.

19.2 Approaches to User Interface Development

An essential function of most technical information systems is to interact with its users. Even a batch system has to have some mechanism for the user to launch a process and complete a process. No matter how well-built an information system's components are, their effectiveness is largely determined by the user interface.

The first step in developing the user interface is to identify where exactly user interaction is needed in a system. One technique adopted by methodologies such as SSADM (chapter 21) is to use process models represented in such specifications such as data-flow diagrams (chapter 13). For each process on a DFD those processes which are essentially human activities are distinguished from those processes which are essentially computer activities. The human related processes are the elements around which an interface needs to be built.

Interaction is normally portrayed in terms of a dialogue between the user and the information system. There is a continuous flow of messages between the user and the information system.

It is useful to distinguish between three major aspects of a dialogue:

1. Content. This refers to the actual messages travelling between user and system.
2. Control. This refers to the way in which the user moves from one dialogue to another.
3. Format. Refers to the actual layout of messages and data on the screen.

Format and control are largely implementation-dependent issues of user interface development. Content should be a relatively implementation-dependent feature. In other words it is not dependent on the hardware or software configuration chosen for the system.

Another way in which we can analyse dialogues is in terms of the four areas of semiotics discussed in chapter 1: pragmatics, semantics, syntactics and empirics. Format, control and content are largely aspects of the syntax of signs — the way in which signs are interrelated in some organised way. Content does however begin to impinge on the semantics of signs — how signs are given meaning. Many of the claims made for icon-based systems, for instance, are that they are in some way more natural, i.e., easier to understand and use, than character-based systems.

19.3 Logical Dialogue Design

Because of the increasing importance of interfaces, great interest has been shown in providing systematic techniques for dialogue design. We illustrate here an approach to user interface development used within the methodology SSADM. Other approaches are available (Schneidermann, 1992). In SSADM the basic unit of processing is the event as identified in the creation of entity-life histories (chapter 16). For each on-line event a dialogue needs to specified.

A logical dialogue outline is developed to represent a dialogue. The outline consists of a diagram documenting the flow of control, the decisions made by the user and by the computer, and a broad description of processing. The diagrams used are similar in notation to conventional flowcharts.

Figure 19.1 illustrates a simple logical dialogue outline for a display customer details event. The column on the left of the diagram indicates data input to the event or output from the event. The column on the right indicates comments on processing. Each decision branch in the dialogue is numbered and commented.

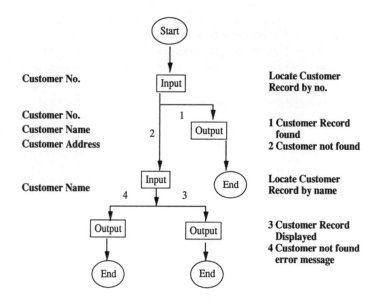

Figure 19.1   A Logical Dialogue Outline

19.4 Types of Interface

In terms of format, Schneiderman (1992) defines five broad categories of interface:

1. Menus. This consists of a displayed list of choices. The user chooses an item from the list either by pressing some key or moving a cursor to the relevant choice and pressing the enter key. Figure 19.2 illustrates a menu which might be used to provide access to a system written for Goronwy Galvanising.
2. Forms. Forms are normally used for data entry purposes, although many systems use such mechanisms for data retrieval also. A form is simply a set of fields laid out on the screen. Each data entry area is normally labelled appropriately. Forms will also have a header line and some area for the display of error messages and prompts. A sample form relevant to the Goronwy system is illustrated in figure 19.3.
3. Command Language. In this form of interface the user enters statements in a formal language in order to carry out functions. Traditional operating systems such as MSDOS use a command language. For instance, to produce a copy of a file one would issue the following statement:

    COPY <file-1> <file-2>

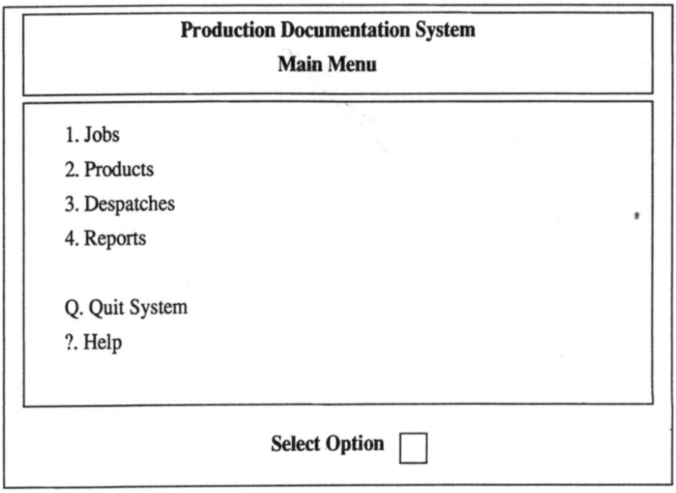

```
┌─────────────────────────────────────────────────────────────┐
│  ┌───────────────────────────────────────────────────────┐  │
│  │           Production Documentation System             │  │
│  │                    Main Menu                          │  │
│  └───────────────────────────────────────────────────────┘  │
│  ┌───────────────────────────────────────────────────────┐  │
│  │   1. Jobs                                             │  │
│  │   2. Products                                         │  │
│  │   3. Despatches                                       │  │
│  │   4. Reports                                          │  │
│  │                                                       │  │
│  │   Q. Quit System                                      │  │
│  │   ?. Help                                             │  │
│  │                                                       │  │
│  └───────────────────────────────────────────────────────┘  │
│                     Select Option  ☐                        │
└─────────────────────────────────────────────────────────────┘
```

Figure 19.2   A Conventional Menu

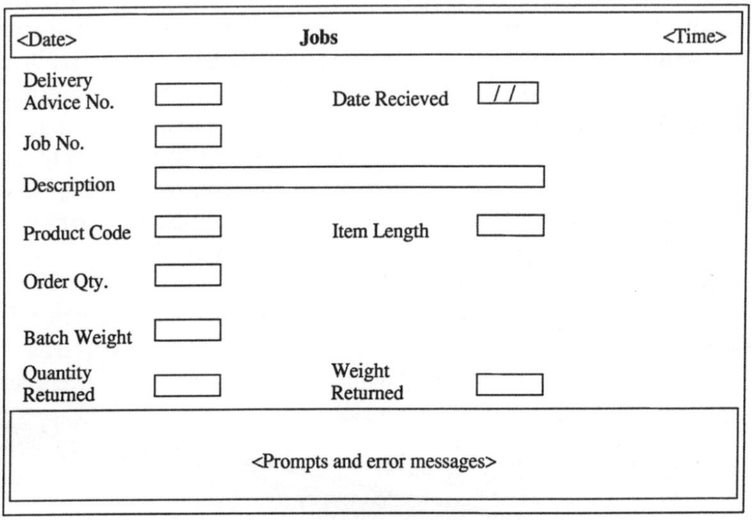

```
┌─────────────────────────────────────────────────────────────┐
│ <Date>                    Jobs                     <Time>    │
│ Delivery                                                    │
│ Advice No. [      ]        Date Recieved  [ / / ]           │
│ Job No.    [      ]                                         │
│ Description [                                    ]          │
│ Product Code [      ]       Item Length    [      ]        │
│ Order Qty.   [      ]                                       │
│ Batch Weight [      ]                                       │
│ Quantity                   Weight                          │
│ Returned   [      ]        Returned       [      ]         │
│ ┌─────────────────────────────────────────────────────────┐│
│ │           <Prompts and error messages>                  ││
│ └─────────────────────────────────────────────────────────┘│
└─────────────────────────────────────────────────────────────┘
```

Figure 19.3   A Data Entry/ Retrieval Form

4. Natural Language. So-called natural language interfaces are not truly natural language in the sense that they will accept everyday English input. They are more accurately described as being restricted English interfaces in that a statement like:

Give me all the salaries of my employees

might be acceptable, whereas the statement:

List my employee's salaries

may not. Such interfaces have achieved some success as front-ends to databases (see Beynon-Davies, 1991).

5. Direct Manipulation. This form of interface is generally associated with icon-based, windows environments (see chapter 10). They are referred to as direct manipulation because the user causes events to happen by manipulating graphic objects via mouse-based actions.

Figure 19.4 illustrates how a system for Goronwy galvanising might run under a windows environment. Here, the user is selecting from a so-called pull-down menu (in fact, two pull-down menus) by placing the cursor (the arrow) over the relevant area of the menu and releasing the mouse button. This action would cause the data entry screen illustrated in figure 19.5 to appear in a window.

From windows-based systems it is a short step to hypermedia systems (see chapter 10). Figure 19.6 illustrates, for instance, how a graphic element might be added to a system built for Goronwy. Here we are producing a histogram of current production. In the near future, many information systems will have interfaces which exploit many other media such as audio and video.

19.5 Guidelines for Interface Design

Whichever format is chosen for an interface the following guidelines are part of established practice:

1. Use consistent and meaningful terminology. This really means applying a consistent and relevant semantics to a particular domain. For instance, if menu selection is chosen:
   a. Use a consistent selection mechanism — numbers, alphabetics, etc.
   b. Title every menu
   c. Align options.
   d. Have no more than seven options per menu.
   e. Have a consistent place for selection entry.
   f. Have a consistent place for error messages.
   g. Organise menus in a hierarchy which emulates the system tasks.

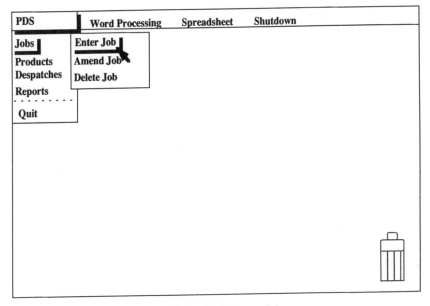

Figure 19.4   Pull-Down Menus

| PDS | Word Processing | Spreadsheet | Shutdown |

Jobs
Products
Despatches
Reports
Quit

Enter Job

| <Date> | Jobs | <Time> |

Delivery Advice No.   Date Recieved

Job No.

Description

Product Code   Item Length

Order Qty.

Batch Weight

Quantity Returned   Weight Returned

<Prompts and error messages>

Figure 19.5   Windowing

2. Design the system for different user-groups. Terms used by a system should be familiar to the proposed group of users. Naive users will need different interfaces to experienced users. For instance, naive users might appreciate selection from a hierarchical system of menus, while expert users might prefer the economy of expression available in command line interfaces.

3. Provide feedback for the User. When the user takes some action provide some indication of the result of that action.

4. Provide dialogues with a well-defined start, middle and end. 3 and 4 have sometimes been discussed under the concept of 'closure'. That is, the importance of showing the user when he has been successful at an operation, or why he has been unsuccessful.

5. Have simple, meaningful error messages.

6. Make it easy to correct a mistake. Allowing the user to backtrack to a previous state is a useful facility.

7. Avoid information overload. Do not clutter screens with too much information.

19.6 Goronwy Galvanising Case Study

Figure 19.7 represents a logical dialogue for the job entry process in the proposed information system. We have used a slightly simpler notation than that discussed in section 19.3. The notation is based on the idea of a state transition diagram as discussed in chapter 16. Note how the closure of the dialogue is maintained by

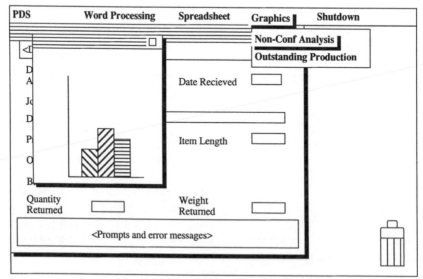

Figure 19.6   A Hypermedia Interface

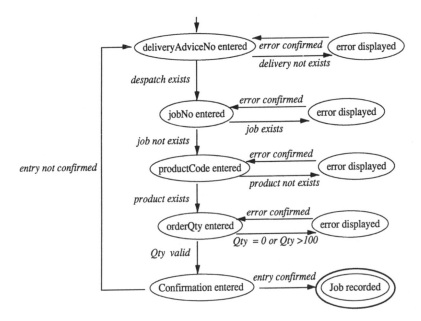

Figure 19.7   A Dialogue Outline for Job Entry

informing the user at each point if an error has been made and returning him to the previous state in the dialogue. Note also that at the end of data entry we request the user to indicate whether he or she wants the record written away (the terminal state), or whether they wish to start again.

Such a dialogue could be implemented in a number of different ways, perhaps using a character-based or a direct manipulation approach.

19.7 Conclusion

User interface development has traditionally been treated as something to be conducted almost as an afterthought on the back-end of any development effort. The data analysis and process analysis is conducted, the system designed, and then some thought is given as to whether the menu items should be numbered or referenced alphabetically.

A number of people are now proposing that the interface is so important that it warrants a place as an equal alongisde data and process analysis. One particularly radical view includes within the realms of interface development the analysis of the informal and formal information systems that determine the direction of technical information systems. We return to this topic in chapter 29.

19.8 References

Beynon-Davies P. (1991). *Expert Database Systems: A Gentle Introduction.* McGraw-Hill, Maidenhead. 1991.

Shneiderman B. (1992). *Designing the User Interface: strategies for effective human-computer interaction.* 2nd Ed. Addison-Wesley. Reading, Mass.

19.9 Keywords

Command Language Interface
Direct Manipulation Interface
Form
Logical Dialogue Design
Menu
Natural Language Interface
User Interface

19.10 Exercises

1. Direct manipulation interfaces have been generally claimed to be easier to use than character-based approaches. Why do you think this is so?
2. User interfaces of the relatively near future are likely to exploit some of the following media: video, animation, photographs and audio. Discuss the application of each of these media in terms of a conventional commercial information system such as the one at Goronwy.
3. What sort of skills will the information systems developer of the future require in the area of the user interface?
4. What sort of interface would you regard as being appropriate for the Goronwy Galvanising system?
5. Produce a logical dialogue outline for the process of issuing a despatch.

Part Four
Methods

Method
Way of doing something, system of procedure, conscious regularity, orderliness.
(_Oxford English Dictionary_)
State of order, rule, regularity, discipline. (_Roget's Thesaurus_)

Whereas a technique is a specific approach to producing some product of information systems development, a method is some organising framework for the application of techniques. In this part of the volume we consider a number of issues which have shaped the way in which information systems development takes place. We begin by considering the important process of analysing the place of infrmation systems within an organisational context. Then we turn our attention to the large number of contemporary technical methodologies available for the construction of large information systems. These methods mainly adhere to the waterfall model of development discussed in chapter 2. We contrast this with a more iterative style of development known as prototyping. Chapter 24 discusses the importance of participation by users in development and chapter 23 looks at the issues of planning strategy for development. Chapter 25 looks at a recent approach to development which attempts to bridge the process and data analysis divide. Chapter 26 looks at the important issue of ensuring that quality is a facet of our information systems.

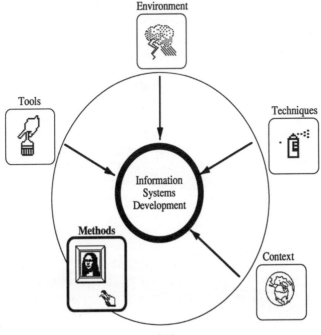

20 Business Analysis

20.1 Introduction

The term business analysis is used in a rather loose sense to describe a vast range of multi-disciplinary activities. We use it here largely to encapsulate what we might describe as the analysis of the informal systems of organisations. That is, the process of analysing the overall objectives and needs of an organisation and identifying the place of the organisation within its environment. The intention is to clearly identify the most fruitful place for technical information systems in some organisation.

Let us first review the distinction between informal, formal and technical information systems. The informal information system of some organisation constitutes a sub-culture where meanings are established, intentions understood, beliefs, commitments and responsibilities are made, altered and discharged (Stamper, 1989). The formal information system constitutes a bureaucracy where form and rule replace meaning and intention. The technical information system automates part of the formal information system. Hence, in a classic office-based organisation the contents of some letter would fall within the domain of the informal information system, the address on the envelope would constitute an element of the formal information system, and the automatic routing of electronic mail would comprise one element of a related technical information system.

In the same way that we distinguish between a formal and an informal information system we may likewise distinguish between formal and informal systems analysis. Formal or 'hard' systems analysis is the process of investigating and documenting the formal information systems of organisations. That is, the system of procedures, rules and regulations present in some organisation. Informal or 'soft' systems analysis is the process of investigating and documenting the informal information systems of organisations. That is, the systems of norms, values, attitudes and beliefs that set the context for formal and technical information systems. It is in this latter domain that the term business analysis deserves its place.

20.2 Soft Systems Methodology

Most of the discussion in this chapter draws upon the work of Peter Checkland and his associates at the University of Lancaster. Over the last decade or so Checkland has been developing the framework of an approach known as soft systems methodology (Checkland, 1987). This method has been adapted to the needs of government

214

departments and renamed Business Analysis Technique (CCTA, 1990). Avison and Wood-Harper (1990) have demonstrated how the techniques of soft systems methodology can lead into conventional 'hard' systems analysis.

Figure 20.1 illustrates the essential elements of the soft systems methodology. We first must have a situation in everyday life which is regarded by at least one person as being problematical. The situation, being part of human affairs, will be the product of a particular history. Facing up to the problem situation are some 'would-be-improvers' of it. These persons are the users of soft systems methodology.

Soft systems methodology follows two interacting streams of enquiry: a stream of cultural enquiry, and a stream of logic-based enquiry. Both streams may be regarded as stemming from the perception of purposeful actions (tasks) in the problem situation and various things about which there are disagreements (issues).

On the right-hand side of figure 20.1 is a stream of enquiry in which a number of models of human activity systems are used to illuminate the problem situation. This is accomplished by comparing the models with the perceptions of the real-world situation. These comparisons serve to structure a debate about change.

The left-hand side of figure 20.1 consists of three examinations of the problem situation. The first exams the intervention itself, since this will inevitably effect some change in the problem situation. The second examines the situation as a 'social system', the third as a 'political system'.

The logic-driven stream and the cultural stream interact. Which selected human activity systems are found relevant to people in the problem situation will be determined by the culture in which it is immersed.

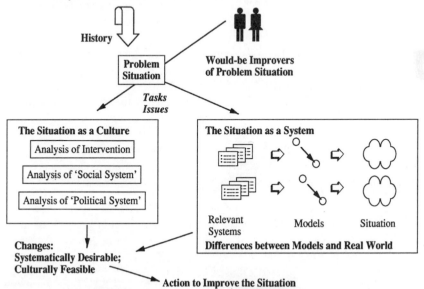

Figure 20.1   Soft Systems Methodology

20.3 The Logic-Driven Stream

The logic-driven stream is undertaken using two major techniques for defining relevant human activity systems: root definitions and conceptual models.

A root definition expresses the core purpose of a human activity system, in terms of input-process-output. Checkland has suggested that most useful root definitions are made out of six elements making up the acronym CATWOE:

C. customers — the victims or beneficiaries of T.
A. actors — those who would do T.
T. transformation — the conversion of input to output.
W. weltanschauung — the worldview which makes T meaningful.
O. owners — those that could stop T.
E. environmental constraints — elements outside the system which it takes as given.

The core of CATWOE is the pairing of transformation with the worldview which makes it meaningful. For any human activity system there will always be a number of different transformations by means of which it can be expressed, these deriving from different interpretations or worldviews of its purpose. The other elements of the mnemonic add the ideas that someone must undertake the purposeful activity, someone could stop it, someone will be its victim or beneficiary, and that the system will take some environmental constraints as a given.

Consider a university. A number of stakeholders exist in this organisation, each with a different worldview as to its purpose. For example, a student's worldview might be characterised as follows:

C. Myself.
A. Other students, lecturers and administrators.
T. The process of attending courses, achieving satisfactory assessments and getting a degree.
W. That higher education is a passage to better job prospects.
O. The lecturers and administrators.
E. The British Higher Education System.

Root definitions provide the material for constructing conceptual models. These represent pictorial representations of key relationships between the minimum necessary activities needed to support the key transformation process. In many respects, the conceptual models of SSM look similar to high-level data flow diagrams except that the arrows represent dependent relationships between activities and not data flow. Figure 20.2 illustrates a simple conceptual model drawn for the Goronwy Galvanising case study.

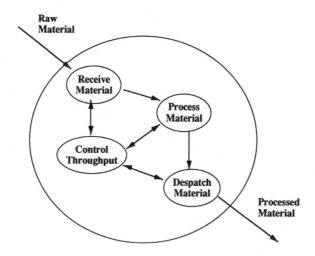

Figure 20.2   Simple Conceptual Model for Goronwy

20.4 The Stream of Cultural Enquiry

The stream of cultural enquiry in SSM comprises three stages known generally as analysis one, analysis two and analysis three.

1. Intervention analysis. Analysing the intervention in terms of three roles:
   a.   The client — the person or perons who caused the study to take place; his or her intentions in causing the study to take place.
   b.   The 'would be problem solver' — their perception of why they wish to do something about the situation in question.
   c.   The problem owner — the problem solver must decide who to take the problem owners to be.
2. Social system analysis. This stage uses a simple model of a social system. It assumes a social system to be a continually changing interaction between three elements: roles, norms and values. Each continually defines and redefines itself in terms of the other two:
   a.   By role is meant a social position which is recognised as being significant in the problem situation.
   b.   A role is characterised by expected behaviours in it, or norms.
   c.   Actual performance in a role will be judged in terms of local standards or values.

3. Political System Analysis. A political system is conceived of as a series of processes by which differing interests reach accommodation. Political analysis is made practical by asking how power is expressed in the situation studied. What are the commodities or embodiments of power used in the situation? (see chapter 29 for more explanation of these concepts)

Each of these three stages of the cultural stream may exploit a diagramming technique known as rich pictures. A rich picture is an attempt to loosely illustrate the cultural context of a problem situation. Figure 20.3 illustrates some of the conventional symbols used to draw rich pictures. Figure 20.4 illustrates a rich picture drawn for the case of Goronwy Galvanising.

20.5 Action Research

Checkland and others have come to see SSM as an example of what they have come to call action research. SSM is designed to help individuals do something about a situation which they regard as in some way unsatisfactory. SSM is therefore a research tool for action.

The two streams of SSM converge in a structured debate concerned with defining changes which will help remove the dissatisfaction. Such changes must be systematically desirable and culturally feasible. The changes must reflect the idea of relevant systems with a cultural context.

20.6 SSM in the Creation of Technical Information Systems

Although SSM is portrayed as a technology-free method of systems thinking, Checkland and Scholes have described the method as particularly applicable to computerised information systems. They discuss how process-based and data-based models of information systems can lead on from the conceptual models of SSM. One methodology specifically designed for computerised information systems work, namely Multiview, explicitly uses this approach (Avison and Wood-Harper, 1990).

20.7 Conclusion

This chapter has concluded that an analysis of the informal system of some organisation is an important first step in any information systems development effort. Methods in this area have to be by their very nature 'soft' or interpretative. The most coherently organised example of methods available is Checklands' Soft Systems Methodology. Some contingency-based methods such as Multiview have incorporated soft systems work.

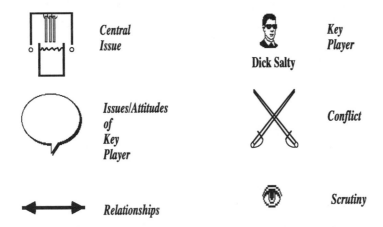

Figure 20.3   Symbols for Rich Pictures

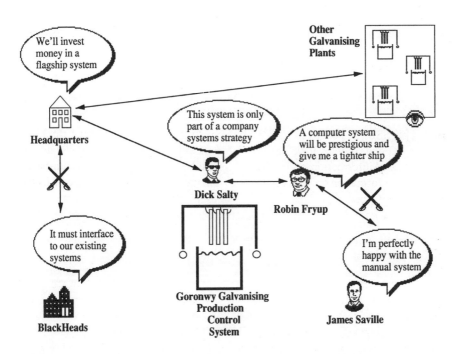

Figure 20.4   A Rich Picture for Goronwy Galvanising

20.8 References

Avison D.E. and Wood-Harper A.T. (1990). *Multiview: An Exploration in Information Systems Development*. Blackwell Scientific Publications, Oxford.

CCTA. *Managing Information as a Resource*. HMSO. 1990.

Checkland P. (1987). *Systems Thinking, Systems Practice*. John Wiley, Chichester.

Checkland P. and Scholes J. (1990). *Soft Systems Methodology in Action*. John Wiley, Chichester.

Stamper R.K. (1989). *Information Management*. Inaugural Address. University of Twente.

20.9 Keywords

Business Analysis
Formal Information Systems
Informal Information Systems
Multiview
Soft Systems Methodology

20.10 Exercises

1. Define the term business analysis.
2. Why do you think there is a demand for business analysts?
3. Define the concept of a human activity system?
4. Explain the major elements of a root definition.
5. What is the purpose of a rich picture?
6. Describe why an analysis of informal information systems is a necessary precursor to the analysis of formal information systems.
7. In what way is Soft Systems Methodology soft?
8. Identify two other major interest groups in a university. Draw up a root definition for each group.
9. Draw a rich picture of a university.
10. SSM is an attempt to reach some form of accommodation between interest groups. Is this always feasible?

21 Large-Scale Methodologies

21.1 Introduction

Part 3 was devoted to describing a number of techniques popular in contemporary systems analysis and design. Presenting the techniques as a relatively discrete set of entities has hopefully emphasised that the individual systems developer can usually select appropriate techniques as and when they are needed during the life-cycle of a particular project. This means that because of the large number of choices available, a large number of possible development methodologies can be created.

Although it is theoretically possible for a development methodology to be made up for each specific project, this is not normally the case in practice. Instead, a standard methodology is applied for all enterprise projects.

In this chapter we examine the need for and composition of a standard methodology. We then discuss the major types of method-making presently available and discuss the framework underlying three popular contemporary methodologies: Structured Systems Analysis (STRADIS), Information Engineering, and SSADM. We conclude with a feature analysis of the three methodologies chosen.

21.2 What is a Methodology?

An information systems development methodology might be defined as being made up of the following primary components:

1. A model of the information systems development process.
2. A set of techniques.
3. A documentation method associated with these techniques.
4. Some indication of how the techniques chosen along with the documentation method fit into the model of the development process.

Given methodologies may also contain the following secondary components:

1. A strategy as to how development projects are to be managed.
2. A strategy for training new users of the methodology.
3. A strategy as to what support tools can be utilised and where.

All methodologies also work within some philosophy which might be defined as the set of assumptions about what constitutes information, an information system,

221

and the place of information systems within organisations. Some include a phase of business analysis (chapter 20).

21.3 Why do we need a Standard Development Methodology?

Any organisation looking to set up a standard methodology for information systems development has a number of available choices:

1. It can develop its own.
2. It can purchase and use one of the many 'off-the-shelf' methodologies.
3. It can purchase an 'off-the-shelf' methodology but adapt it to its own purposes.

A standard development methodology is normally employed for a number of reasons. Some of the claims are outlined below:

1. People employ a methodology because they believe that it is likely to produce a better end-product than produced via an ad-hoc approach. In other words, better information systems are held to result from methodology-driven work.
2. Developers do not need to spend valuable time creating a new methodology for each new project. Instead, they can become skilled in the application of techniques within one overarching framework.
3. New members of the development team are more easily trained in the process of systems development.
4. Some people have claimed that the use of a methodology reduces the level of skills required by developers. This improves development by reducing its cost.
5. The application of a standard methodology makes project management and the estimating of project time that much easier.
6. A standard methodology facilitates communication not only between development staff, but also with end-users.
7. Standard methods encourage the automation of the development process.
8. The improved systems specifications and production of detailed documentation associated with the use of a methodology makes the maintenance and enhancement of information systems that much easier.

21.4 The Growth of Methodology

Methodologies have arisen from two sources: the commercial world and the academic world.

In the commercial world, methodologies arose out of consultancy work in information systems development. In the early days, information systems consultancies sold solely the skills of individual developers to client organisations. Each consultant employed his own favourite techniques in his own preferred ways. This made communication between developers somewhat difficult, and the problem of controlling such ad-hoc development even more difficult. Most consultancy organisations came to realise that the methodology of information systems development was one of their most important assets that had to be produced as a product, made consistent, marketed, maintained and continually developed.

Academic methodologies started life as research vehicles in universities and other research centres. The main aim of such methodologies was to build techniques upon sound theoretical concepts. Two areas which have proven academic roots is the idea of soft systems analysis (chapter 20) and the important emphasis on user participation (chapter 24) in the development process.

21.5 A Typology of Methodologies

It is useful to classify the vast array of modern methodologies under three major headings: data-driven methodologies; process-driven methodologies; and integrative methodologies. Although data-driven and process-driven methodologies may be seen as precursors of the integrative stream, many contemporary methodologies still very much fall into either the data-driven or process-driven camp.

Data-driven methodologies are those which have primarily arisen out of an overriding interest in database development. Process-driven methodologies have arisen out of an interest in modelling the functional transformation of data within organisations. As a general abstraction, it is probably true to say that the process-driven approach has had strong support from American software companies and their European associates, while the data-driven approach has had its strongest impact in western Europe.

In recent years, most of the proferred methodologies have attempted to integrate the data and process elements of information systems development. Methodologies like SSADM are clearly in this camp as are the recent attempts at object-oriented analysis and design (chapter 25).

A number of other features have been discussed in the context of comparing methodologies (Fitzgerald *et al.*, 1985) such as:

1. General philosophy - the set of principles underlying a methodology. For instance, whether the methodology takes an objectivist or subjectivist view of reality (see chapter 24).
2. The general model of the development process supported. For instance, whether the methodology adheres to a waterfall, prototyping, evolutionary or hybrid model of information systems development (chapter 2).
3. The techniques used. For example, E-R diagrams, DFDs, action diagrams, etc. (part 3).
4. The place of automated support within the methodology. Whether both front-end and back-end CAISE tools exist to support the activities of the methodology (chapter 8).

5. The intended scope of the methodology. Whether it incorporates business analysis (chapter 20) as well as information systems development. Whether the methodology expects the production of computerised systems. Whether the methodology is defined for use on large or small projects.
6. The expected and actual users of the methodology. For instance, whether the methodology is designed solely for use by information system professionals or not. Whether user participation (chapter 24) is expected. How much actual practical experience the methodology has been exposed to.
7. The major product produced by the methodology. For instance, whether the methodology stops at design, or whether a working system is expected as output.

In the sections which follow we briefly describe three contemporary methodologies: STRADIS; Information Engineering; SSADM. Our aim is mainly to illustrate the distinction between process-driven, data-driven and integrative methodologies. Discussion of participative methodologies (chapter 24) and object-oriented approaches (chapter 25) is deferred to other chapters. We conclude with a discussion of where each methodology lies on the seven feature dimensions listed above.

21.6 Structured Systems Analysis (STRADIS)

In this section we discuss the basis of a methodology primarily due to Gane and Sarson (1977) but also expounded in the work of Yourdon, Constantine, De-Marco and Myers (Yourdon and Constantine, 1979) (De-Marco, 1979) (Myers, 1979). The methodology STRADIS has been developed over a number of years on a practical basis in the United States. Very little has been written on the detailed steps of the method, although commercial variants such SADT (Structured Analysis and Design Technique) are commonplace. Structured Systems Analysis contains most of the classic elements of a process-driven approach.

21.6.1 The Structure of Structured Systems Analysis

Gane and Sarson distinguish between four major stages of information systems development: initial study, detailed study, defining and designing alternative solutions, and physical design. The initial study stage is a cut-down version of the feasibility study stage described in chapter 2. Detailed study is similar in objectives to analysis, stage 3 is similar to design and stage 4 is similar to implementation.

Figure 21.1 illustrates the basic elements of stages 2 to 4 of Structured Systems Analysis. We have also incorporated the contributions of Yourdon, Constantine, DeMarco and Myers into the discussion.

The main technique used is data flow diagramming (chapter 13). We first document as much as we can about the existing system as a set of current physical data flow diagrams. We then abstract out the implementation detail from such diagrams to produce a set of current logical data flow diagrams. The next step is to identify significant areas on the DFDs that may be amenable to change with the introduction of computing technology. These domains of change direct us to produce a set of new logical DFDs. Incorporating implementation detail we produce a set of new physical DFDs.

Alongside the data flow diagramming the developers will be producing and amending a data dictionary (chapter 14) and an associated set of process descriptions (chapter 15) in structured English. The data dictionary will be suitably normalised to design file structures for the new information system.

The eventual set of DFDs will be used to drive the production of structure charts (chapter 18) through transfrom or transactional analysis. Structure charts constitute the program designs for the new system, and along with process descriptions, are expected to further drive the production of pseudocode.

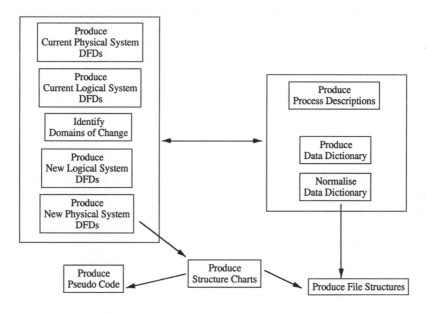

Figure 21.1   Structured Systems Analysis

21.7 Information Engineering

The concept of Information Engineering is generally attributed to the work of James Martin and Clive Finkelstein (Finkelstein, 1989). Information Engineering may be seen as an evolutionary development from an earlier methodology known as D2S2 (Macdonald and Palmer, 1982). In its present form information engineering is clearly a sophisticated methodology which displays many of the elements of integrative approaches. The general philosophy of the method however still displays its origins in a data-driven tendency.

Information engineering has been developed specifically with automation in mind. It is a methodology constructed from a set of integrated, graphical techniques which contribute to defining a model of a given information system. This model is held in an active encyclopedia which is used to:

1. Store all the information relevant to a given development project.
2. Control consistency and mapping between the various techniques.
3. Produce, via a system generator, major parts of the working information system automatically.

21.7.1 The Structure of Information Engineering

Figure 21.2 illustrates the concept of information engineering as a set of building blocks, each representing a technique employed.

The horizontal building blocks represent the fundamental analysis, design and implementation techniques of the methodology. The vertical blocks represent strategies for shortening the project life-cycle:

1. The blocks all rest on an enterprise or business model established by a process known as business strategy planning. This model establishes the mission, objectives and goals of the enterprise.
2. The next block represents information strategy planning. This constitutes a top-down analysis of business objectives, their information needs and priorities, the types of data that must be kept, the functions making up the business, and how all these pieces relate.
3. The third block consists of data modelling and process modelling. Data modelling creates a broad, overview E-R model (chapter 12). Process modelling breaks down broad business functions into specific business processes, identifies interdependencies between processes, and what data is needed to support processes (chapter 23).
4. The fourth block is data structure design which creates the preliminary database design and attempts to make it as stable as possible.
5. A technique known as action diagramming is used to specify the procedures that act on the database. These diagrams are drawn in such a way that they can be converted directly into templates for 4GL programs (chapter 7).
6. For large, heavy-duty applications the application might have to be designed with distribution in mind. Physical tuning of the database may also need to be considered.
7. Module design and 3GL coding (chapter 4) can be used particularly where performance and efficiency is critical.

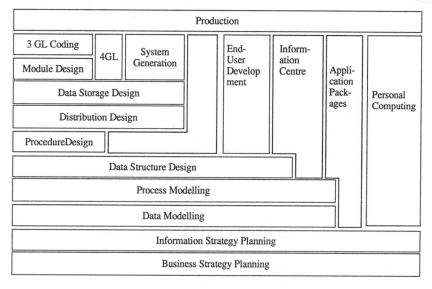

Figure 21.2   Information Engineering

Essential to the concept of information engineering is a set of alternative fast-development paths that exploit fourth generation technology. The diagram in figure 21.2 shows the earliest points at which it is reasonable to break out of the standard development cycle and proceed directly to working systems.

21.8 SSADM

In 1980 a British information systems consultancy, Learmonth and Burchett Management Systems (LBMS) were invited to work with the Central Computer and Telecommunications Agency (CCTA) of the UK government in carrying out a joint project to develop a standard analysis and design methodology for public sector organisations (Cutts, 1990). This resulted in SSADM (Structured Systems Analysis and Design Method) which has now undergone a number of versions - Version 4.0 being the latest. SSADM is an open standard, i.e., it is freely available for use in public and private sector industry. The methodology is now mandatory procedure for most public sector computing projects. Many commercial organisations are now also established users of the methodology.

SSADM is a classic example of an integrative methodology. It attempts to encompass the use of process analysis techniques with data analysis techniques in one unified framework (Ashworth and Goodland, 1990).

21.8.1 The Structure of SSADM

SSADM (version 4) is organised into five clearly defined modules (Eva, 1992). These modules are further subdivided into stages, steps and tasks:

1. Feasibility Study. The feasibility module consists of a single stage — stage 0, feasibility. This stage constitutes a high-level analysis and design exercise. It is undertaken in order to determine whether or not a system can in fact meet business requirements.
2. Requirements Analysis. This module consists of two stages:
   a. Stage 1, investigation of current environment. Used to identify the current business environment and system in terms of major processes and data structures.
   b. Stage 2, business system options. Used to generate up to six possible logical models of possible systems.
3. Requirements Specification. This module consists of a single stage — stage 3, definition of requirements. During this stage more detailed documentation of requirements takes place.
4. Logical System Specification. This module consists of two stages:
   a. stage 4, technical system options. This produces specifications pertaining to the technical and development environments for up to six options. One of the options is selected.
   b. Stage 5, logical design. This represents the logical design of update processes, enquiry processes and dialogues.
5. Physical design This module consists of a single stage — stage 6, physical design. It takes the logical specifications produced from module 4 and creates a physical database design and a set of program specifications.

Figure 21.3 summarises the interaction of these stages as a loose overview data flow diagram.

Each stage can be broken down into more detail in terms of:

1. The set of tasks to be performed in each stage.
2. The set of techniques to be used in each stage.
3. The inputs to the stage, and the outputs from each stage.

Figure 21.4 illustrates how we might draw a level 1 diagram for module 1 of SSADM. Essentially the feasibility study is a quick review of SSADM used to identify the key problems and benefits of the proposed system. Steps 010 And 020 involve drawing DFDs and LDSs (Logical Data Structures — SSADM's term for E-R diagrams) which document the major logical requirements. Steps 030 and 040 involve refining a number of business and technical options with possible project plans.

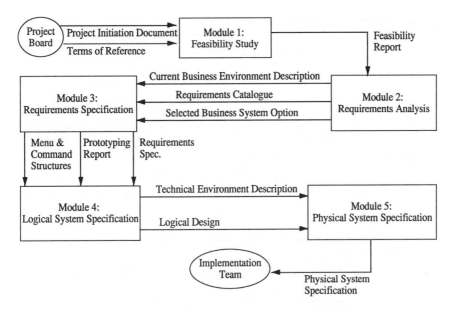

Figure 21.3   Overview Diagram — SSADM

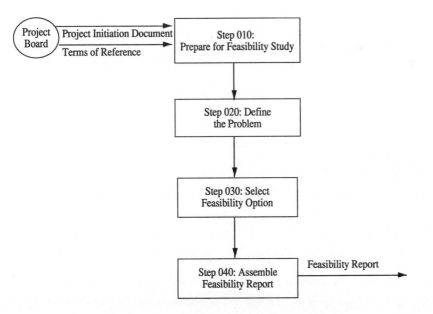

Figure 21.4   Module 1 — Feasibility Study

21.8.2 SSADM in the Development Life-Cycle

There are stages which need to come before and after an SSADM project. The ideal predecessor to the SSADM feasibility study is a business analysis stage (chapter 20) as well as the development of a corporate information systems strategy (chapter 27). This will identify and prioritise candidate information systems, each of which will move through the SSADM life-cycle in turn. The progression from physical design to implementation is deliberately left unspecified because of the variety of technical environments used. However, SSADM is increasingly being used in conjunction with RDBMS (chapter 6) and fourth generation tools (chapter 7). The CCTA is encouraging suppliers of such products to develop interface guidelines to SSADM, which describe how the step from physical design to implementation should be taken (Haigh, 1991).

The SSADM manuals do not cover all aspects of the work required to implement the five stages of the method. For instance, it does not include a project management method or procedures for quality control (chapter 26). However, it provides 'hooks' to other methods such as PRINCE: a project management method (chapter 28).

21.9 A Feature Analysis

We list some of the general comments we can make on the methodologies in terms of the features outlined in section 21.5:

1. General philosophy. All the methodologies considered in this chapter adhere to an objectivist view of reality. In other words, they assume that there is a reality that is the same for everyone. The task of the information systems developer is to abstract key elements of this reality in an information system. Two other methodologies — ETHICS (chapter 24) and SSM (chapter 21) — take a much more subjectivist view of reality. In other words, they make the assumption that reality is a social construction. That the task of the information systems developer is to negotiate an information system. That an information systems project is a reality constructing process.

2. All three methodologies adhere to a waterfall-like model of information systems development. However, Information Engineering encourages the use of prototyping (chapter 22) as a parallel stream of development and SSADM in its current version acknowledges the benefits of prototyping as a requirements elicitation tool.

3. Information Engineering and SSADM use a battery of similar techniques although IE tends to emphasis the importance of data analysis. STRADIS tends to concentrate around the use of DFDs and data dictionaries.

4. All three methodologies offer some form of automated support. Many integrated project support environments have been designed specifically for SSADM. IE is presently supported by two CAISE workbenches: Information Engineering Facility and Information Engineering Workbench.

5. All three methodologies were originally designed for large-scale computer projects. However, SSADM does offer a cut-down version known as micro-SSADM for personal computing projects and IE specifically identifies personal computing as a fast strategy for producing systems. SSADM does not currently include a business analysis stage although a methodology based on SSM can be used to front-end an SSADM project. IE specifically includes a strategic and business planning stage within its framework.

6. All three methodologies are designed for use mainly by information systems developers. No precise figure is available for the actual users of SSADM, IE or STRADIS.

7. IE specifically addresses working systems. SSADM and STRADIS stop at design.

21.10 Conclusion

Future methodologies are likely to develop in a number of directions:

1. Methodologies are likely to increasingly emphasise the importance of the front-end stages of development: strategic information systems planning and requirements analysis. No concensus has yet been reached as to the most effective techniques for these stages. Strategic Planning is discussed in chapter 23.

2. Future methods are likely to look for increased levels of abstraction. To this end, methods basing themselves around the object-oriented paradignm look likely to be influential (see chapter 25).

3. There is likely to be a growing emphasis on contingent methods. That is, methods which include techniques for determining the best way to tailor a method to particular circumstances. In this light, we discuss a contingency approach known as Multiview in chapter 24.

4. Debate continues still as to the standard methodology to be used within the European Community — to be known as EuroMethod. At the time of writing, the main contenders are the UK's SSADM and the French methodology Merise.

21.11 References

Ashworth C. and Goodland M. (1990). *SSADM: a practical approach*. McGraw-Hill, London.

Cutts G. (1990). *Structured Systems Analysis and Design Methodology*. 2nd Ed. Blackwells Scientific, Oxford.

DeMarco T. (1979). *Structured Analysis and System Specification*. Prentice-Hall, Englewood-Cliffs, NJ.

Eva M. (1992). *SSADM (Version 4) - A User's Guide*. McGraw-Hill, London.

Finkelstein C. (1989). *An Introduction to Information Engineering: from strategic planning to information systems*. Addison-Wesley, Sydney.

Gane C. and Sarson T. (1977). *Structured Systems Analysis: tools and techniques*. Prentice-Hall, Englewood-Cliffs, NJ.

Fitzgerald G., Stokes N., Wood J.R.G. (1985). Feature Analysis of Contemporary Information Systems Methodologies. *The Computer Journal*. (28). 223-30.

Haigh J. (1991). Feats of Design. *Government Computing*. Sept. 20-22.

Macdonald I.G and Palmer I.R. (1982). System Development in a shared data environment - the D2S2 methodology. In Olle T.W., Sol H.G. and Verryn-Stuart A.A. (Eds) *Information Systems Design Methodologies: a comparative review*. North-Holland, Amsterdam.

Macdonald I.G. (1986). Information Engineering: an improved, automatable methodology for the design of data sharing systems. In Olle T.W., Sol H.G. and Verryn-Stuart A.A. (Eds). *Information Systems Design Methodologies: improving the practice*. North-Holland, Amsterdam.

Myers G. (1979). *Structured Design*. Van Nostrand, London.

Yourdon E. and Constantine L. (1979). *Structured Design: fundamentals of a discipline of computer program and systems design*. Prentice-Hall, Englewood-Cliffs, NJ.

21.12 Keywords

Information Engineering
Methodology
SSADM
STRADIS

21.13 Exercises

1. List the three most important problems in information systems engineering that you believe methodologies address.
2. Methodologies constrain. Discuss the consequences of this statement.
3. Discuss the relationship between CAISE and the methodologies movement.
4. Discuss whether a methodology like SSADM is suitable for PC-based projects.
5. Is a large-scale methodology applicable to the Goronwy Galvanising project?

22 Prototyping and Evolutionary Development

22.1 Introduction

In chapter 2 we discussed the waterfall model of information systems development. This model is generally held to be an excellent vehicle for the production of large-scale information systems from well-defined environments. A well-defined environment is usually one in which there is either some manual system waiting to be computerised, or there is an existing computer system that has to be overhauled.

However, the waterfall model has proven difficult to apply in ill-defined environments. An ill-defined environment is one where there are probably no existing manual procedures. There may not even be a clear idea of what is required from an information system. For such environments, a more iterative approach to systems development is required. This approach, which we shall refer to as prototyping, is the topic of the first half of this chapter.

22.2 What is prototyping ?

Prototyping is essentially the process of building a system in an iterative way. Normally using a fourth generation language or environment, the information systems engineer, after some initial investigation, constructs a working model which he demonstrates to the user. The engineer and the user then discuss the prototype, agreeing on enhancements and amendments. The ease of use of most 4GLs means that the engineer can quickly make the suggested improvements in the working model. This cycle of inspection-discussion-amendment is repeated several times until the user is satisfied with the system.

22.3 An Example of Prototyping

Consider the case of building an information system for the motor claims insurance business discussed in section 1.5. At present, the company runs an entirely manual operation. There is also very little experience of computers in the company. In this type of setting it is very difficult to establish a reasonable set of requirements for the proposed technical information system. Staff at the company have very little idea of the potential of the technology. It would therefore seem reasonable to build a small initial prototype to give them a feel for the functionality and potentiality of the system. A single data entry screen perhaps emulating their existing claims form would be a useful start. The next step might be to build a simple report from the data entered via the screen. The whole purpose of the exercise is to get the company to think about its business and how it might be computerised.

22.4 Types of Prototype

It is useful to distinguish between two major types of prototype:

1. A prototype designed to test out some aspect of a proposed information system. In this category we may distinguish between:
   a. Mock-up. A single-screen or multi-screen model of how a significant part of the proposed system (usually the user interface) will work.
   b. Research Model. An investigation into parts of a system which will prove crucial, e.g., to test the performance of a particular module.
   c. Implementation Model. An invesigation into the different ways that a system may be implemented in terms of languages, DBMS, hardware, etc.
2. A prototype which by incremental refinement will form part of the finalised information system. It is this form of prototype which has received the most attention in recent years.

22.5 Benefits of Prototyping

The main benefit of prototyping is that it allows users to refinetheir ideas on what a system should look like. Prototyping allows users to be wrong. The fact that users can change their minds is a recognised and encouraged part of the process. As a result of this, the engineer gets a better understanding of what the user wants, and the information systems engineer gets a clearer idea of the requirements in the domain. The primary objective of prototyping is hence to clarify requirements. Prototyping eliminates suprises at the end of the development cycle, as users have seen and agreed what will be delivered.

It is also claimed that prototyping increases productivity. This it can do in a number of ways. For instance, the improved quality of requirements can have definite returns in shortening the back-end of a project - particularly in areas such as testing and maintenance. Also, substantial parts of a prototype may be suitable as a base for the final system, thus cutting down the effort involved in testing.

22.6 Problems with Prototyping

The major problem with prototyping lies in identifying precisely what it is. Is protoyping a suitable basis for system production, or should it be used solely as a means for system specification?

The latter view of prototyping is prevalent in many other professions, e.g., mechanical engineering. It is taken for granted in mechanical engineering that the prototype will eventually be thrown away. In information systems engineering, there is much discussion as to whether the prototype should itself become part of the final system.

If the implementation tool being used is sufficiently powerful and flexible to make lower-level coding unecessary, there may be a strong case for effectively implementing a prototype. What often happens however, is that prototyping initiates the 'prefab' problem. That, because the user wants the system quickly, the prototype is implemented on a temporary basis. Many important things are left undone, e.g., proper recovery and restart procedures, proper test planning, proper sizing, etc. As with post-war prefabricated housing, the intention is to replace the prototype with something more substantial quite soon. However, because of other issues, the implemented prototype, with all its pressing problems, remains in production.

The nature of prototyping, where documentation follows on from the development, rather than coming before it, means that there is also the risk of a prototype continuing into production undocumented. Associated with this is the problem that large-scale prototypes can become unmanageable through repeated iterations. The lack of documentation and repeated changes can so affect the system that the time taken to make further changes increases unacceptably.

Over a period of years, the cumulative effect of modifications to a traditional system can make it harder and harder to implement further changes as the initial sound structure of the system becomes more and more compromised. A prototype taken through to implementation may show similar characteristics, as it has been subject to repeated change during development. The difference is that the system derived from a prototype is already several years 'old' when implemented.

Perhaps the greatest problem however is that, due to the open-ended nature of the exercise, there is great difficulty in providing accurate estimating and resource planning for prototyping. This is a serious problem given that most commercial software projects have to justify themselves financially.

22.7 Rapid vs Constrained Prototyping

The problems with prototyping have forced many persons to the conclusion that prototyping should never be used instead of good project management. Prototyping may well alter the project life-cycle, especially because it facilitates iterative improvement. What it does not do is replace the project life-cycle. There is still a need for strong project management and the application of a structured systems analysis and design methodology.

Many people have therefore proposed that prototyping should be located within structured development as a means primarily of generating user requirements. Consequently, at some stage in a project protoyping would be terminated, probably at the stage at which the user requirements document is produced. This we might call constrained prototyping.

However, the weight of these statements clearly varies with the size of a project. For small-scale projects, particularly one-man projects, the overheads associated with a waterfall approach may be too great. This is because the waterfall model, and methodologies based on this approach, have been built primarily as a means of coordinating the work of large teams of information systems engineers. For small-scale projects the idea of rapidly producing versions of systems for users to criticise may be extremely productive. This we might call rapid prototyping.

A third approach which we shall call evolutionary development has developed in recent years. This attempts to integrate elements of rapid prototyping and constrained prototyping.

22.8 Evolutionary Development

Evolutionary development embodies the idea of building a system by small, incremental steps, each of which forms a working, delivered system. Crinnion (1991) also discusses the way in which each step should be sufficiently small to be managed as a prototyping project.

This idea attempts to encompass the problems of change within organisations. One phenomenon noted by most information systems practitioners is that providing a working information system for some organisation usually serves to widen the perception of the application of information technology within that organisation. This means that further information systems will need to address these changes in perceptions.

The assumption then is that business information systems should evolve with an organisation. The analogy is clearly with biological organisms rather than human artefacts. A technical information system must adapt to changes in its formal and informal environment.

The rise of the PC and the increasing adoption of LANs in organisations has encouraged the idea of evolutionary development. Many organisations are now providing workstations for their employees on which are sited productivity tools such as word-processing, spreadsheet and database software. Links between such software take the place of much of the workload of custom-built application systems.

22.9 Conclusion

Prototyping is an approach to information systems development which has had its greatest support from the tools available on PCs and PC networks. It has particularly proven itself on small-scale projects with a short development time-scale. Recently prototyping has been resurrected with the emergence of object-oriented technology (chapter 5) and the idea of software reuse.

22.10 References

Crinnion J. (1991). *Evolutionary Systems Development: a practical guide to the use of prototyping within a structured systems methodology*. Pitman, London.

22.11 Keywords

Constrained Prototyping
Evolutionary Development
Prototyping
Rapid Prototyping

22.12 Exercises

1. Prioritise the main advantages of prototyping.
2. Prioritise the main disadvantages of prototyping.
3. Contrast prototyping with the waterfall model of development.
4. Prototyping is good for small-scale, PC-based applications, but bad for large-scale, mainframe-based applications. Discuss.
5. In your opinion, how might prototyping be used in the Goronwy Galvanising project?

23 Information Management

23.1 Introduction

In recent years it has become clear that information is a resource of high value to organisations. In this sense, information is viewed as a corporate asset and therefore must be managed in the same way as any other organisational resource.

In other words, information resource management pertains to data in the same way as human resource management pertains to people. Data, like people, are subject to sound management principles. They are subject to organisation, planning, control, inventory, cost-accounting and budgeting.

In this chapter we concentrate on one facet of information management known as strategic data planning (Martin, 1982). A more business-oriented and less technically-oriented discussion of information management is provided by Galliers (1987).

23.2 Data Inventories

Commercial companies are generally very good at collecting and securing data. Large corporations spend millions of pounds on this process. However, there is much evidence that many companies are very poor at getting information back to users needing to make business decisions. Companies have got into the habit of storing data without maintaining records of its location. In this sense data can become a liability rather than an asset. Until a company actually does something with the data it collects it is merely paying out for input and storage.

One of the main aims of information management is therefore to build and maintain a data inventory: a record of all the date collected by the company (CCTA, 1991). This has a number of important benefits:

1. The company can use the inventory to ensure that data entered is not duplicated throughout the organisation.
2. The inventory can be used to rationalise the storage of data.
3. The inventory can be used to plan for the collection of data for competitive advantage.

23.3 Competitive Advantage

Information management has emerged as a discipline for managing not only the data needed to support the activities of an organisation, but also for planning the use of information for competitive advantage. The aim of information resource management is to develop a complete corporate information architecture. This architecture defines the structure of a company's data and the global processes that use this data. It defines a data and process model for the entire enterprise.

Figure 23.1 illustrates the extending role of organisational data. No longer is it sufficient to see data merely as a means of handling the routine, administrative tasks of the organisation. Data can also be used in a more proactive role as a means of strategically improving the market share of a company or planning tactics to deal with immediate changes in the environment of an organisation. Earl (1989), for instance, cites numerous examples of the way in which data embodied in information technology can take on a more strategic and tactical role.

Information

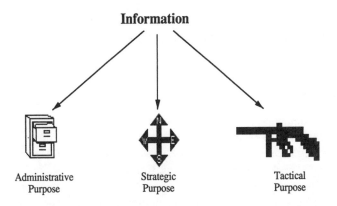

| Administrative | Strategic | Tactical |
| Purpose | Purpose | Purpose |

Figure 23.1   Information for Competitive Advantage

23.4 Building a Corporate Information Architecture

A corporate information architecture comprises an enterprise activity model and an enterprise data model suitably packaged together in some organisational framework (see figure 23.2). A number of stages have been identified as important in building such an architecture:

1. Gaining Management Commitment. Management must be committed to, and involved in, the management of the information resource. Managers must set both the short-term and long-term information needs of the organisation. They must set priorities based on these needs and establish plans for achieving goals. They must also allocate budgets to carry out such plans.

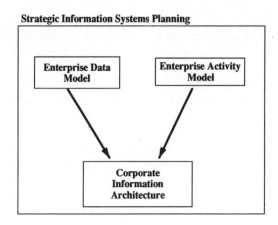

Figure 23.2   Strategic Information Systems Planning

2. Development of the global information plan. This is done top-down, in much the same way as one would develop any information system. Two global models are developed: an enterprise activity model and an enterprise data model. From these two models a plan is developed by grouping data into subject databases and systems.
3. Development of detailed information plans. For each subject database and system, a detailed plan is constructed for the information system's development, implementation and maintenance.
4. Two organisational developments go hand-in-hand with this planning exercise: the development of a data administration function and the creation of an information centre.

23.4.1 Developing an Enterprise Activity Model

An enterprise activity model is a high-level description of the activities of some organisation. It is built in a number of steps:

1. List the functional areas of the business. E.g., finance, personnel, sales, distribution, etc.
2. Identify the processes involved in each functional area. For instance:
   a.   Finance: financial planning, capital acquisition, funds management.
   b.   Sales: territory management, selling, sales administration, customer relations.
   c.   Personnel: Personnel planning, recruiting, compensation planning.
   A large, complex, organisation may have as many as 30 functional areas, each having as many as 10 processes.

3. Identify, for each process, the typical activities needed to run each process. There are typically 5 to 30 activities for each process. E.g., for a purchasing process we might have the following activities:
   a. Create requisitions for purchase.
   b. Select suppliers.
   c. Create purchase orders.
   d. Follow up the delivery of items on purchase orders.
   e. Process exceptions.
   f. Prepare information for accounts payable.
   g. Record supplier performance data.
   h. Analyse supplier performance.

All this should sound somewhat familiar. Enterprise activity modelling is fundamentally an attempt to apply the partitioning process characteristic of techniques such as data flow diagramming to the global aspects of an organisation's information. This is in contrast to a subset of an organisation's activity to which they are normally applied. High-level DFDs (chapter 13) can therefore form a useful part of the documentation of the corporate information architecture.

23.4.2 Developing an Enterprise Data Model

Alongside a process picture of the organisation, we need a data picture of the organisation. This enterprise data model is built in the following way:

1. For each functional area of the organisation, identify the entities of interest to that function. For instance, purchasing might be interested in the following entities: Part, Supplier, Requisition, etc.
2. From the entire list of entities cluster the entities into subject databases. Subject databases relate to the classes of data of interest to the organisation rather than to conventional information system applications.

A technique such as E-R diagramming (chapter 12) and data dictionaries (chapter 14) are of obvious relevance to this process. In a sense, what we are attempting to do in constructing an enterprise data model is to draft an entity model for the entire organisation. From such a global data map we then derive an appropriate structure for integrated databases.

23.4.3 Group Subject Databases into Information Systems

This step involves plotting subject databases from our enterprise data model against the processes derived from our enterprise activity model. This is fundamentally a larger scale version of the entity life history matrix as discused in chapter 16. For example, consider the matrix below:

Databases Processes	Customers	Suppliers	Sales	Employees
Accounting	X	X		X
Purchasing		X		X
Selling	X		X	
Customer Relations	X		X	
Personnel Planning				X

From this matrix, we can identify clusters of entities and processes which could usefully form the basis for information systems. This means rearranging the order of either processes and/or subject databases on the two axes until some form of aggregation occurs.

23.5 Data Administration

Once a corporate information architecture has been implemented in some form, there still remains the problem of administering the data on a day-to-day basis. The effective management of the data resource begins with the establishment of a formal data administration function. The data administration function must manage data resources, data integrity and security and data access.

1. Data resources. Administration of data begins with an inventory of data resources. In its simplest form, the inventory comprises a list of the existing data with a record of who owns or who is responsible for the data, and where it is located. This list must be supplemented by a set of activity and data models which represent corporate information policy. All of this material constitutes meta-data. Data administration manages the data about data of relevance to an organisation.
2. Data Integrity and Security. Data must be secured against unauthorised access. Authorised access to data must also be controlled if the integrity of data is to be maintained. Data integrity and security are essential to ensure the privacy of personal data.
3. Data Access. Data administration must ensure that data is available when and where it is needed.

23.6 Data Protection

The data administration function must also ensure that any data held by an organisation complies with national legislation. In the UK, for instance, the Data Protection act of 1984, lays down a number of duties upon any organisation using computerised data:

1. All systems holding data of a personal nature must be registered with the data protection register.
2. A person must be nominated to whom all requests for information should be directed.
3. Data has to be obtained lawfully and fairly. The sources of data have to be disclosed.
4. Personal data can be held only for lawful purposes.
5. When processing data, all relevant data has to be included and all irrelevant data has to be excluded. The data must be accurate.
6. It is unlawful to keep data in a personal identifiable form longer than is necessary.
7. There is a legal duty to protect data from unauthorised access.
8. A data subject has the right of access to data held about him.

Many other European countries such as those in Scandinavia and the EC also have data protection legislation in place.

23.7 The Information System as a Competitive Weapon

Recent studies have shown that information systems offer an oppurtunity for competitive advantage. Ives and Learmonth (1984) define an application as being strategic if it changes a company's product or the way a firm competes in its industry. They use the idea of a customer resource life-cycle to identify potential strategic applications. This model considers a firm's relationship with its customers and how this relationship can be changed or enhanced by the strategic application of IT.

The customer resource life-cycle is discussed as a cycle of 13 stages:

1. Establish Requirements. To determine how much of a resource is required.
2. Specify. To detail the attributes of the required resource.
3. Select a Source. Locate an appropriate source for the resource.
4. Order. To order a quantity of the resource from the supplier.
5. Authorise and Pay. Before a resource can be acquired, authority for the expenditure must be obtained and payment made.
6. Acquire. To take possession of the resource.
7. Test and Accept. The customer must verify the acceptability of the resource before putting it to use.
8. Integrate. The resource must be added to an existing inventory.
9. Monitor. Ensure that the resource remains acceptable while in inventory.
10. Upgrade. If requirements change, it may be necessary to upgrade resources.
11. Maintain. To repair a resource, if necessary.
12. Transfer or dispose. Customers will eventually dispose of a resource.
13. Account for. Customers must monitor where and how money is spent on resources.

Ives and Learmonth give examples of the strategic application of information technology at each of these stages. For instance, a Swedish dairy cooperative produces for their retailers pro-forma orders detailing estimated requirements. The customer then has the option of using the prepared orders or changing them. Such orders assisted the retailer at both the specification and requirements stage of the customer life-cycle.

23.8 Conclusion

Information management has developed around one particular technical information systems tool, the database. Only with the rise of database systems and their central place in modern-day information systems have issues such as the ownership and exploitation of corporate data come to the fore. Data and database administration have now become accepted roles in the modern information systems department.

Recently, the term information management has been used to include the management of information systems, particularly the planning of strategic IT. We consider this issue again in chapter 27.

23.9 References

CCTA. (1991). *Information Resource Management*. HMSO, London.

Earl M.J. (1989). *Managament Strategies for Information Technology*. Prentice-Hall, Hemel Hempstead, UK.

Ives B and Learmonth G.P. (1984). The Information System as a Competitive Weapon. *CACM*. 27(12). 1193-1201.

Galliers R. (1987). *Information Analysis: Selected Readings*. Addison-Wesley, Sydney.

Martin J. (1982). *Strategic Data Planning Methodologies*. Prentice-Hall, Englewood-Cliffs.

23.10 Keywords

Competitive Advantage
Corporate Information Architecture
Data Inventory
Enterprise Activity Model
Enterprise Data Model
Information Resource Management
Strategic Data Planning

23.11 Exercises

1. Is information really a resource in the same way as plant and machinery?
2. What sort of tools would be needed to develop enterprise data models effectively?
3. What sort of organisational problems might arise in developing a corporate information architecture?
4. What advantages can be gained from a large organisation like the UK National Health Service developing a corporate information architecture?
5. Consider the customer resource life-cycle of a university. What applications might be used to add value to its service?
6. Other countries such as Sweden and Holland have data protection legislation in place. Investigate how their laws compare with the UK case.
7. Identify some ways in which IT can be used for competitive advantage in Goronwy Galvanising.

24 Participative Development

24.1 Introduction

The idea of participative development in information systems is similar to the idea of participative development in the world of architecture. Architectural design was traditionally seen to be the prerogative of the architect as technical expert. In response to some of the dismal social failures of the architecture of the 1960s and early 1970s a reaction has occurred in British architecture in recent years. The so-called community architecture movement has placed greater emphasis on the role of the architect as facilitator.

24.2 Five Key Assumptions

Participation has not been heavily emphasised in British information systems development. This is primarily because conventional systems development practice is founded on a number of key assumptions about the nature of reality (Hirschheim and Klein, 1989):

1. Objective Reality. Most systems design techniques treat the real world as a given. They assume that there is one reality that is measurable and the same for everyone.
2. Objective Management. Management is assumed to lead an organisation via clearly defined system objectives designed to improve organisational efficiency.
3. Technical Expertise. The primary role of the information systems developer is to be expert in the technology, tools and methods of information systems development.
4. Reality Modelling. Information systems development is the task of designing systems that model reality. Information systems are cast as utilitarian tools for management to achieve their ends.
5. Organisational Consensus. Organisational 'politics' are irrational and interfere with maximum efficiency and effectiveness. As such, they are treated as external to the realms of consideration.

In essence these assumptions are based on a limited conception of the culture of organisations. In the tradition of systems theory (Silverman, 1976), organisations are generally presented in the information systems literature as well-structured formal information systems. The application of computerised information systems occurs within a relatively well-bounded area of this formal domain.

24.3 A Critique of Assumptions

The assumptions described above are clearly open to a critique from a sociological position:

1. Subjective Reality. Reality is socially constructed. Reality is a continuing negotiation between actors in the social world (Berger and Luckman, 1971).
2. Subjective Management. Management frequently do not have any clearly defined goals. They may also hold objectives which conflict with organisational effectiveness.
3. Human Expertise. Most systems analysts find themselves doing more human-related work than technical-related work (Beynon-Davies, 1990). Technical expertise is often used more as a vehicle for exercising power over users than as a tool for improving organisational efficiency (Markus and Bjorn-Anderson, 1987).
4. Reality Shaping. Systems design is usually about modelling one particular group's conception of reality — i.e, some sub-group of management. This conception may conflict with the perceptions and expectations of other organisational groups. Information systems development is not simply 'engineering'. It is as least as much organisational innovation (Keen, 1977).
5. Systems Conflict. Organisational 'politics' are the stuff of which information systems are made. The management (not necessarily the resolution) of organisational politics is probably one of the best ways of improving organisational effectiveness (Keen, 1981).

Any formal information system takes its context or direction from the informal information system that surrounds it (chapter 1). The informal information system sets the shape of the organisational reality. It determines the shape of management objectives and determines the direction of organisational 'politics'.

What is interesting is how the assumptions about reality are a reflection of a country's socio-political environment. Systems development in Britain under the Thatcherite ethos clearly emphasised technical rationality and consequently low participation. In the Scandinavian countries, however, trade unions have for many years been actively involved in determining the direction of information technology (Bjerknes *et al.*, 1988).

24.4 Scandinavian Systems Development

For a number of years, the Scandinavian countries of Norway, Sweden and Denmark have taken a particularly humanistic view of technical information systems. Trades Unions have long been seen to be central to the information systems development process. The strength of trades unions backed by national legislation has meant that employees have been able to negotiate satisfactory agreements with their employers over work practices. Unions have been able to fund their own independent research projects and educational programs in new tehnology. This has given workers increased understanding of the technology and enabled them to become actively involved in decisions relating to the design and implementation of technical information systems (Bjerknes *et al.*, 1988).

24.5 Computer Supported Cooperative Work

The idea of participative development has a clear relationship with an area concerned with exploring how computers can be used to facilitate the coordination and cooperation of work groups. Computer supported cooperative work (CSCW), at least in its Scandinavian guise, takes a libertarian view of technical information systems. The conventional model of information systems within organisations is as mechanisms for control. CSCW emphasises the use of information systems as a means for bringing groups together to work more effectively.

The end-product of much CSCW research is groupware — computer software which facilitates group interaction. One cogent example of groupware is the information lens project at MIT (Williams, 1990). Information lens provides intelligent tools to help manage large streams of electronic messages. Information lens helps users to find information, file, sort and prioritise their messages. Using representations similar to those discussed in section 9.7, users can get the system to automatically sift electronic mail. Junk mail can be automatically discarded; priority mail can be filed in various folders.

Groupware has begun to infiltrate the marketplace under the banner of workflow applications such as Lotus Development's Notes. Workflow applications automate business processes that involve comunication between individuals. A simple example is that of processing an expenses request. Using such an application the employee will fill in a standard expense request form on the screen and send it via electronic mail to his immediate superior for approval. If the amount is over a certain figure, a copy will be automatically sent to the regional manager for independent approval. The whole transaction is completed on screen and the expenses are finally credited to the employee's bank account electronically.

24.6 Socio-Technical Design

In Britain, probably the most influential of the attempts to introduce user participation into information systems development is the work of Enid Mumford (1983) at the Manchester Business School.

Mumford has distinguished between three different levels of user participation:

1. Consultative Participation. Decision-making is still in the hands of systems analysts, but there is a great deal of staff at every level.
2. Representative Participation. A design group is formed made up of representatives of all grades of staff with systems analysts. The representatives however are selected by management.
3. Consensus Participation. A design group is formed as in 2, but representatives are elected by staff and given the responsibility to communicate group decisions back to staff.

Mumford has developed a methodology for participative development out of her work on socio-technical systems. The methodology is called ETHICS (Effective Technical and Human Implementation of Computer Systems). The objective of ETHICS is to design a new form of work organisation with the dual objectives of improving job satisfaction (the social system) and work efficiency (technical system).

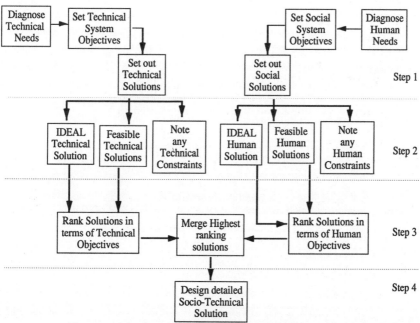

Figure 24.1   The ETHICS Method

The ETHICS method is laid out in figure 24.1. The steps of the methodology are laid out below:

1. The diagnosis of technical and human needs is undertaken primarily by collecting and analysing questionnaire data. This data is used to determine the fit between the present work situation and a valued work situation in terms of a typology of needs. Both job satisfaction objectives (such as provide work variety, and performance incentives) and efficiency objectives (such as improve level of customer performance) are then constructed.
2. In step 2 we set out a range of technical and social alternatives. We then assess each alternative in terms of human advantages and disadvantages and technical advantages and disadvantages.
3. In step 3 we rank each technical and human alternative in terms of their ability to meet both human and technical objectives. We choose the highest ranking human and technical alternative that are compatible.
4. Develop detailed socio-technical design.

24.7 An Example of the Application of ETHICS

Mumford provides a case study of a customer orders and accounts system which was analysed by the ETHICS approach, and from which a new social and technical system emerged.

The basic technical system involved orders clerks filling out order forms, accounts clerks updating customer ledgers and any problems being resolved by lots of paper-passing. The social system represented a clear distinction between orders clerks and accounts clerks, each accounts clerk working across a number of different customer accounts, and problems being resolved by two senior clerks.

The motivations for change were both technical and social. Examples of technical problems were orders incorrectly filled out, customer ledgers incorrectly updated, slow methods of resolving problems. Examples of social problems included high absenteeism, high staff turnover, and some 'industrial vandalism'.

Results from the job satisfaction questionnaire identified low job satisfaction in the present work situation as a result of piece-work, lack of overall picture, individual isolation, low status, and poor prospects for advancement. The valued work situation was characterised in terms of more responsibility, group working, more important work and better opportunities for advancement.

After the study was complete a new work and technical system was put into place. The technical system constituted terminal input of orders, batch update of a central database and regular reports output from the system. The social system was changed to small work groups of 5 clerks, each work group handling orders and accounts for a group of customers. The group handled customer problems thrown up by printouts.

24.8 Conclusion

ETHICS is certainly an improvement over traditional non-participative development. There is an assumption made however that some form of compromise between
social and technical systems can be made. It assumes that there need not be conflict
between human needs and technical needs. In many situations where perhaps job
losses are inevitable this assumption is not tenable.

Certain authors such as Winograd and Flores (1986) have begun to question the
traditional rationalisic conception of computing. They would like to emphasise a
more positive facilitation role for computers. Enhancing group communciation and
coordination is one embodiment of this idea.

24.9 References

Berger P. and Luckman T. (1971) *The Social Construction of Reality.* Penguin,
Harmondsworth.

Bjerknes G., Ehn P. and Kyng M. (1988). (Eds.) *Computers and Democracy: A
Scandinavian Challenge.* Gower, Oxford.

Markus M.L. and Bjorn-Anderson N. (1987). Power Over Users: its exercise by
systems professionals. *CACM.* 30(1). 498-504.

Mumford E. (1983). *Designing Participatively.* Manchester Business School Press,
Manchester.

Silverman D. (1976). *The Theory of Organisations.* Heinemann, London.

Williams D. (1990). New Technologies for Coordinating Work. *Datamation.* May
15. 92-96.

Winograd T. and Flores F. (1986). *Understanding Computers and Cognition: a new
foundation for design.* Ablex Publishing, Norwood, N.J.

24.10 Keywords

CSCW
ETHICS
Groupware
Participative Development
Workflow Applications

24.11 Exercises

1. Over the last decade in particular, users have become much more expert at using
    information systems. In what way do you think does this end-user movement
    have a bearing on participative development.

2. Which approach to development is more suited to participation: prototyping or the waterfall approach?
3. Given the current political and economic climate in Western Europe would you expect participation rates to increase or decrease?
4. A technical information system represents an implementation of a social reality. Discuss.
5. In what way might SSADM be adapted to the participative approach?
6. How much of a standard commercial information system might be classed as groupware?
7. How might participation be relevant to the Goronwy project?

25 Object-Oriented Development

25.1 Introduction

Object-Oriented (OO) is definitely the current thing to be. Systems analysis, systems design, programming, and most recently database systems have all been caught up in the crest of this new wave. Roger King (1988) has even written an article entitled — My Cat is Object-Oriented. The implication being that if his cat is OO then he is far more likely to be able to sell it!

The main aim of the chapter is to portray how conceptual modelling as applied to database systems can move relatively painlessly into the domain of OO. We will discuss how OO analysis, an approach primarily directed at the building of applications in procedural or object-oriented languages, is equally relevant to the development of database systems.

25.2 Streams of OO Analysis

Most paradigms (chapter 2) are based on a small number of firmly held principles. One of the principles which is adopted in most of the contemporary literature on OO is that the objective of OO development is to heal the contemporary divide between process analysis methods and data analysis methods.

Proponents of OO rightly point to the deficiencies of each of the contemporary approaches to information systems development. Process analysis methods based around techniques such as data flow diagramming and functional decomposition (see part 3 section 2) over-emphasise the functional or dynamic side of information systems and under-emphasise the structural or static side of information systems. In contrast, data analysis methods (see part 3 section 1) based around such techniques as entity-relationship diagramming and normalisation over-emphasise data and under-emphasise process.

Since objects have both a structural (data) and behavioural (process) aspect (chapter 5), any analysis method based on such concepts should reflect the integrative emphasis of objects. However, it is interesting to note that few of the proposed OO methods divorce themselves entirely from the 'structured' battles of the 1980s. Most of the current OO methods pay lip-service to having some ancestry in the process-oriented or data-oriented traditions. What we might call process-directed OO methods build objects out of clusters of behaviours or functions (Gibson, 1990). In contrast, data-driven OO methods start with an analysis of structure and introduce functions later (Coad and Yourdon, 1991).

25.3 Entities to Objects

Entity modelling as we have described it in chapter 12 has much in common with object modelling (Blaha *et al.*, 1988). In this section we consider some of the common threads between entity and object modelling and discuss some proposals for extending entity modelling into an object modelling approach.

In chapter 12 we defined an entity as being some thing of interest to an organisation which has an independent existence. This abstract definition can serve equally well for defining objects. The major difference between entities and objects lies in the way we apply these constructs in the modelling process. Entities are primarily static constructs. An entity model gives us a useful framework for painting the structural detail of a database system. In other words, an entity model translates into files and relationships between files in some database system.

Objects however have a more ambitious purpose. An object is designed to encapsulate both a structural and behavioural aspect. In other words, an object model gives us a means for designing not only a database structure but also how that database structure is to be used. An object model not only models files, it also models constraints and transactions.

The easiest way to begin to build an object model is to exploit some of the inherent strengths of entity modelling and extend them with behavioural abstractions.

25.4 Object Models

An object is a package of data and procedures. Data are contained in attributes of an object. Procedures are defined by an object's methods. Methods are activated by messages passed between objects.

In chapter 5 we distinguished between between an object and an object class. An object class is a grouping of similar objects that define their attributes and methods. Objects are instances of some class. They have the same attributes and methods. In other words, object classes define the intension of the database — the central topic of database design. Objects define the extension of a database — the central topic of database implementation.

The primary reason for defining objects in this manner is that they should display a property known as encapsulation, sometimes known as information hiding. This is the process of packaging together of both data and process within a defined interface and controlled access across that interface.

25.4.1 Behavioural Mechanisms

Two major types of behavioural mechanism need to be documented in the design of a database system: constraints and transactions. Constraints define allowable states

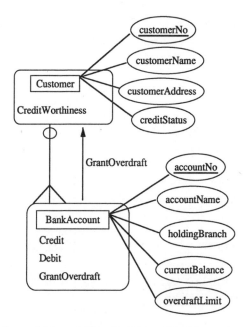

Figure 25.1   A Simple Object Model

of a database. Transactions are the means of causing changes to a database.

Constraints and transactions are therefore interdependent. Constraints determine the acceptable behaviour of transactions. Transactions are the means of activating constraints.

This interdependence is reflected in an object model. Transactions are represented usually by messages between objects. Constraints are generally embedded in the methods pertaining to objects.

We have defined three methods for the object class in figure 25.1: Credit, Debit and GrantOverdraft. Methods provide the link between data and transactions. In a truly OO manner transactions impact upon data (attributes) through messages. Credits and debits, for instance, are messages which activate the methods of the object class and update the balance attributes of object instances.

Methods may also be used to incorporate integrity constraints. Hence the GrantOverdraft method might incorporate a check on a person's credit-worthiness. This would mean sending a message to another object and receiving some reply. Figure 25.1 illustrates a message dependency (indicated by a labelled arrow) between a Customer class and a BankAccount class.

25.4.2 Primary Methods

Every class object has associated with it four primary methods: create, delete, amend and retrieve — sometimes referred to as constructor, destructor, modifier and selector methods (Booch, 1990) (see figure 25.2). These correspond to the classic file maintenance operations implemented in most DBMS.

Because of their ubiquity such methods are usually left off the diagrams pertaining to object models. However, if constraints are attached to such methods then the primary method concerned should be displayed on the object diagram.

For instance, we might attach an existence constraint to the create method of the class BankAccount to the effect that:

> a bankaccount should not be created for a non-existent customer

We might also attach a similar type of constraint to the delete method of the customer class to the effect that:

> a customer object should not be deleted until all associated bankaccount objects have been deleted.

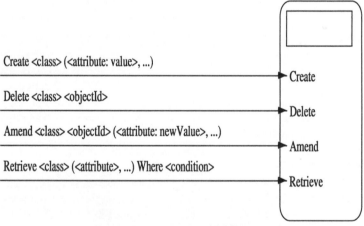

Figure 25.2   Primary Methods

25.4.3 Secondary Methods

An object class may have several secondary methods defined within it. Secondary methods are always written on the object diagram.

Figure 25.3, for instance, illustrates how generalisation might be applicable to the BankAccount domain. Note how we have defined two methods — Credit and Debit - to be relevant to the superclass object BankAccount. The other methods — GrantOverdraft and IncreaseRate — are specific to the individual sub-class objects.

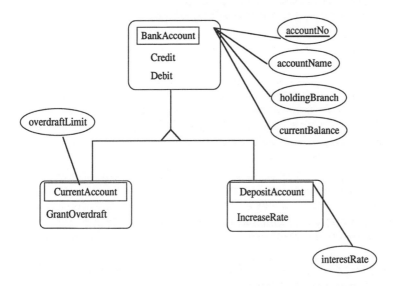

Figure 25.3   Generalisation

25.5 Stages in OO Analysis

OO analysis is strongly iterative in nature. Although the technique can be described in terms of the following stages, the process is one of successive refinement with numerous feedback loops (Booch, 1990):

1. Identify object classes
2. Identify attributes
3. Identify relationships
4. Identify messages/methods

In most traditional approaches to database design, process concerns are introduced either as a means of validating entity models, or as a means of recording physical design decisions against entity models.The main benefit that OO analysis offers database design is the ability to integrate, at the logical level, behavioural with structural concerns.

25.6 Accommodation to the Relational Data Model

Object models are conceptual models. In other words they are meant to be implementation-independent. Having said this, in much the same way that entity models are naturally implementable in entity-relationship databases, object models are most naturally implementable in OO databases. However, the level of abstraction built into object models means that like entity models, object models can be accommodated to relational schema. Some of the steps involved are indicated below:

1. Each object becomes a relation.
2. The entity ID becomes the primary key of the relation.
3. All other attributes become non-key data-items of the table.
4. Each 1:M association between objects is implemented via a foreign key (entity ID) at the many end of a relationship.
5. Optional status at the many end of an association means that the foreign key should be declared null.
6. Superclasses and subclasses form separate relations with the same entity ID.
7. Inheritance can be simulated via views (Kung, 1990).
8. In the near future many of the features of methods will be implementable in the extended integrity language of SQL. For the moment, constraints need to be implemented in code written in some host language such as C or some applications building tool such as ORACLE's SQL*FORMS.
9. Messages translate into major transactions. Primary or secondary methods without constraints can be implemented in the basic file maintenance primitives of SQL. Complex transactions involving the activation of numerous constraints will need to be produced in a host language.

25.7 An Object Diagram to an SQL-Based Relational Database System

In this section we discuss how the object model discussed in previous sections can be used to produce a design for an integrated database. The object model, at least as far as the database is concerned, would achieve its most natural implementation in an OODBMS. However, in this section we discuss a relational (SQL) implementation of object modelling concepts.

The object diagram in figure 25.3 can be used to design a relational database for customers and accounts information according to the steps described in the previous section. The relational schema is given below as a series of ANSI SQL create table statements (Beynon-Davies, 1991):

```
CREATE TABLE Customers
(customerNo CHAR(10) NOT NULL,
  customerName CHAR(20) NOT NULL,
  customerAddress CHAR(20),
  creditStatus CHAR(5))
```

```
PRIMARY KEY (customerNo)
CREATE TABLE BankAccounts
(accountNo CHAR(10) NOT NULL,
  accountName CHAR(20) NOT NULL,
  customerNo CHAR(10) NOT NULL,
  holdingBranch CHAR(20) NOT NULL,
  currentBalance NUMBER(8,2))
PRIMARY KEY (accountNo)

CREATE TABLE CurrentAccounts
(accountNo CHAR(10) NOT NULL,
  overDraftLimit NUMBER(6,2))
PRIMARY KEY (accountNo)
FOREIGN KEY (accountNo IDENTIFIES BankAccounts,
DELETE OF accountNo RESTRICTED,
UPDATE OF accountNo CASCADES)

CREATE TABLE DepositAccounts
(accountNo CHAR(10) NOT NULL,
  interestRate NUMBER(2))
PRIMARY KEY (accountNo)
FOREIGN KEY (accountNo IDENTIFIES BankAccounts,
DELETE OF accountNo RESTRICTED,
UPDATE OF accountNo CASCADES)
```

Also, we can simulate inheritance between the class BankAccount, and the class DepositAccount, by using the following view:

```
CREATE VIEW DepositAccount AS
SELECT B.accountNO, holdingBranch, interestRate, currentBalance
FROM BankAccounts B, DepositAccounts D
WHERE B.accountNo = D.accountNo
```

A similar view can be built for the class CurrentAccount. We can simulate the method Credit with the following SQL script:

```
/* CREDIT.SQL */
UPDATE BankAccounts
SET currentBalance = currentBalance + &1
WHERE accountNo = &2
```

Where &1 and &2 are parameters to be passed to the transaction.

25.8 An Object Diagram to an OO Database

Because of the mathematical simplicity of their underlying data model, relational databases have proven to be extremely successful at supporting standard data processing applications such as accounting, payroll and personnel. A number of emerging non-standard applications in areas such as office automation, knowledgebase systems and computer aided design, however, have caused many people to reassess the position of the relational data model for database management. Such non-standard applications demand the support of complex objects such as documents, rules and graphics. Although powerful, the relational data model is generally considered insufficient for supporting this new object-orientation.

To illustrate the idea of an OO database we use an approach based on binary relations as discussed in chapter 9. A binary relational schema for the application discussed in previous sections is given below:

        BankAccount AKO Object
        Customer AKO Object
        Customer Holds BankAccount
        Customer HASA customerName
        Customer HASA customerAddress
        Customer HASA creditStatus
        BankAccount HASA accountName
        BankAccount HASA currentBalance
        CurrentAccount AKO BankAccount
        DepositAccount AKO BankAccount
        CurrentAccount HASA overdraftLimit
        depositAccount HASA interestRate
        customerName TYPE CHAR(20)
        customerAddress TYPE CHAR(50)
        creditStatus TYPE NUMBER(1)
        accountName TYPE CHAR(20)
        overdraftLimit TYPE NUMBER(5)
        interestRate TYPE NUMBER(4,2)

Note that we have not specified any identifiers for objects. These have been assumed to be system-generated. The notion of primary and foreign keys are no longer relevant. Note also, we have not specified any methods in the above schema. These might be represented by rules as described in section 9.5.

25.9 The Goronwy Galvanising Case Study

In chapter 12 we developed the entity model (figure 25.4) for the Goronwy Galvanising application. To extend this into an object model we need to define

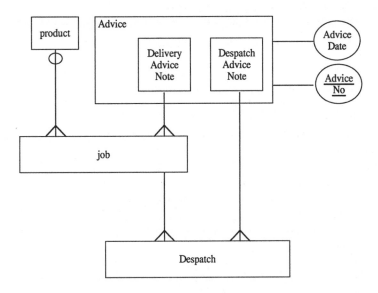

Figure 25.4   Entity Model for Goronwy

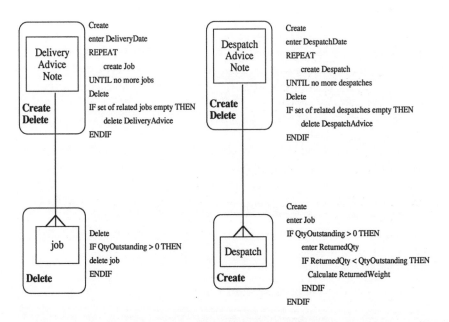

Figure 25.5   Some Primary Methods

interfaces for each object. Figure 25.5 illustrates four simple interfaces for despatch advices, delivery advices and jobs. Note how we have used a form of structured English (chapter 15) to specify the methods.

25.10 Conclusion

We summarise the discussion below:

1. Entity models, as represented by entity-relationship diagrams, can evolve into object models, as represented by object diagrams.
2. Object models are equivalent to entity models plus two additional sets of abstraction mechanisms:
   a. Structural abstraction such as generalisation and aggregation.
   b. Behavioural abstraction such as methods and messages.
3. Object models provide a new dimension for database design. They allow the integration of process analysis with the proven traditions of data analysis.
4. Object models can be used to develop the newer OO databases, the more conventional databases such as relational systems, and hybrids such as OO extensions to relational systems. An accommodation process for relational schema has been discussed.

25.11 References

Beynon-Davies P. (1991). *Relational Database Systems*. Blackwell Scientific, Oxford.

Blaha M.R., Premerlani W.J. and Rumbaugh J.E. (1988). Relational Database Design Using an Object-oriented Methodology. *CACM*. 31(4). 414-427.

Booch G. (1990). *Object-Oriented Design with Applications*. Benjamin-Cummings. Redwood City, Calif.

Coad P and Yourdon E. (1991). *Object-Oriented Analysis*. 2nd Ed. Prentice-Hall, Englewood-Cliffs, NJ.

Gibson E. (1990). Born and Bred: Object Behaviour Analysis. *BYTE*. Oct. 245-254.

King R. (1988). My Cat is Object-Oriented. In Kim W. and Lochovsky F. *Object-Oriented Languages, Applications and Databases*. Addison-Wesley. Reading, Mass.

King R. and McLeod D. (1985). Semantic Data Models. In Bing Yao S. (Ed.) *Principles of Database Design. Vol. 1: Logical Organisations*. Prentice-Hall, NJ.

25.12 Keywords

Abstraction
Constraints
Entity

Entity Type
Generalisation
Inheritance
Method
Message
Object
Object Class
Primary Method
Secondary Method
Transactions

25.13 Exercises

1. How do you think entity life histories might be useful in the analysis of methods?
2. Discuss some possible relationships between object modelling and formal methods.
3. Databases are an attempt to separate data from process. Object-oriented systems are an attempt to integrate data with process. Is this a step back, or a step forward?
4. Draw an object diagram for the small system described in section 5.6.
5. What sort of problems might you envisage in querying an object-oriented database?
6. Define an interface for the object Product in the Goronwy Galvanising application.

26 Quality Assurance

26.1 Introduction

Quality assurance or software quality assurance has been defined as a planned and systematic pattern of all the actions necessary to provide adequate confidence that software conforms to established technical requirements (Chow, 1985). The key ideas of quality assurance are:

1. Comprehensiveness. Quality assurance is not restricted to the function of a software quality group or phase. It includes all the necessary activities that contribute to the quality of software throughout the entire life-cycle of a project.
2. Planning. The emphasis is on a systematic plan to achieve the objectives of software quality. The quality of a piece of software is not left to the efforts of individuals.
3. Relativity. The notion of quality is relative to some requirements. There is no absolute sense of quality. The purpose of quality assurance is not to guarantee 100% reliability or zero defect software. It is rather to increase confidence that every reasonable effort has been made to ensure the quality of the end-product. Quality therefore equals conformance to requirements, not excellence.
4. Cost. When purchasing any product, the level of quality of a product is usually reflected in its price. Hence, software quality involves increased cost. Product quality is therefore wholly a matter of customer choice. It is essential at the requirements analysis stage for the analyst to identify appropriate customer quality needs.

26.2 Information Systems Areas

Quality assurance is therefore a topic that involves many different information systems areas. First, although a definition is provided above, there is no ready agreement on a definition of software quality, not to mention how to measure it. Second, since quality must be built into the product from day one of a project, quality assurance must include a consideration of sound techniques of construction. Third, in most large-scale projects, quality cannot be assured without effective management. Fourth, the availablity of tools for information systems development and project management is critical to the success of quality assurance. Fifth, quality is a concept that has organisation-wide implications. Quality assurance has to be planned for and implemented within the environment of a given organisation.

264

In this chapter we illustrate how quality can be effected in two ways: first by the use of software metrics; and second through the adoption of peer group review.

26.3 Software Metrics

A software metric is a number extracted from a software product. Metrics are used in a number of ways: to provide feedback to staff on the quality of their work; to monitor the structural degradation of a system during maintenance; to aid costing and estimating software projects.

Some of the main classes of software metrics are given below:

1. Function-based metrics. These are metrics used primarily for project estimation. Probably the best known function-based metric is associated with an estimating technique known as function-point analysis. Function-point analysis is conducted by project managers by counting the features of some functional specification such as the number of entities or processes. These counts are then inserted into an algebraic expression that produces what is called a function point count. Function point counts and actual costs of projects are stored in a historical database. These figures are used to produce a statistical estimate for the current project.
2. System design metrics. These metrics are extracted from design notations such as structure charts (chapter 18). They are usually calculated by counting features such as the size of a module's interface or the number of calls that a module makes. These metrics are used as a measure of the amount of coupling between the modules of a system (chapter 18). Good designs exhibit a low measure of coupling.
3. Control-flow metrics. These metrics are usually extracted from detailed program designs or program code. They are based on counting features in the control flow of a program or module, such as the number of decision statements. Control-flow metrics are particularly useful for measuring the readability and testability of modules.
4. Source-code metrics. These metrics are based on counting features in source code such as the number of identifiers and operands. They have been used to measure the readability of programs, as an estimate of the number of residual errors, and as an estimate of the amount of debugging that a module requires.

Metrics do not need to be as sophisticated as some of the ones indicated above. In one company known to the author, the most useful metrics collected were the number of errors identified in events known as structured walkthroughs.

26.4 Structured Walkthroughs

A structured walkthrough is a group review of any product of software development prior to its release into the project life-cycle. Its is also referred to as a peer group review, team debugging or ego-less programming.

Walkthroughs can take place at various stages in a project. During analysis, such items as E-R diagrams and DFDs might be subject to review. During the design phase a review of structure charts might be considered. At the implementation phase, walkthroughs of programs and the associated documentation are essential.

Yourdon (1978) has maintained that structured walkthroughs have a number of tangible and intangible benefits:

1. Correctness. Organisations that subject all systems to stringent walkthroughs reportedly reduce the program error-rate from an average of three to five defects per hundred lines of code to a more manageable average of three to five defects per thousand lines of code.
2. Standards. Walkthroughs are a useful way of establishing and enforcing standards for the analysis, design, coding, testing and documentation of computer systems.
3. Readability. Walkthroughs improve the readability of programs and systems documentation, thereby aiding the process of software maintenance.
4. Training. Walkthroughs have the effect of passing on good organisational practices to new company personnel.
5. Insurance. Walkthroughs disseminate information about systems throughout the organisation, thus offsetting the problems of high staff turnover.

A structured walkthrough is usually a group effort, with several people serving different roles within the team. A team might consist of a presenter, a coordinator, a scribe, a maintenance critic, a standards critic, and one or more user representatives.

1. The presenter is normally the creator of the product being reviewed. His or her role is to lead the team through an examination of the product.
2. The coordinator organises all the activities that should occur prior to a walkthrough. For example, the coordinator must ensure that each team member receives a copy of the product to be reviewed prior to the walkthrough.
3. The scribe records the proceedings, and eventually forwards a report to management summarising the team's findings.
4. The maintenance critic inspects the product for any source of future maintenance problems.
5. The standards critic ascertains that the product adheres to organisational standards.
6. User representatives verify that the product performs as requested.

Even though each team member has a primary role, all team members are equally accountable in terms of examining the quality of the system and offering comments and criticisms. The responsibility of the team is to give an accurate appraisal of the product being reviewed. The participants should identify defects, but they should not attempt to correct them. Correction is the sole responsibility of the presenter.

During the walkthrough, participants are required to remain as objective as possible. In particular, they should remember to evaluate only the product itself, and not the person presenting it. A walkthrough can easily degenerate into heated and destructive argument if criticism becomes personal. Moreover, the participants should remember that in system development there are many 'correct' solutions to the same problem. Participants should therefore not try to impose their own preferred solution on the problem under consideration.

The outcome of the walkthrough is the walkthrough report prepared by the scribe. This report comes in two parts: a summary and an issues list.

On the summary, all participants sign the report to indicate that they are in agreement with the decisions made. At the bottom of the summary the final verdict is given. The product is accepted as is with minor revisions or it is rejected. Rejection can be broken down into three categories:

1. The product has so many serious flaws that it must be completely rebuilt.
2. The product needs major revisions.
3. The review was incomplete and must continue.

The second page of the report, the issues list, details all the problems that need attention. As the problems are corrected, they are checked off this list by the team member assigned to monitor progress.

Managers are expected to receive at least a copy of the summary. In contrast, the issues list is primarily for the benefit of the presenter. A sample walkthrough report is illustrated in figure 26.1.

26.5 Quality Assurance and the Organisation

The quality ethic has become influential in business circles ever since the Japanese demonstrated the marketability of the concept. In organisations whose primary business is the production of information systems the question of quality is influenced by a number of issues:

1. Project Management. It is argued that an effective project manager will build into his monitoring process clear checkpoints for assessing the quality of a developing information system. This is discussed in more detail in chapter 28.
2. CAISE. Many argue that CAISE tools offer the developer a route to better quality systems because fewer errors are likely to occur between stages such as design and implementation.

3. Formal Methods. The advocates of formal methods would claim that this approach offers a key to quality in the sense that an implementation can be proven to meet its specification.
4. Object-Orientation. Object-oriented languages foster the reuse of code. Building an information system from well-proven parts is likely to lead to increased quality.

26.6 Conclusion

Quality assurance is a series of activities, standards and procedures which ensure that software is developed that meets user requirements. The concept of quality and the process of assuring quality are many-faceted beasts which affect all aspects of information systems development, from systems analysis and design through programming to configuration management. In a sense, the issue of quality is central to the professionalisation of information systems engineering which we discuss in chapter 30. Some notion of the distinction between a good and bad system is intrinsic to the rationale behind engineering disciplines.

One of the main lessons being learnt is that quality cannot be grafted onto a system at the end of its development. Quality is, above all, about people. A continuing commitment to produce quality information systems and provide a quality service is needed from people at all levels in information systems engineering.

**Walkthrough Report
Summary**

Product: Edit Personnel Record   Date: 2/3/90
Presenter: P.Beynon-Davies   Start: 9.30
                                                     End: 11.30

Coordinator: R.Coles

Scribe: G.Evans

Other Participants: P.Davies

Issues List

1. Non-Standard variable names.

2. Non-meaningful error messages

Figure 26.1   A Walkthrough Report

26.7 References

Chow T.S. (Ed.). (1985). *Software Quality Assurance: A Practical Approach*. IEEE Computer Society Press, Siver Spring, MD.

Ince D. (Ed.). *Software Quality and Reliability: Tools and Methods*. Chapman and Hall, London. 1991.

Yourdon E. (1988). *Structured Walkthroughs*. Yourdon Press, New York.

26.8 Keywords

Quality Assurance
Software Metric
Structured Walkthrough

26.9 Exercises

1. One man's idea of quality is another man's idea of shoddy workmanship. Discuss.
2. Discuss whether a metric of quality is feasible?
3. Discuss whether a metric of quality is desirable?
4. In what ways do you think structured walkthroughs engender a quality ethic in project teams?
5. What disadvantages might be associated with structured walkthroughs?
6. How do you think standards affect quality and quality assurance?
7. Discuss the need for a quality control department in large information systems development organisations.
8. Discuss how the issue of quality might affect the Goronwy Galvanising project.

Part Five
Environment

Environment
Surrounding objects or circumstances. (*Oxford English Dictionary*)
Encompassment, containment, medium, atmosphere, background. (*Roget's Thesaurus*)

In this part we discuss some organisational issues which supply the environment for any information systems development effort. We first examine some of the economic and organisational changes which have affected information systems engineering in recent years. Next, we consider the important issue of appropriate ways to manage information systems projects. Finally, we examine the social dimension of information systems and make the important point that any information systems development effort is as much a social as it is a technical exercise.

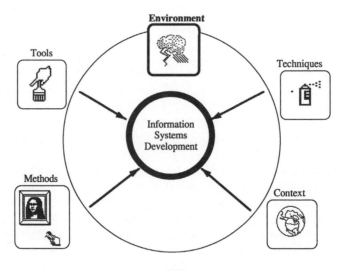

27 The Organisation of Information Systems Engineering

27.1 Introduction

Throughout this work we have primarily portrayed information systems engineering as a discipline servicing the information technology needs of some organisation, frequently some business organisation. In this chapter we turn attention to information systems engineering as an organisation in itself. We first look at the contemporary place of information systems engineers in national economies. Then we look at various models of how information systems engineering can and should be organised. We conclude with the idea of planning strategically for information systems.

27.2 The Service Sector

Information systems are primarily part of the service sector of the economy. Information technology provides a service which facilitates the running of other organisational functions. One of the notable facets of the change in employment patterns over the last thirty years has been the rise of the service sector. The share of service in total employment in the UK economy increased from 49% to 63% between 1966 and 1983. The share of manufacturing declined from 37% to 27% in the same period. Within the service sector, the most rapid growth in employment has been in the office-based private services such as financial, business and professional services (Barras and Swann, 1983).

Information systems people either work for one of the providers of IT or for one of the established users of IT. IT providers may be subdivided into electronics, products and systems industries such as aerospace, defence systems and computer hardware manufacturers, and IT services such as software houses and consultancies. IT users may be subdivided into industrial users, such as the manufacturing, engineering or process industries, or service users, such as retailing, finance and local or central government.

No published statistics exist for the current population of IT staff in the UK. However, in 1986, Connor and Pearson estimated that there were approximately 200,000 professional IT staff in the UK. One-third worked in the electronics industries, while two-thirds worked in computer-related occupations. The majority were under 35, few were women. Connor and Pearson estimated that this population would rise to 260,000 by 1990.

What is interesting is that the majority of IT employers recruit experienced staff to replace leavers and to expand their IT activities. The prime source of new staff for IT skills is the higher education system. Only a minority of organisations recruit school leavers or retrain existing staff.

Although recessions such as the UK recession of 1980-1982 and the current recession reduce the demand for IT staff, there is little expectation of a long-term fall in the demand for IT staff. Throughout the developed world the application of IT is seen as an essential ingredient of economic success. Having said this, the nature of information technology has changed and is changing. It is to this change, particularly in the nature of Information Systems organisations, that we now turn.

27.3   The Traditional Information Systems Services Department

Because of the exigencies of building and running information systems on large, centralised mainframes, the conventional information systems services department has always been structured as a hierarchy:

1. At the bottom of the hierarchy lie the operating staff. These staff are generally expected to maintain the operation of the centralised mainframe.
2. Next in the hierarchy come the programmers. These may be organised in groups such as maintenance programers and development programmers. Development programmers develop new applications. Maintenance programmers repair and extend existing applications.
3. Systems analysts are the next rung in the hierarchy. These are persons primarily involved in the analysis and design of information systems. It is these persons alone who make contact with end-users.
4. Many organisations segment staff further in terms of project teams of analysts, programmers and sometimes operators. The topic of project team organisation will be discussed in more detail in chapter 28. We only wish to say here that each project team will be headed by a project manager.
5. The data processing centre will be headed by at least one person, probably called the DP manager. In a particularly large organisation there may be a number of intermediate managers, such as operations managers, development managers and maintenance managers, each coordinating a particular aspect of information systems work.

27.4 Pressures for Change

During the 1970s and 1980s a number of pressures have forced some radical changes on information systems departments. The first pressure we might call the rise of the end-user movement. The increasing infiltration of PCs into organisations has meant that computing power can be sited where it is required; PC packages such as spreadsheets and word-processing software have been specifically written for the end-user; end-users have consequently gained more experience of computing and are consequently much more confident in expressing their needs. The second major pressure we might call the integration movement. The developing use of databases (chapter 6), and in particular the database approach (part three, section 1), has meant that organisations have to plan for and manage data at a corporate level.

27.5 The Information Centre

In response to some of the pressures described above, many modern DP departments have cast themselves either entirely or in part as information centres. An information centre is a corpus of DP expertise whose role is to service other departments which are heavily involved in handling a large proportion of their DP themselves. This is in marked contrast to the traditional DP department which is a monopoly controlling all organisational computing.

The information centre is normally implemented by setting up a specialised group of information systems people devoted to the use of fourth generation technology (chapter 7). Users are given training in the use of business software such as spreadsheets, DBMS, and word-processing packages. Information centres are also founded in distributed computing (chapter 3) — siting computing resources where they are needed. This primarily means connecting up personal computers, minicomputers and mainframes in an effective organisational network.

All this means that there is a consequent change in the role of DP staff. The traditional distinction between systems analysts and programmers becomes eroded. There is also a corresponding broadening of the technical and business expertise of computing staff. The change is from a systems analyst's technical role to a business analyst's company role.

The information centre also stimulates a change in the relationship between end-users and engineers. End-users become much more involved in their own computing and are expected to solve most of the standard problems themselves. The systems engineering department now casts itself more as a consultancy centre, or centre of excellence, for information technology. Advising, training and helping users to perform their own DP work.

27.6 The Changing Division of Labour

The traditional division of labour in information systems work is a four-fold one: project managers, systems analysts, programmers, and operations staff. With the rise of different organisational structures such as the information centre a greater diversification of information systems staff has ensued. We now have job-titles such as:

1. Analyst/Programmer. A person who takes on the role of both systems analyst and programmer for given projects.
2. Database Administrator. People tasked with monitoring a given database running under a given DBMS.
3. Data Analysts. Personnel tasked with planning and monitoring the data requirements of organisations.
4. Business Analysts. People whose expertise is much more in traditional business areas such as accountancy or administration than in the technical areas of information systems.

Figure 27.1 plots some key job titles on the dimensions of business and technical knowledge.

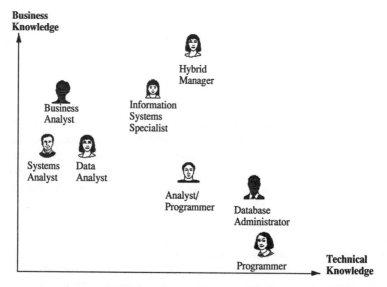

Figure 27.1   Changing Roles of IS Personnel

27.7 Five Levels of Maturity

There is a growing consensus that information systems organisations exist on one of five levels of 'maturity':

1. Initial Level. There is no formal method, no consistency, no standards on how information systems should be built. Every software developer considers himself or herself to be an artist or craftsman.
2. Repeatable Level. There is some consensus within the organisation as to the appropriate way to develop information systems. No attempt has been made however at formalisation or documentation of procedure. Success largely depends on the intuitive skills of project managers.

3. Managed Level. There is a formal, documented process for developing information systems and managing their development. The organisation continually refines and updates its methods.
4. Measured Level. The organisation has instituted software metrics for measuring the process of developing information systems and its associated products.
5. Optimising Level. The organisation uses the measurements from the previous level to improve the development process.

The first three levels are obviously designed to encourage the use of systematic approaches to information systems development (chapter 21). The last two are obviously designed to foster the exploitation of software metrics (chapter 26).

What is interesting is that organisations that have not attained level three cannot make effective use of CASE (chapter 8) or technologies like OOA, OOD and OOP (chapter 25). Coad and Yourdon (1991) quote a survey which reported that in the late 1980s 87% of US software organisations were at level one, 10-12% at level two and only 1% at level three.

27.8 Strategic Information Systems Planning

The questions of appropriate organisation and the exploitation of information systems are necessarily interlinked. Remenyi (1991) defines strategic information systems planning (SISP) as a process of establishing a programme for the implementation and use of information systems in such a way that it optimises the effectiveness of an organisation's information resources and uses them to support the objectives of the whole organisation. This idea is obviously related to that of information management discussed in chapter 23. The products of SISP will typically include both a short-term (12-18 months ahead) and long-term (3-5 years ahead) plan for the use of and development of information systems

Traditional information systems planning either occurs in isolation from business planning or is produced as a reaction to changes in business policy. In true SISP, business and information systems planning are intertwined. Each is dependent on the other.

A large number of conceptual frameworks now exist for SISP, such as competitive advantage and crtitical success factors. Competitive advantage comes in three forms:

1. Cost advantage. Aspects involved in improving overall efficiency.
2. Differentiation. Aspects which help to distinguish a company's product from its competitors, e.g., better quality relative to price.
3. Location. Placing distribution, marketing and information outlets where required.

Any organisation needs to identify areas in which it has relative superiority, and to use that superiority to create barriers to entry as well as to launch strategic offences in its marketplace. One popular method of achieving this uses the concept of a critical success factor (CSF). A CSF is a factor which is deemed crucial to the success of a business. CSFs are those areas that must be given special attention by management. They also represent critical points of leverage for achieving competitive advantage. For example, in the case of Goronwy Galvanising CSFs might be the speed of turnaround back to the customer, its ability to respond quickly to changes in customer requirements, or the cost/quality balance of its products. The adoption of information technology can affect each of these CSFs. IT can be used to speed up the scheduling of the Galvanising process, rapidly change customer order details, and cause improvements in the throughput of material through the plant.

27.9 Conclusion

Some people have proposed that information systems development can be placed on the same footing as manufacturing. This is unlikely to be feasible. A factory is a mechanism for producing many discrete units with exactly the same qualities. Information systems, usually by their very nature are unique. This is analagous to saying that every product off a production line will be different.

Although the principles of automation can undoubtedly be applied to certain areas of the development process, areas such as analysis will probably always remain craftsman-like activities. It is therefore more accurate to make the analogy between engineering disciplines such as civil and structural engineering than it is with manufacturing. In this sense, information systems engineering is seen as critical to building an effective infrastructure for organisational activity. We shall return to this issue in the concluding chapter.

27.10 References

Barras R. and Swann J. (1984). The Adoption of Information Technology in the UK. Technical Change Centre, London.

Coad P. and Yourdon E. (1991). *Object-Oriented Design*. Yourdon Press, Englewood Cliffs, NJ.

Connor H. and Pearson R. (1986). IT Manpower into the 1990s. Institute of Manpower Studies, London.

Remenyi D. (1991). *An Introduction to Strategic Information Systems Planning*. NCC/Blackwell, Manchester.

27.11 Keywords

Information Centre
Information Services Sector
Strategic Information Systems Planning
Critical Success Factor

27.12 Exercises

1. Discuss whether the information services sector will continue to expand.
2. What sort of future is there for the information systems specialist?
3. Is it sensible to equate the maturity of information systems organisations purely with the adoption of software metrics?
4. Discuss whether there is a future for the large, centralised information systems department.
5. What sort of critical success factors are relevant to a university?
6. Identify the critical success factors for Goronwy Galvanising.
7. Suggest an appropriate organisation for information systems work within the owning company of Goronwy.

28 The Management of Information Systems Projects

28.1 Introduction

In this chapter we address the issues of managing information systems projects. We define a project loosely as being any concerted effort to develop an information system.

The issue of project management can be divided into three interrelated areas: project planning, project organisation and project control. Project planning involves determining as clearly as possible the likely parameters associated with a particular project. Project organisation concerns how to structure staff activities to ensure maximum effectiveness. Project control concerns ensuring that a project remains on schedule, within budget and produces the desired output.

Project management has a clear overlap with the issue of quality assurance (chapter 26).

28.2 Project Failure

The business of information systems development is at least 40 years old, but managers of development departments still have to face many project failures. One of the biggest causes of systems failures is the project end-date cast in stone. The problem is that a software project is frequently and mistakenly seen as analogous to a traveller getting from one part of the country to another. However, the traveller has three advantages over the information systems developer:

1. The distance between geographical points is known.
2. The best route between points is easily worked out using readily available maps.
3. The traveller may have done the journey, and many like it, before.

In the systems development world:

1. The distance to be travelled is seldom known.
2. The route used is often untried and there is little basis for assessing whether it is optimal.
3. The project manager has never trodden the path before.

For these reasons there is a modern tendency to encourage systems development organisations to keep detailed records of past projects. In a sense, a map of the geography of an organisation's systems development needs to be built up. No two projects will be entirely the same. But keeping track of how much time, effort and resources have gone into projects is an essential base from which to plan future projects.

28.3 Project Planning

The classic questions of project planning are: what, who, when, how, and progress?

1. What. The product or output must be defined and the project must be broken down into a series of tasks. Adherence to a standard model of information systems development, as described in chapter 2, clearly aids this process. Standards to be used in the project, such as appropriate notations, must also be identified.
2. Who. Staff must be assigned to the project and responsibilities identified. The most popular method of estimating the amount of staff needed for a project is to use experts who have conducted similar projects in the past. Another approach is to estimate the size of the proposed product and derive a staff estimate from this figure by the application of an appropriate formula.
3. When. Milestones must be identified and schedules established. Most experts recommend that a software project be divided into sequential phases and a milestone or control point established at the end of each phase.
4. How. A budget for the project must be constructed and resources must be allocated to the project. The likely cost of the project must be calculated and a case made for a budget for the project.
5. Progress. An effective mechanism for monitoring the progress of projects must be established. Milestones can be used as points of audit to ensure that standards are being adhered to and the project is on schedule.

28.4 Project Planning

The conventional way of planning a project is to segment a project into a number of stages, each of which can be managed independently (Parkin, 1980). Each of these stages is further broken down into a series of tasks or activities.

One popular method of representation is to lay out a project in diagrammatic form as a network. Developed in the late 1950s, this is known as the critical path or PERT (Programme Evaluation Review Technique) method.

Figure 28.1 illustrates how a small project such as that involved in building a system for Goronwy Galvanising might be laid out. The nodes represent stages, the arrows represent predecessor/successor relations between stages. Each stage can be

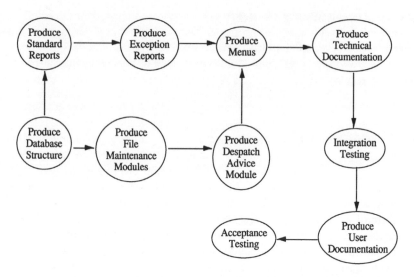

Figure 28.1   A Simple PERT for the Goronwy Project

further expanded as a diagram indicating the dependencies between activities.

An estimate is then made of the resources required to achieve each task — usually expressed in the number of man-days required. The sum of these man-days, plus a contingency factor for emergencies, is the estimated time required for each stage. Conducting this calculation for each stage will give the manager an idea of the overall man-days required. Since man-time is the also the most significant cost-factor, this calculation will give the manager an idea of total approximate cost.

For each activity the earliest possible start date is calculated on the basis of a schedule assigned to predecessors. A latest completion date is also calculated for each activity on the basis of the scheduled start dates for each of the activity's successors and the target completion date for the overall project. The difference between the calculated time available to complete an activity and the estimated time required to complete it is known as an activity's float. If the float is zero, the activity is said to be critical, since any delay in completing it will cause a delay in completing the final project.

This estimating approach described above is usually complicated by the fact that since no two information systems projects are ever the same there is an inherent uncertainty associated with the time required for each activity. Brooks (1979) has also discussed how using man-days, man-weeks or man-months as the central unit of estimating and scheduling can be misleading. It is tempting to infer that the progress of a project improves with the number of men assigned to it. Because of the increased communication between team-members, Brooks makes a cogent case for reversing this inference. He summarises his argument in the statement: "adding manpower to a late software project makes it later".

28.5 The Organisation of Projects

Project organisation is the issue of how to organise staff so that they produce the desired output. Essentially there are three alternatives in organising staff (Daly, 1979) (see figure 28.2):

1. Project Organisation. Here staff are organised within project boundaries. This form of organisation encourages quick decision-making, minimises interfaces between staff and generates high identification with projects among staff. The disadvantages are that it works well only for small projects, the economies of scale are low, and the sharing of expertise across projects is minimal.
2. Functional Organisation. Here staff are organised according to functional responsibilities, each function supporting a number of different projects. This form of organisation generates economies of scale, promotes the growth of specialists, and reduces the effects of staff turnover. The disadvantages are that it generates lots of communication across projects, it decreases the number of people with a general feel for projects, and reduces the cohesion of given projects.
3. Matrix Organisation. Here staff are mixed across project and functional divisions. The basic organisation is functional, but a project organisation is imposed under a series of project managers. The advantages of this approach are that short-term objectives (the success of a project) are maximised via the project organisation whereas long-term objectives (such as promoting special-ism) are maximised via the functional division. The major disadvantage is that project and functional needs may conflict in some organisations.

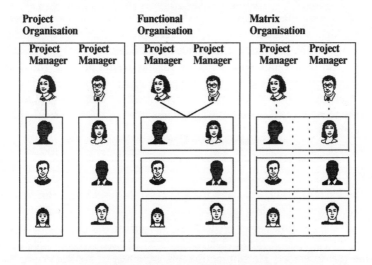

Figure 28.2   Forms of Project Organisation

28.6 Project Control

The aim of project control is to ensure that schedules are being met, that the project is staying within budget and that appropriate standards are being maintained. The most important objective of project control is to focus attention on problems in sufficient time for something to be done about them. This means that continual monitoring of progress must take place.

The primary document used for the evaluation of progress is the progress report. This contains information on time estimated for each activity plotted against actual time spent. Another useful measure is an estimate as to the percentage of completeness of a project.

Time actually spent on a project is usually collected via weekly time-sheets. Such time-sheets normally indicate the tasks performed and their duration.

Many automated tools are now available to aid the project manager. Plans can be created using a graphics approach as described in section 28.4, and estimates associated with each activity. Time-sheet data can then be fed into the system and progress reports automatically generated. Some packages even allow the manager to perform 'what-if' reasoning on the project model. A schematic data flow diagram for this process is presented in figure 28.3.

Progress reports can be used either by management reviews or project audits. Management reviews are scheduled opportunities for project managers to appraise themselves of the accomplishments and problems associated with a given project. Project audits are formal events scheduled into the life-cycle of a given project in

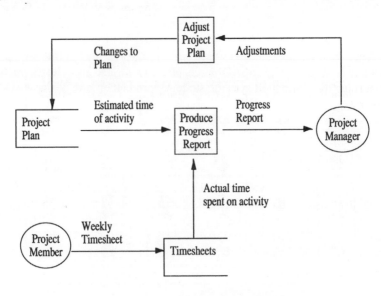

Figure 28.3   A Project Control System

which an independent audit team examines the documentation associated with a given development effort and interviews key team members.

Large-scale projects in particular may institute a change control mechanism. This involves setting up a systematic mechanism for handling all changes to a developing piece of software. Normally a change management committee is instituted for decision-making and a change management procedure is established. The essence of this procedure is to ensure that each version of a product can be uniquely identified.

28.7 PRINCE

The acronym PRINCE stands for PRojects IN Controlled Environments. PRINCE is a structured method for project management originally developed from a government-sponsored initiative in the 1970s which resulted in the method known as PROMPT (Bentley, 1992). PRINCE provides the following components:

1. A method for defining the organisation structure for a project.
2. It defines the structure and content of project planning.
3. It defines a set of controls and reports which can be used to monitor whether a project is proceeding to plan.
4. It actively encourages the monitoring of quality (chapter 26).

The application of PRINCE revolves around identification of the products which are to be produced by a project. Identification of products leads to identification of activities needed to produce them. Such activities then trigger off the planning stage and are used to define the mechanisms for ensuring quality.

PRINCE has been designed to be used particularly with the information systems development methodology SSADM (chapter 21). It also has clearly specified relationships to information systems strategy formulation and business analysis (chapter 27).

28.8 Conclusion

Even though many systematic techniques have been suggested for the process of project management, project management is still very much an art rather than a science. Projects are about people. The social dimension of information systems projects is the topic of the next chapter. Also, the one-off nature of most information systems projects also makes them far more difficult to manage than most engineering projects. This we discuss in chapter 30.

28.9 References

Bentley C. (1992). *Introducing PRINCE: The Structured Project Management Method*. NCC Blackwell, Oxford.

Brooks F.P. (1979). *The Mythical Man-Month*. Addison-Wesley. Reading, Mass.

Daly E.B. (1979). Organising for Successful Software Development. *Datamation*. December. 107-116.

Keen J.S. (1987). *Managing Systems Development*. (2nd Ed.). John Wiley, Chichester.

Parkin A.F. (1980). *Systems Management*. Edward Arnold, London.

28.10 Keywords

PERT
PRINCE
Project
Project Management

28.11 Exercises

1. At what point do you think a critical mass is reached in terms of project group size?
2. Discuss three of the main problems arising in the management of large project groups?
3. Which form of organisation do you think is most prevalent in information systems departments: project organisation; functional organisation or matrix organisation?
4. What sort of timings, effort and resource information should be kept in an organisation's project experience-base?
5. Even the most carefully planned of projects fail. Suggest some reasons.

29 The Social Dimension of Information Systems Development

29.1 Introduction

Students of computing have traditionally been criticised for their lack of interpersonal skill. The stereotypical computer studies student is generally regarded as a good technician but a poor communicator; better at working alone than in teams; more comfortable at the keyboard than talking to people about their work. As a result, software companies frequently complain that they would rather employ arts graduates and train them to a required level of expertise than employ computing students. As DeMarco and Lister (1987) cogently put it:

> "The business we're in is more sociological than technological, more dependent on worker's abilities to communicate with each other than their abilities to communicate with machines ..The main reason we tend to focus on the technical rather than the human side of work is not because it's more crucial, but because it's easier to do...Human interactions are complicated and never very crisp and clean in their effects, but they matter more than any other aspect of the work."

Clearly therefore, there is a need to address this problem by directing more attention to the interpersonal side of information systems development.

In this chapter we illustrate how material from the behavioural sciences can be used to redress some of the technicist imbalance in computing. The general premise is that a mapping between social science concepts and information systems problems is possible and indeed desirable.

29.2 Concepts

Concepts are the means by which we define and understand reality. Richer concepts mean a clearer definition of what we mean by reality. An appreciation of some concepts borrowed from social science is an effective tool in the armoury of any systems analyst. In a sense, this idea is a development of something known as the Sapir-Whorf hypothesis (Whorf, 1956). This hypothesis states that a person's understanding of the world is dictated by the language he uses. Hence, for instance, one's understanding of the word information has an important bearing on the way in which one approaches information systems engineering (chapter 1).

Social science has at least as many concepts as computing science. We shall only consider a relatively small subset here: culture, social group, norms, roles, status, power and authority. The major analogy we wish to make is between the systems analyst and the social anthropologist (Beynon-Davies, 1990). The activity of systems analysis, investigating and documenting the workings of some existing or required information system, has much in common with the activity of investigating and documenting the life of some society or social group.

29.3 Culture

The first concept to define is that of a culture. A culture is the set of behaviours expected in a social group. A social group is any collection of people who regularly interact with one another. It is a truism that any long-standing social group develops its own expected set of behaviours. Such expectations are known as norms in the jargon of social science.

The pervasiveness of culture can be demonstrated by a simple social experiment. Assuming you are sitting close to someone, turn to that person and stare into their eyes. Count the seconds before you smile and avert your gaze.

What you should have experienced is a cultural expectation or norm. There is a certain length of time, give or take a few seconds, that you are expected to gaze into somebody else's eyes. This varies from total strangers who are expected only to engage in the briefest of glances, through friends where a certain amount of eye contact is encouraged, to lovers where it is expected to be a major activity.

But what does the concept of culture provide for us as systems analysts at work in business organisations? The answer is that every organisation has its own particular culture. When a person starts work for an organisation he or she has to learn the expected set of behaviours. A systems analyst has to continually learn the expected behaviour of the organisation he is called in to work with.

The organisational culture may have a lot to do with national differences. Hence, a Japanese-owned company is likely to expect different work patterns of its staff than a British-owned company. Cultural differences, however, will exist between different organisations of the same nationality and even between divisions, departments and levels within one company. DeMarco and Lister (1987) give a good example of the way in which a particular group of software testers developed their own culture.

Stamper (1988) has exploited a useful typology of the components of culture for evaluating the impact of innovations (of which technical information systems are a part) on organisations. The typology is presented below:

1. Interaction. Verbal and non-verbal communication.
2. Association. Social relationships.
3. Subsistence. Physical livelihood.

4. Sexuality. Gender.
5. Territoriality. Division of space.
6. Temporality. Division of time.
7. Learning. Education and training.
8. Play. Recreation and fun.
9. Defence. Protection against the elements and other groups.
10. Exploitation. Tools, technology, systems and their uses.

He describes the technique, which he calls evaluation framing, in terms of the following steps:

1. Select a simple taxonomy of behaviour (like the one above).
2. For any innovation classify its main impacts on each of the areas of behaviour.
3. Search for secondary effects under each of the headings taking the main impact as the starting point.
4. Remember that primary, secondary and even tertiary effects can arouse strong feelings in organisations and these feelings will determine the acceptability of a particular innovation.
5. Estimate, where appropriate, the costs and benefits of the proposed changes from the points of view of the various interest groups within an organisation.

Take the introduction of an office automation system into a previously non-computerised administrative department. Interaction is likely to change as much of the communication will be expected to take place via the formal information system. This will affect social relationships. Subsistence and sexuality behaviours will be transformed as job specifications change. The location of computing terminals and the scheduling of work will impact upon the areas of territoriality and temporality. Learning about technical information systems might affect the enjoyment or satisfaction associated with work. The new technology may extend the exploitation afforded to the department and also raises the problems of establishing defensive strategies in areas such as information privacy and access.

29.4 Roles

People make behaviour. But people package behaviour in collections which social scientists call social roles. The analogy here is clearly with the acting profession. To paraphrase Shakespeare — 'All the world is a stage, and we are merely players'. In other words, we all take on a number of different roles throughout our lifetime, and for each role different expectations are involved. Checkland has used the concepts of role and norm in his stage of social systems analysis within SSM (chapter 20).

The role of systems analyst is a particularly ambivalent one. Expectations of the systems analyst held by management may frequently conflict with expectations of the systems analyst held by other social groups in an organisation. People frequently hold a technicist image of the systems analyst — believing him or her to be looking for purely technical solutions to organisation problems. As a result, many groups will choose not to cooperate fully with the analyst.

Much systems analysis can be seen as an attempt to reconcile the expectations of various social groups impinging on a given information system. Many information systems projects have failed because they have made an unhappy compromise between these differing expectations.

29.5 Status

A complementary concept to that of social role is that of social status. A person's status implies some form of position is a social hierarchy. The formal hierarchy of an organisation may not be the most important one to know about. There are frequently one or more informal hierarchies which are more effective in organisation terms. Such hierarchies, for instance, frequently stimulate camouflage. Many people put up a 'front' in organisations to preserve their informal status. They may tell you that the organisation functions in this way, when in fact it functions entirely differently.

29.6 Power and Authority

Power is the ability of a person or social group to control the behaviour of some other person or social group. Authority is legitimated power. The exercise of power is accepted by those over whom it is exercised. Organisational politics is the embodiement of power-play within some organisation.

In many organisations there will be a mismatch between naked power and authority. Manager A may be the person in whom formal power is invested. Manager B however has the recognised authority, and it is this manager who actually controls staff.

There is a tendency to conceptualise power as a commodity owned by a particular individual or group. Power and authority are however not static entities. Power and authority are relationships between individuals and groups. They are fluid entities that are continuously negotiated within organisations. Any information systems development project taking more than a few months to complete is almost certain to ride the stormy sea of internal power struggles.

Land (1976) portrays information systems projects in terms of stakeholders. A stakeholder is someone with a vested interest in an information systems project. Some stakeholders will have made an investment in the project in the hope of increasing their power base. Others will have a stake in the failure of the project.

As we mentioned in chapter 1, it is naive to assume that information systems and information system engineers can remain aloof from organisational politics. Organisational politics are frequently the life-blood of information systems. Power is probably of even more importance to the analysis of informal information systems than it is to the analysis of formal information systems. Both the soft systems school of Checkland (chapter 20) and the socio-technical school of Mumford (chapter 24) tend to underemphasise the crucial role of power in information systems projects.

29.7 Goronwy Galvanising

Let us make the social organisation at Goronwy more concrete by providing three short sketches of key players in the systems project: Richard Sawyer, Robin Fryer and James Richards. These represent stereotypes of users. The sketches are presented below.

> **Richard Sawyer**. Richard is a systems consultant from the headquarters of the owning company. Richard feels his remit is to manage the quality control of the project. The systems consultancy division never code systems themselves. They are expected, however, to oversee all systems development within the parent company.
>
> **Robin Fryer**. Robin is the works manager at Goronwy. Robin wants a computer system to enhance the prestige of his brand-new plant. If the system is seen to be successful then it will probably be demanded by other galvanising plants. Robin is also of the impression that a computer system will give him a 'tighter ship'.
>
> **James Richards**. James is the production controller at Goronwy. James will eventually be given responsibility for running the information system. He is however less than happy with the project. He feels that the system is unlikely to be worthwhile. He's perfectly happy with the existing manual system.

An exercise in organisational analysis might then portrayed in the following terms:

> You are a contractor brought in to develop a micro-based system for production control. Richard and Robin have already discussed the proposed system in depth, and Richard has produced an initial requirements analysis/ system specification which he presents to you at the first development group meeting. Produce, in writing, a brief description of how you think the development will progress. In particular, address the following questions:

1. What do you think your role is going to be?
2. What role do you think Richard, Robin and James will take?
3. Who do you think is the best person to talk to concerning how the system should look?
4. What problems do you expect to encounter?

5. How do you think the new system will be used?

Using some of the concepts discussed in this chapter, this is left as an exercise for the reader.

29.8 Conclusion

An appreciation of the social side of information systems development is necessary for any information systems specialist. We might concretise this by saying that an analysis of informal information systems is a necessary precursor to an analysis of formal information systems. Such an analysis cannot satisfactorily take place without some basic conceptual hooks. It has been the aim of this chapter to intruduce a basic set of such hooks.

29.9 References

Beynon-Davies P. (1990). The Behaviour of Systems Analysts. *The Computer Bulletin*. March. 21-23.

DeMarco T. and Lister T. (1987). *Peopleware: Productive Projects and Teams*. Dorset House, New York.

Land F. (1976). Evaluation of Systems Goals in Determining a Design Strategy for a Computer-based Information System. *Computer Journal*. 19(4). Nov. 290-294.

Stamper R. (1988). Analysing the Cultural Impact of a System. *International Journal of Information Management*. (8). 107-122.

Whorf B.L. (1956). *Language, Thought and Reality*. MIT Press, Cambridge, MA.

29.10 Keywords

Authority
Culture
Norm
Power
Role
Social Group
Status

29.11 Exercises

1. An informal information system is made up in part of norms. A formal information system is made up in part of rules. Discuss the distinction between a norm and a rule.
2. Discuss some of the ways systems development staff maintain power over users.
3. In what way does computer jargon establish a reality in which information systems development takes place?
4. In chapter 12 we defined an entity as being 'something of interest to an organisation'. Who determines what is of interest?
5. The term 'user' is frequently used in a derogatory way by technical staff. Discuss this tendency in the light of the concepts of role and status.
6. Analyse an information system known to you in terms of major stakeholders.
7. Discuss how software testing can be considered a social practice.

30 The Nature of Information Systems Engineering

30.1 Summary

The area of information systems is a large and ever-expanding field. Our main aim in writing this revised edition has been to provide as much of a framework as possible for introducing the vast range of material now published on information systems and information systems development.

We began this work by examining some of the assumptions underlying the contemporary practice of information systems. In particular we attempted a definition of information and information systems which includes a frequently neglected component, people (chapter 1). This lead to a three-fold division of information systems: informal information systems, formal information systems, and technical information systems. Most of the contemporary practice of information systems is directed solely at technical information systems. The important context of human interaction within organisations is frequently ignored.

It is useful to divide information systems engineering, particularly for the purposes of explanation, into three sub-disciplines: software engineering, information engineering and knowledge engineering.

Software engineering has traditionally taken a rather process-directed approach to information systems. Structured development, discussed here under the umbrella of software engineering, can now be considered as accepted practice in the industry. Formal methods and object-oriented analysis, design and programming are now elements receiving the most attention in the software engineering literature.

Information engineering takes a data-based approach to information systems development. Built upon the successful exploitation of database design techniques it has heavily influenced the idea of managing information as a corporate resource and strategic information systems planning.

Knowledge engineering is very much associated with expert systems in particular and knowledgebase systems in general. Given the fact that all information systems development can be considered knowledge intensive, it is not suprising to note a recent convergence between conventional information systems work and knowledgebase systems work.

We have used a simple model of technical information systems (chapter 3) to order particularly the material on tools and techniques. We divided a technical information system into four main components: a user interface subsystem, a control subsystem, a process subsystem and a data subsystem. Some tools, such as database systems (chapter 6) are designed primarily to attack one of these subsystems. Other tools, such as high-level programming languages (chapter 4), have been used to build all aspects of technical information systems.

There has been something of a split in the information systems world between techniques primarily directed at designing suitable data structures (data analysis techniques: part 3 section 1) and techniques primarily directed at designing suitable processes (process analysis techniques: part three, section 2). This split in techniques has prompted a similar split in methodologies. Hence some methodologies like Information Engineering are heavily influenced by data analysis while others such as STRADIS are heavily influenced by process analysis (chapter 21). Attempts such as Object-Oriented approaches have set out to bridge this divide (chapter 25).

In its infancy, information systems development was an area staffed primarily by mathematicians and physicists using high-level programming languages on large, centralised mainfames. In its developing guise information systems engineering is an area staffed by people with a range of different competences, using a range of different software on a range of different hardware platforms (chapter 27). The days of the 'pure' information system and 'pure' information specialist are gone. The days of hybrids — people, software and hardware has arrived.

30.2 Engineering

In most people's minds the concept of engineering is equated with the application of scientific principles to the construction of artefacts such as buildings and bridges. This straightforward characterisation of engineering as science is one which has influenced much of the movement attempting to place information systems work on an engineering footing.

However, it is interesting that traditional engineering disciplines such as civil and structural engineering have long cast doubt over the purely scientific nature of the discipline. Petrowski (1985), for instance, quotes the following as a generally accepted definition of structural engineering:

> "Structural engineering is the science and art of designing and making, with economy and elegance, buildings, bridges, frameworks, and other similar structures so that they can safely resist the forces to which they may be subjected."

The important part of this definition is that structural engineering is seen to be as much art as science. Elegance of design is given equal footing with economy of design. The principles of aesthetics are at least as important as the principles of mechanics.

What is also interesting is the emphasis on safety. This is resonant of much of the discussion in software engineering, particularly in the area of safety critical systems.

The ability to formally prove that an application meets its specification is seen to be important in certain applications such as military command and control systems.

However, perhaps the most important reason that information systems work has been portrayed as engineering is that it is inherently bound up with the attempt to place the information systems specialist on a professional footing.

30.3 The Profession of Information Systems Engineering

The ubiquity of modern information systems has caused a debate within the community involved in their development about the status of their work. Societies like the British Computer Society (BCS) and the American Institute of Electronic Engineers (IEEE) have attempted to cast information systems engineering as a true profession in much the same guise as lawyers, accountants, architects and the medical profession. As a practical step towards this goal, members of the BCS now have a route to chartered engineering status.

A formal scheme for professional development constructed by the BCS has also been adopted by many large IT using organisations such as BP, British Gas and ICI. The scheme is built on an industry structure model which defines some 40 roles in computing management, system development, technical support, auditing and training. Each role can have a number of experience levels. At each experience level there is a description of the type of work done, the experience and skills expected and the training needed to prepare a person for the next level. A European Informatics Skills structure based upon this model is being positioned to support the mobility and transfer of IT skills in the single European market.

A profession might be defined as a group of persons with an accredited corpus of specialist knowledge. Professions usually revolve around a formal body invested with the powers of conferring entrance to the profession. As a consequence, the same body is entrusted with ensuring that only 'qualified' persons enter the profession. The main arguments for professional status are that in a time of increasing disquiet over the quality of information systems, a body such as the BCS can guarantee persons able to build quality systems.

The main practical problem in turning information systems engineering into a profession is the fact that as little as 20% of the persons involved in IT belong to bodies like the BCS. At the time of writing, only as few as 50 or so companies nationally are involved in the BCS professional development scheme.

Another problem is that there is little agreement about the corpus of knowledge making up information systems engineering. As we shall in the next section, there is a big question about whether purely technical knowledge is sufficient.

30.4 The Information Systems Specialist

Institutions like the British Computer Society have recently become interested in broadening the skills expected of information systems engineers. The idea of a hybrid manager has been much discussed (Palmer, 1990). The term hybrid manager was coined by Michael Earl to define a manager who combines information systems and business skills (Earl, 1989):

> "People with strong technical skills and adequate business knowledge, or vice versa...hybrids are people with technical skills able to work in user areas doing a line or functional job, but adept at developing and supplementing IT application ideas."

Skyrme and Earl (1990) identify five crucial competences of hybrid managers:

1. Knowledge of information technology for appreciating strategic information systems opportunities within business.
2. General business knowledge for appreciating the use of information systems within relevant business situations.
3. Organisation-specific knowledge cumulated in line-management.
4. Managerial skills, particularly communication and social skills.
5. Personality traits such as being outgoing and people-oriented.

In a sense, the idea of hybrids is merely echoing a sentiment first expressed by Stamper in the 1970s:

> "The demands of society and the opportunities of technology are now changing so quickly that we must learn to construct organisations that are responsive to our needs. Organisations cannot be left to evolve; as far as it is possible they must be designed. Many people are working on these problems: managers, administrators and staff specialists. In one way or another they are all trying to make organisations use information effectively. It is information that holds organisations together and drives them along. What we urgently need therefore, are information specialists who are as thoroughly acquainted with the information needs of organisations as they are with the capabilities of modern information technology" (Stamper, 1973).

Stamper generalises the concept of business and social knowledge from purely the manager to all information systems engineers.

30.5 The Management of Information

Probably one of the major reasons that information systems engineers must change is that the discipline must abandon an overly simplistic model of information and information systems.

In chapter 23 we discussed the concept of information resource management - the idea that information is a resource that has to be managed by organisations. Boland (1987) has recently criticised what he sees to be a number of inherent assumptions underlying this discipline. He casts his argument in terms of five fantasies; a number of metaphors which we take too literally in information systems work:

1. Information is structured data. Information is an object to be manipulated. This implies that information can be divorced from its meaningful interpretation by human beings.
2. An Organisation is information. Systems designers believe that they can orchestrate organisational life through the manipulation of structured data. The organisation is portrayed purely in terms of a model of rational decision-making.
3. Information is power. Power is portrayed as a commodity held in the hand of certain organisational groups. This fantasy glorifies the role of the systems designer as an allocator of power. Power is more accurately portrayed as a relationship between groups and individuals.
4. Information is intelligence. This equates to an idea popularised by H.A.Simon that information as structured data and programs as technologies for moving through a problem space equals intelligence.
5. Information is perfectable. That there is some possible state where perfect information is feasible.

Boland summarises this trend as the progressive removal of the human actor from consideration as he struggles to make sense of the world and produce social reality through dialogue. In constrast, he argues that:

> "Designing an information system is a moral problem because it puts one party, the system designer, in the position of imposing an order on the world of another."

This is of course similar to defining organisational information systems purely in terms of technical information systems (chapter 2). Bowden (1992) believes it is the result of taking an analogy too far or too literally. Information is treated as a physical thing. It is treated as a fourth resource to go with human, material, and financial resources (chapter 23). But information is not physical and hence must be managed differently than conventional resources.

30.6 Technical Information Systems

Not only do we need a hybrid conception of information and the information systems specialist, hybrids are also likely to invade the realms of technical information

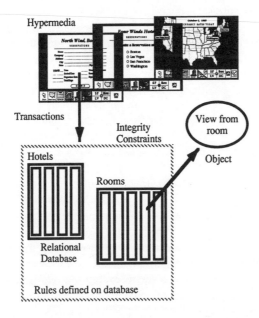

Figure 30.1   A Technical Information Sytem of the Near Future

systems. Figure 30.1 is meant to illustrate the possibilities for information systems development in the short to medium term future. Information systems of the future are likely to be built using hybrid architectures. Although many of the streams discussed in chapter 3 propose themselves as overarching formalisms, it is unlikely that any single approach will offer the information systems builder all the tools he needs. Hybrids will exploit the strengths of each of the various paradigms and site each approach at strategic points within the information systems building effort.

Relational databases are probably likely to remain at the heart of the information systems effort, if only because they have proven extremely flexible tools for data management (chapter 6). Object-orientation will certainly have a part to play, particularly in the declaration of complex data types and their associated methods (chapter 5). In our example, a panoramic view data type is declared on a column of the rooms table. This might allow customers to see an image of the view from a particular room at a particular hotel. Integrity constraints are likely to be expressed in something like logic, probably in the guise of declarative extensions to the existing SQL standards. In this sense, they will constitute knowledgebase systems as discussed in chapter 9. Declarative 4GLs and CAISE tools (chapter 8) are likely to be the major implementation mechanisms for the information systems of the future. User interfaces are almost certainly going to be multi-media in flavour (chapter 10). We can expect graphics, sound and video to be important parts of future information systems.

30.7 Conclusion

Our aim in writing this work was to portray, in as straightforward a manner as possible, some of the diversity which makes up modern information systems development. We believe that such development can be cast as an engineering discipline in the sense that it might be defined as:

> Information systems engineering is the science and art of designing and making, with economy and elegance, technical information systems that support the activity of particular organisations.

Information is however a far more complex entity than the material with which structural engineering has to work. It is impossible to divorce information from the process of human interpretation. Information systems are primarily human activity systems.

The information systems engineer must be well-versed in the capabilities of the increasing array of tools for building technical information systems. He or she must be aware of appropriate techniques for recording the decisions of analysis and design. He must be exposed to a range of methods or frameworks for employing the techniques. But perhaps most of all he must be aware that he works within the constraints of a social environment and that an analysis of informal information systems is a necessary prerequisite for formal analysis work.

To use the framework of semiotics discussed in chapter 1, most information systems work has been devoted to an analysis of form rather than content (Beynon-Davies, 1992). Most information systems work has fallen into the areas of empirics and syntactics. Until recently, little attention has been paid to the pragmatic and semantic nature of information systems work. This volume is a small attempt to redress some of this imbalance.

30.8 References

Beynon-Davies P. (1992). The Realities of Database Design: an essay on the sociology, semiology and pedagogy of database work. *Journal of Information Systems.* 1(2). 207-220.

Boland R.J. (1987). The In-Formation of Information Systems. In Boland R.J. and Hirschheim R.A. (Eds) *Critical Issues in Information Systems Research.* John Wiley, Chichester.

Bowden D. (1992). What Kind of Resource is Information? *Computer Bulletin.* 4(2). April. 6-7.

Earl M.J. (1989). *Management Strategies for Information Technology.* Oxford University Press, Oxford.

Palmer C. (1990). Hybrids - A Growing Initiative. *The Computer Bulletin.* 2(6). August.

Petrowski H. (1985). *To Engineer is Human: The role of failure in successful design.* Macmillan, London.

Stamper R.K. (1973). *Information in Business and Administrative Systems.* Batsford, London.

Skyrme D.J. and Earl M.J. (1990). Hybrid Managers: what should you do? *The Computer Bulletin.* 2(4). May.19-21.

30.9 Keywords

Hybrid Manager
Information Resource Management
Information Systems Engineering

30.10 Exercises

1. Discuss what steps you think are necessary to put information systems engineering on a professional footing.
2. Investigate the state of information systems engineering in other countries such as the USA, Sweden, and Japan.
3. Is the trend towards greater diversity of skill demanded of the information systems specialist a restriction on the development of a profession?
4. Consider one application known to you in terms of the hybridisation of technology. How do you think this application will be built in ten years, time?
5. How do methodologies fit in with the push for professionalisation?

Selected Solutions

Many of the exercises in the chapters of this book are deliberately open-ended. Here we present solutions only to those exercises where an answer is relatively closed.

Chapter 5: Object-Oriented Programming Languages

1. Claim, Vehicle, Client, ThirdParty, Solicitor, InsuranceBroker.
2. E.g., Claim: openClaim; resolveClaim; printClaim, etc.
3.

```
TYPE
        Claim = OBJECT
        claimNo: INTEGER;
        clientNo: INTEGER;
        description: STRING;
        resolutionFlag: STRING;
        CONSTRUCTOR Init(initClaim, initClient: INTEGER, initDesc:
        STRING);
        PROCEDURE resolveClaim;
        PROCEDURE PrintClaim;
END;

CONSTRUCTOR
Claim.Init(initClaim, initClient: INTEGER, initdesc STRING);
BEGIN
        claimNo := initClaim;
        clientNo := initClient;
        description := initDesc;
        resolutionFlag = 'N'
END;

PROCEDURE Claim.PrintClaim;
BEGIN
        WRITELN (clientNo);
        WRITELN (claimNo);
        WRITELN(description);
END;
```

```
PROCEDURE Claim.resolveClaim;
BEGIN
        resolutionFlag := 'Y';
END;
```

11. DeliveryAdvice, DespatchAdvice, Despatch, Job, Product.

Chapter 6:   Databases, DBMS and Data Models

1. CREATE TABLE Brokers(brokerNo CHAR(4), brokerName CHAR(20), brokerAddress CHAR(30), brokerTelNo CHAR(12))
2. ALTER TABLE Policies ADD(brokerNo CHAR(4))
3. INSERT INTO Brokers VALUES('0007', 'Roger Rabitt', 'ToonTown', '111222'))
   INSERT INTO Policies VALUES('3333', '1234', '30-JAN-93', '30-JAN-94', 50, 'Standard Life'))
4. SELECT * FROM Policies P, Brokers B WHERE P.brokerNo = B.brokerNo AND brokerName = 'Roger Rabitt'
5. CREATE VIEW rabitt AS SELECT * FROM Policies P, Brokers B WHERE P.brokerNo = B.brokerNo AND brokerName = 'Roger Rabitt'
6. GRANT SELECT ON rabitt TO jones
7. Information on delivery advices, job sheets and despatch advices.
8. List all jobs outstanding, List all jobs despatched.

Chapter 9: KnowledgeBase Systems

1. Policy ASSOC Holder
   Policy HASA startDate
   Policy HASA renewalDate
   Policy HASA premium
   Holder HASA holderName
   Holder HASA holderAddress
   Holder HASA holderTelNo
   StandardLife AKO Policy
   StandardBuildings AKO Policy
   StandardContents AKO Policy
   2001 ISA StandardLife
   5432 ISA Holder
   etc.

2. Planet HASA size
   Planet HAS orbit
   Moon HASA parentBody
   Sol ISA Sun
   Earth ISA Planet
   Juno ISA Moon
   etc.

3. IF A ISA Male
   AND C mother B
   AND C mother A
   THEN A brother B

   IF A ISA Male
   AND C father B
   AND C father A
   THEN A brother B

6. UnitTrust AKO Investment
   Shares AKO Investment
   Investment PARTOF InvestmentPortfolio

Chapter 10: Normalisation

1. Figure S.1

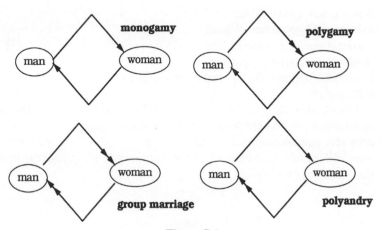

Figure S.1

2.
Marriages(<u>man</u>, woman)
Marriages(man, <u>woman</u>)
Marriages(<u>man</u>, woman)
Marriages(<u>man</u>, <u>woman</u>)

3. Figure S.2
Towns(<u>town</u>, population)
Managers(<u>managerNo</u>, managerName)
Cinemas(<u>cinemaCode</u>, cinemaName, town, managerNo)
Films(<u>filmNo</u>, filmName)
Venues(<u>cinemaCode</u>, filmNo, takings)

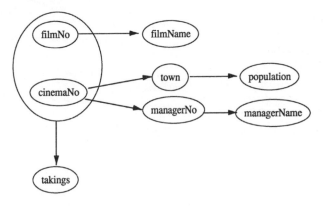

Figure S.2

6. Figure S.3
Doctors(<u>doctorNo</u>, doctorName)
Patients(<u>patientNo</u>, patientName, dateOfAdmission)
Schedule(<u>doctorNo</u>, <u>patientNo</u>)
Operations(<u>operationNo</u>, operationDate, operationTime, patientNo)

This is an interesting problem in that it highlights the need for non-functional dependencies in database design. A non-functional dependency exists between doctorNo and operationNo in that for every doctorNo there are potentially many operationNos, and vice versa, for every operationNo there may be more than one doctorNo relevant.

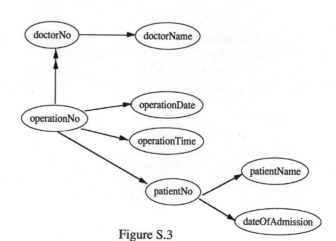

Figure S.3

8. Figure S.4
   Employees(<u>NINo</u>, address, telNo, wage, patternNo, currentShiftNo)
   Shifts(<u>shiftNo</u>, startHour, endHour)

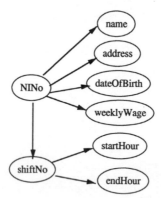

Figure S.4

Chapter 12: E-R Diagramming

1. Figure S.5
2. Horses(horseName, father, mother, dateOfBirth, sex)
3. Figure S.6
4. Figure S.7
6. Figure S.8
8. Figure S.9
9. Figure S.10

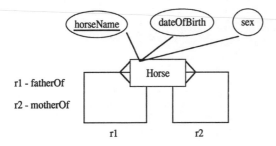

Figure S.5

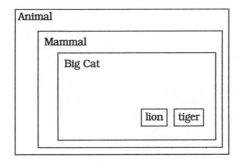

Figure S.6

Figure S.7

Figure S.8

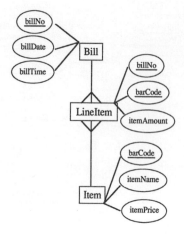

Figure S.9

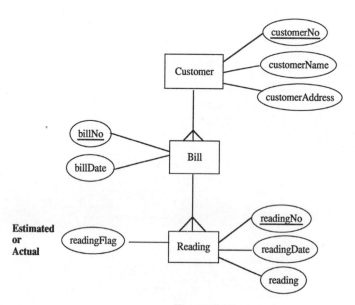

Figure S.10

Chapter 13: Data Flow Diagramming

1. Figure S.11
2. 2-dimensional interconnection is more easily shown on a diagram. Descriptive information is included in the symbols of a diagram. Diagrams require less effort to produce, and are easier to understand.

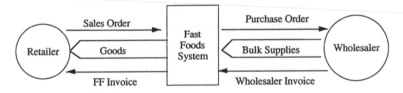

Figure S.11

3. This DFD does not tell you much. The data flow names and process name are too general to be useful. An unlabelled DFD. The process does not seem to be doing much to the transaction flow.
4. Besides the flow and process names being unmeaningful, levels 1 and 2 do not balance. H goes into process 1.2 and comes out again. Flow E is nowhere to be seen on level 2.
5. External entities merely define the boundaries of information systems. Entities on E-R diagrams define the important data structures for an information ·system.
6. Contents being moved would be a goods flow. Inventory would be a data flow.
7. Without it we would not be able to encompass increasing detail and complexity.
8. Information is data interpreted by actors in some context (see chapter 1).
9. Figure S.12.

Accept Delivery

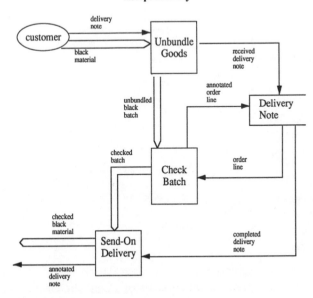

Figure S.12

Chapter14:   Data Dictionaries

1. textbook = contentsList + {chapter}+ index
   chapter = chapterTitle + {section}
   section = sectionHeading + {page}
   page = header + {line} + footer
2. dictionary = contentsList + {flow} + {process} + {dataStore}
   flow = flowName + flowDescription + {fromProcess} + {toProcess}+ {dataStructure}
   process = processName + processDescription + {inboundFlow} + {outboundFlow}
   dataStore = dataStoreName + dataStoreDescription + {inboundFlow} + {outboundFlow} + datDescription + (volume) + (access)
3. The sign '+' is not a summation operator; it is a concatenation operator. Hence 10 = 5 + 5 is wrong in BNF; 55 = 5 + 5 is right.
4. **Processes**
   check credit status
   determine discount
   create purchase order
   despatch goods
   Flows
   sales order
   prepayment request
   validated sales order
   discounted sales order
   order information
   credit status
   customer status
   goods information
   purchase order
   bulk supplies
   delivery note
   wholesaler invoice
   goods
   shipping note
   FF invoice
   Stores
   retailers
   sales orders
   goods

5. **Process Name**: Despatch Goods
   Inbound Flows: Bulk Supplies, Delivery Note, Wholesaler Invoice
   Outbound Flows: Goods, Shipping Note, Invoice
6. FFInvoice = invoiceNo + customerName + customerAddress + (despatchDate)
   + {productNo + productDescription + qtyOrdered + unitPrice + orderValue}
   + totalValue *invoice sent to retailer with shipping note and goods*

Chapter 15: Process Descriptions

1. There are two possible meanings:
a. Customers with more than £1000 in their deposit account and an average current account balance exceeding £100 OR persons who have been customers for more than 5 years.
b. Customers with more than £1000 in their deposit account AND persons with an average current account balance exceeding £100 or who have been customers for more than 5 years.

2.
a. IF depositBalance > 1000
   AND averageCurrentBalance > 100
   THEN customer is entitled to free banking

   IF customer has been with bank for more than 5 years
   THEN customer is entitled to free banking

b. IF depositBalance > 1000
   THEN customer is entitled to free banking

   IF averageCurrentBalance > 100
   OR customer has been with bank for more then 5 years
   THEN customer is entitled to free banking

3. Figure S.13

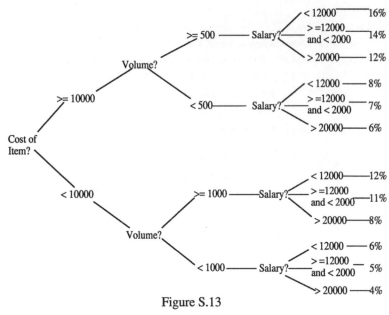

Figure S.13

4. Figure S.14
5. Produce Despatch Advice

BEGIN
    Produce despatch advice header; get Job
    DO WHILE not end of Jobs
    IF completionIndicator = 'Y' and totalWeight < 20 tonnes **THEN**
    BEGIN
        Produce despatch line
        totalWeight = totalWeight + batchWeight; get next Job
    END
    ENDIF
    ENDDO
    IF totalWeight < 20 tonnes **THEN** get first Job
    DO WHILE not end of Jobs
    IF qtyOutstanding > 0 and totalWeight < 20 tonnes **THEN**
    BEGIN
        Produce despatch line
        totalWeight = totalWeight + batchWeight; get next job
    END
    ENDIF
    ENDDO
produce report footer
END

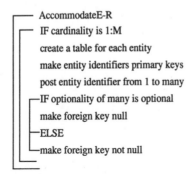

Figure S.14

Chapter 16: Entity Life-Histories

1. Figure S.15
2. Figure S.16

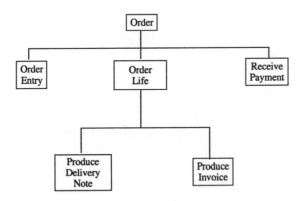

Figure S.15

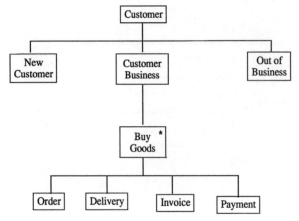

Figure S.16

3. Figure S.17
4. Figure S.18
5. Figure S.19
6. Figure S.20
8. Figure S.21
9. Figure S.22

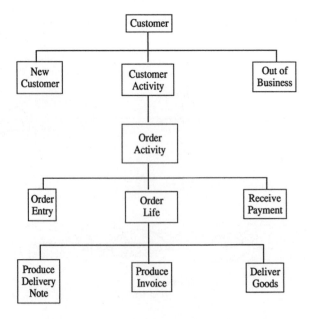

Figure S.17

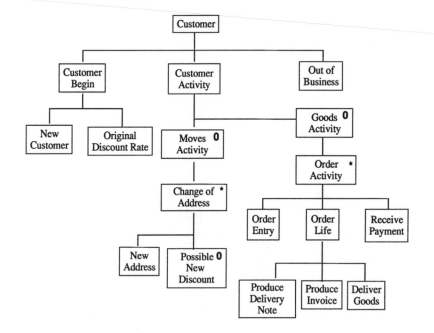

Figure S.18

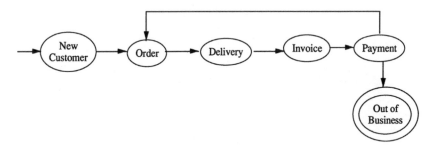

Figure S.19

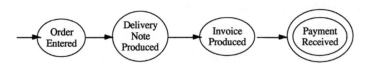

Figure S.20

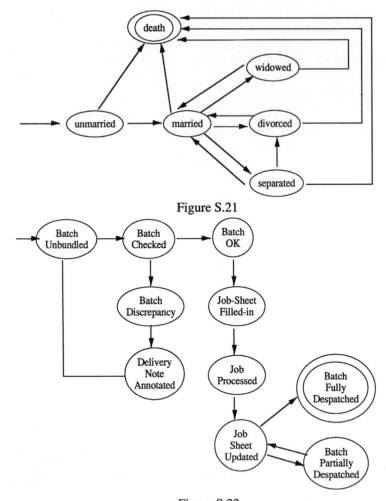

Figure S.21

Figure S.22

Chapter 17: Formal Specification

1.

a. $\forall (X) (\text{lifePolicy} (X) \Rightarrow \text{insurancePolicy} (X))$

b. $\forall (X) (\text{insurancepolicy}(X) \Rightarrow \text{lifePolicy} (X) \wedge \text{vehiclePolicy}(X))$

3.

DeliveryAdvices = DeliveryAdviceNos → Jobs-SET

DespatchAdvices = DespatchAdviceNos → Despatches-SET

Products = ProductCodes → Jobs-SET

Despatches = JobNos → Despatches-SET

4.

despatchJob (jb : JobNo)
EXTERNAL WR DeliveryJobs, DespatchJobs : Jobs
PRE-ASSERTION jb ∉ DespatchJobs ∧ jb ∈ DeliveryJobs
POST-ASSERTION DespatchJobs = DespatchJobs' ∪ jb ∧ DeliveryJobs =
DeliveryJobs' − jb

Chapter 18: Structured Program Design

4. Figure S.23

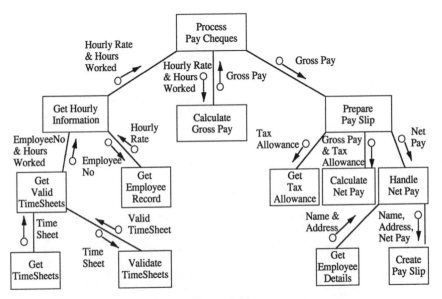

Figure S.23

Chapter 19: User Interface Development

5. Figure S.24

Chapter 20: Business Analysis

9. Figure S.25

Chapter 25: Object-Oriented Development

4. Figure S.26

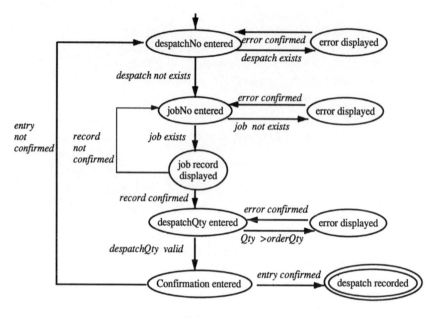

Figure S.24

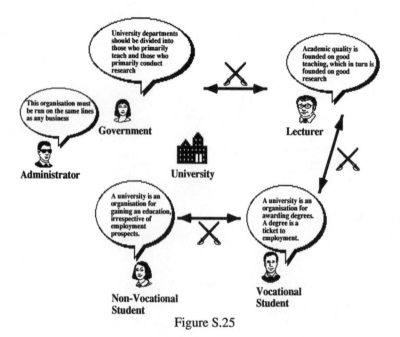

Figure S.25

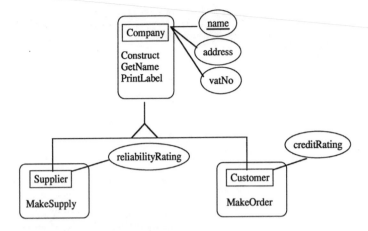

Figure S.26

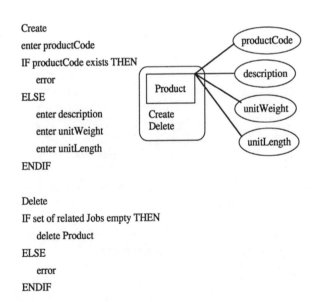

Create
enter productCode
IF productCode exists THEN
    error
ELSE
    enter description
    enter unitWeight
    enter unitLength
ENDIF

Delete
IF set of related Jobs empty THEN
    delete Product
ELSE
    error
ENDIF

Figure S.27

A Dictionary of Information Systems Engineering

Abstraction	The process of modelling 'real-world' concepts in a computational medium.
Accommodation	The process of producing a relational schema from an E-R diagram or determinancy diagram.
Active Data Dictionary	A data dictionary at the heart of a relational DBMS. Designed to buffer users and application programs from base tables.
AKO (A-Kind-Of)	A relationship between two objects. One object being the super-class of the other object.
Artificial Intelligence	A discipline originally charged with attempting to emulate aspects of human intelligence in a computational medium.
Assembly Language	A low-level form of programming language. The lowest form of symbolic programming.
Assertion	A statement of truth.
Attribute	A property of an entity.
Authority	Legitimated power.
Balancing	Ensuring that the symbols at various levels in a DFD hierarchy match.
Back-End CAISE	CAISE tools for implementation and maintenance.
Binary Relation	A relationship between two objects.
Black Box	A highly cohesive module that can be used to build low-coupled systems.
Block	A section of program code.
BNF	Backus-Naur Form. A meta-language originally designed for the specification of programming languages.
Bracketing notation	A notation for representing the structure of a relational schema.
Business Analysis	A term used in this work to include the analysis of the informal systems of organisations.

Candidate Key	A column or group of columns which could act in the capacity of a primary key.
CAISE	Computer Aided Information Systems Engineering. *See CASE*
Cardinality	The number of instances of an entity involved in a relationship.
CASE	Computer Aided Software Engineering.
Central Transform	The process identified in structured design, around which a structure chart is built.
Cohesion	A function of how closely the elements within a single module are related together.
Command Language Interface	A form of user interface driven by commands typed by the user.
Competitive Advantage	A term used to describe the advantage gained in competition from certain types of IT application.
Component-CAISE (C-CAISE)	A CAISE environment put together via an assembly of standaloneCAISE tools.
Computer Supported Cooperative Work	A term used to describe attempts to augment group activity with computer systems.
Condition	A selection statement.
Connection	Any reference from one module to something defined in another module.
Constrained Prototyping	A form of prototyping in which a prototype is primarily used to generate system requirements.
Constraint	A rule for maintaining integrity of a database.
Context Diagram	The top-most DFD in a DFD hierarchy.
Control Structure	A term used to encompass loops, sequences and selection statements.
Control Subsystem	That part of a technical information system devoted to controlling the interaction of process, data and user interface elements.
Corporate Information Architecture	A term used to encompass an enterprise activity model and an enterprise data model.
Couple	A data item that moves from one module to another.
Coupling	A measure of the degree of interdependence between modules.
Critical Success Factor	A CSF is a factor which is deemed crucial to the success of a business.

Cursor	A construct used to interface between the file-at-a-time processing characteristic of query languages such as SQL and the record-at-a-time form of processing characteristic of most third generation languages.
Culture	A set of behaviours expected in a social group.
Data	Facts about some aspect of the real world.
Data Analysis	A term generally used to encompass techniques such as E-R diagramming and normalisation.
Data Definition	That part of a data model which specifies the principles involved in creating data structures.
Data Dictionary	A repository of metadata.
Data Element	An atomic piece of data.
Data Flow	A pipeline of data.
Data Flow Diagram	DFD. A diagrammatic representation of data flow.
Data Integrity	That part of a data model which specifies inherent integrity rules.
Data Inventory	A term used in IRM to describe the entire collection of information sources owned by some organisation.
Data Item	*see Data Element*
Data Manipulation	That part of a data model which specifies the principles for manipulating data structures.
Data Model	An architecture for data as in the relational data model. Also used to specify a set of business rules.
Data Modelling	*see Data Analysis*
Data Store	A repository of data.
Data Structure	An aggregation of data elements.
Data Subsystem	That part of a technical information system devoted to managing data needs.
Database	A shared repository of organisational data.
Database Management System	A shared set of facilities for accessing a database.
Decision tree	A hierarchical representation of process logic.
Decision table	A matrix-like representation of process logic.
Declaration	A program statement normally used to assign some data type to program variables.
Degree	*see Cardinality*
Dependency	*see Determinancy*
Dependent data-item	That data item which is determined by some other data-item.

Determinant data-item	That data-item which determines some other data-item.
Determinancy	Some directed association between data items.
Direct Manipulation Interface	A type of interface in which graphics and pointing devices provide the major means of communication with information systems.
Domain	The pool of values associated with the columns of relations.
De-normalisation	The process of moving back from third normal form.
Embedded SQL	SQL embedded in some host language such as C.
Empirics	The physical characteristics of the medium of communication.
Encapsulation	Packaging data and behaviour within an object.
Enterprise Activity Model	A process model which plots the dynamics of some entire corporation.
Enterprise Data Model	A data model which plots the data needs of some entire corporation.
Entity	A thing of interest which can be uniquely identified.
Entity Integrity	An inherent integrity rule of the relational data model.
Entity Life History	A representation of the flow of events affecting an entity.
Entity Life History Matrix	A matrix which plots entities against events.
Entity Type	A categorisation of entities.
ETHICS	A methodology for participative development. Derived from the work of Mumford on socio-technical systems.
Event	Some real-world happening.
Evolutionary Development	A style of development which proposes that an information system evolve from a number of smaller projects.
Existential Quantifier	With existential quantification, only some of the instantiations need to be true for the proposition to be true.
External entity	Something, lying outside the context of a system, which is the net originator or receiver of system data.
First Normal Form	A relational database is in first normal form if it has no repeating groups.

Foreign Key	A column or set of columns which refers to the primary key of a table in a relational database.
Formal Information System	At the formal level of some organisation are the explicitly recognised precepts of behaviour which may be a part of the wider culture in which the organisation operates; on the other hand they may be expressed in the rules, regulations and official structure of authority.
Formal Methods	The application of mathematics to the specification of information systems.
Fourth Generation Language	A term generally used to refer to a programming language with enhanced data management facillities.
Frame	A packet of knowledge.
Front-End CAISE	CAISE tools for analysis and design.
Function	A one-to-one mapping between objects.
Functional determinancy	Data item A is said to functionally determine data item B if for every value of data item A there is one, unambiguous, value for data-item B.
Generalisation	The process of building hierarchies of object classes.
Groupware	A term used to describe a class of software used to augment group interaction.
HASA	A relationship between an object and a property of the object.
Hardware	A general term for computing machinery.
High-Level Language	A term generally used as a synonym for third-generation language.
Human Activity System	The class of systems to which computing is generally applied. Such systems have an additional component added to the conventional input-process-output model of systems: people. Human activity systems consist of people, conventions and artefacts designed to serve human needs.
Hybrid Manager	A manager who combines business and personal skills with technical skills.
Hype Curve	A way of describing the progression of hype associated with most new developments in computing.

Hypermedia	Hypermedia is the approach to building information systems made up of nodes of various media connected together by a collection of associative links
Hypertext	A subset of hypermedia concentrating on the construction of loosely connected textual systems.
Information Centre	A centre of information systems excellence.
Information Engineering	A term generally used to encompass a global concern with the management of information in organisations. Also used to refer to a specific development methodology.
Information Resource Management	The process of building and managing a corpo rate information architecture.
Information Services Sector	That part of the economy devoted to the production and maintenance of information systems.
Information Systems Engineering	A term used in this work to represent the science and art of designing and making, with economy and elegance, technical information systems that support the activity of particular organisations.
Integrated-CAISE (I-CAISE)	A CAISE environment made up of a series of closely-coupled CAISE tools.
Imperative Language	The most popular group of programming languages for commercial information systems work.
Informal Information System	At the informal level, an organisation will gradually evolve complex patterns of behaviour which are never formulated, but which must be learnt by newcomers.
Information	Data placed within some meaningful context.
Information Management	The discipline of managing data for administrative, strategic and tactical advantage. Also sometimes used to encompass Strategic Information Systems Planning.
Information Society	A term originally coined by Daniel Bell to indicate a change from a primarily goods-producing to an information-based society.
Inheritance	A subclass is said to inherit all the instance variables and methods of its superclass.
Instance	A specific occurrence of an object.

Invariant	Invariants state what must be true for a particular application throughout the life of the application.
ISA	A relationship between an object and an object class.
Knowledge	Knowledge is derived from information by integrating information with existing knowledge. Knowledge might be pragmatically defined as facts, rules and inference.
Knowledge Elicitation	The process of collecting the knowledge relevant to some domain.
Knowledge Engineering	A term generally used to denote the discipline devoted to building knowledgebase systems.
Knowledge Representation	The process of mapping the knowledge of some domain onto a computational medium.
KnowledgeBase System	A computer system which emulates the knowledge in some domain.
Levelling	The process of producing a hierarchically organised set of DFDs.
Logical Dialogue Design	The process of laying out a dialogue in implementation-independent terms.
Loop	An iterative programming construct.
Machine Code	The lowest level of programming language.
Membership class	*see Optionality*
Menu	A list of options from which the user selects.
Meta-CAISE	A term used to describe CAISE tools that are able to construct other CAISE tools.
Method	The routines associated with an object are referred to as an object's methods.
Methodology	An information systems development methodology might be defined as being made up of the following primary components: 1. A model of the information systems development process; 2. A set of techniques; 3. A documentation method associated with these techniques; 4. Some indication of how the techniques chosen along with the documentation method fit into the model of the development process.
Message	To make an object perform one of its methods we have to send an object a message
Module	*see Black Box*

Multimedia	Information systems constructed from various different media: text, data, sound, graphics, video, etc.
Multiview	A contingency based methodology.
Natural Language Interface	A restricted English interface usually to databases.
Non-loss decomposition	A step by step approach to normalisation in which a universal relation is fragmented by a series of relational projects.
Norm	A social expectation of behaviour.
Normalisation.	The process of producing a series of relations free from update anomalies.
Object	A thing of interest specified both structurally and behaviourally.
Object Class	A generalisation of a group of objects.
Object Model	An entity model with behavioural abstraction.
Object-Oriented	A much-used term, most sensibly used to describe any computing area which uses the concept of objects.
Optionality	The participation of an entity in a relationship.
Overview Diagram	A DFD which details the major processes, flows, stores and entities involved in some system.
Participative Development	A style of development which places great emphasis on user-involvement.
PARTOF	A relationship of aggregation.
Passive Data Dictionary	A term normally used to refer to a repository of design information.
PERT	A technique for graphically representing a project.
Physical Data Dictionary	A data dictionary recording implementation information.
Polymorphism	The ability to send the same message to objects of different classes and thus to have this message interpreted differently.
Post-Assertion	A post-assertion describes a condition that is intended to hold after a process is executed.
Power	Power is the ability of a person or social group to control the behaviour of some other person or social group.
Pragmatics	The study of the general context and culture of communication. The shared assumptions underlying communication and understanding.

Pre-Assertion	A pre-assertion describes a condition that is expected to hold before a process is executed.
Primary Method	Four major primary methods associated with any object: constructor methods; destructor methods; transform methods and retrieval methods.
PRINCE	A government-sponsored project management method.
Process	A transformation of incoming data flow to outgoing data flow.
Prototyping	A form of development in which some model of the eventual system is built.
Psuedo-code	A form of process description close to actual program code.
Primary Key	A unique identifier for the rows of a table.
Procedure	A module of program code.
Process Description	A description of process logic.
Production Rule	An IF-THEN construct used to represent knowledge in a knowledgebase system.
Project	An operator of the relational algebra. Produces a subset of the columns of a table.
Project Management	A term used to encompass every consideration pertaining to the planning and monitoring of projects.
Quality Assurance	Quality assurance is a planned and systematic pattern of all the actions necessary to provide adequate confidence that software conforms to established technical requirements.
Quantifier	Quantifiers are used to indicate how many of a variable's instantiations need to be true for the whole of the proposition to be true.
Query Language	A software tool specifically designed to query databases.
Rapid Prototyping	A form of iterative development in which a prototype is refined into an eventual system.
Referential Integrity	An inherent integrity constraint of the relational data model. A foreign key must either be null or the primary key of a table.
Relation	A disciplined table. A table which obeys restricted number of rules.
Relational Algebra	The manipulative part of the relational data model.
Relationship	An association between two or more entities.

Report Generator	A software tool specifically designed for the production of reports.
Role	People package behaviour in collections which social scientists call social roles.
Schematic Logic	A form of process description available in JSP.
Screen Painter	A software tool specifically designed for producing data entry and retrieval screens.
Second normal form	A second normal form database is free from part-key dependencies.
Secondary Method	Any method associated with an object which is not primary.
Semantic Data Model	A data model having a rich set of constructs for modelling the 'real world'.
Semantic Net	A technique used mainly in AI and cognitive psychology for representing relationships between concepts.
Semantics	The study of the meaning of signs. The association between signs and behaviour.
Semiotics	The discipline devoted to the study of signs.
Sequence	An ordered list of program instructions.
Set	A collection of items with no duplicates.
Sign	A sign can be considered as a relationship between a symbol, a concept and a referent.
Sink	*see External Entity*
Social Group	A social group is any collection of people who regularly interact with one another.
Soft Systems Analysis	Informal or 'soft' systems analysis is the process of investigating and documenting the informal information systems of organisations.
Soft Systems Methodology	Over the last decade or so Checkland has been developing the framework of an approach known as soft systems methodology
Software Metric	A software metric is a number extracted from a software product. Metrics are used in a number of ways: to provide feedback to staff on the quality of their work; to monitor the structural degradation of a system during maintenance; to aid costing and estimating software projects.
Software Problem	A term used to encapsulate all the problems experienced in the development of information systems.

Software Engineering	Software engineering is the systematic application of an appropriate set of techniques to the whole process of software development.
Source	*see Sink*
Spiralist Model	A hybrid model of software development proposed by Boehm.
SQL	Structured Query Language. The major interface to relational databases.
Status	A person's status implies some form of position is a social hierarchy
Strategic Data Planning	*see Information Resource Management*
Strategic Information Systems Planning	A process of establishing a programme for the implementation and use of information systems in such a way that it optimises the effectiveness of an organisation's information resources and uses them to support the objectives of the whole organisation.
SSADM	Structured Systems Analysis and Design Method. A UK government standard methodology for systems development.
Statement	A coherent unit of program code.
STRADIS	A methodology proposed by some of the founders of structured analysis, Gane and Sarson.
Structure Chart	A diagrammatic representation of a hierarchy of program modules.
Structure Diagram	A graphical technique for representing process and data structures in JSP.
Structured Analysis	An attempt to separate the logical from the physical description of systems.
Structured Design	A term used by Yourdon and Constantine to include their discussion of coupling, cohesion and the derivation of structure charts.
Stuctured English	A constrained subset of English used for process description.
Structured Language	A language which adheres to the tenets of structured programming in providing facilities for modularisation and clear programming.
Structured Programming	A disciplined programming philosophy based upon firm notions of appropriate syntax for procedural programming languages.
Structured Prototyping	A form of prototyping melded with structured development. *See Constrained Prototyping*

Structured Walkthrough	A group review of any product of the development process.
Syntactics	The logic and grammar of sign systems.
System	A system might be defined as a coherent set of interdependent components which exists for some purpose, has some stability, and can be usefully viewed as a whole
Table	*see Relation*
Technical Information System	A term used in this work to indicate computerised information systems.
Third normal form	A relational database is in third normal form if it is free from file maintenance anomalies.
Transaction	Some event which changes the state of a database.
Universal Quantifier	With universal quantification, all instantiations of a variable within some domain of interest must be true for the proposition to be true.
User Interface	A term generally used to encompass all facets of human communication with computing devices.
User Interface Subsystem	That part of a technical information system concerned with interfacing with the user.
VDM	Vienna Development Method. A style of formal methods.
Waterfall Model	One of the most prevalent models of software development. It proposes a sequence of clearly defined stages.
Workflow Applications	Software specifically designed to handle the flow of documents amongst groups of users.
Z	A style of formal methods.

Index